The Non-Runner's Marathon Trainer

David A. Whitsett
Forrest Dolgener
Tanjala Mabon Kole

McGraw·Hill

New York   Chicago   San Francisco   Lisbon   London   Madrid   Mexico City
Milan   New Delhi   San Juan   Seoul   Singapore   Sydney   Toronto

Library of Congress Cataloging-in-Publication Data

Whitsett, David A.
     The non-runner's marathon trainer / David A. Whitsett, Forrest A.
Dolgener, Tanjala Mabon Kole.
        p.   cm.
    ISBN 1-57028-182-3
     1. Marathon running—Training.   I. Dolgener, Forrest, 1946–.
II. Kole, Tanjala Mabon, 1958–.   III. Title.
GV1065.17.T73W55   1998
796.42′52—dc21   97-49288
                                   CIP

    19 20 21 22 23 24 25 26 QWD   13 12 11 10

ISBN 1-57028-182-3

McGraw-Hill books are available at special quantity discounts to use as premiums and
sales promotions, or for use in corporate training programs. For more information, please
write to the Director of Special Sales, Professional Publishing, McGraw-Hill, Two Penn
Plaza, New York, NY 10121-2298. Or contact your local bookstore.

This book is printed on acid-free paper.

Contents

Foreword

Neither of us remembers exactly how it began. All we know is that in the spring semester of 1985 we taught for the first time what the students at the University of Northern Iowa now call "the marathon class." We called it a seminar in Fitness and Mental Health and we had 14 students enrolled, none of whom had ever run more than three miles. The students could take the three credit hours they received in either psychology or physical education because these are the two departments in which we teach. Beginning in January, the class met twice a week for 15 weeks and the students ran 6 days each week in addition to attending class twice a week. Forrest taught one of the classes each week and lectured on such topics as cardiovascular functioning, proper hydration and nutrition. Dave taught the other class session and talked with the students about believing in themselves and using mental imagery to get through the long tough training days. The students ran on their own or in small groups and we all did the week's longest run together on Saturday mornings. In the first week of May, when the training was done, we took them to Des Moines, Iowa to participate in the 26.2 mile Drake Relays Marathon. They all finished.

As a condition of enrolling in the course, the students had agreed to be participants in our research, so they participated in stress tests on a treadmill, kept a detailed daily log of their experiences and filled out several psychological questionnaires. Our data showed that they had improved in both physical fitness and self-esteem during the semester. When the students finished the marathon they were thrilled with their accomplishment and we were equally thrilled to have been part of their success. We agreed that we would like to teach the course again and try to get more students involved.

We have taught the course four more times since then, in 1988 with 25 students, in 1990 with 40, in 1993 with 72, in 1995 with 52 and we are teaching it again in 1998 with over 50 students as this book goes to press. Our participants have ranged in age from 18 to 55. Well over half of them have been women. Almost none had ever run more than three miles prior to training with us. Every time, all of the students have finished the marathon, (with one notable exception...more on him later) and every time it has had the same exhilarating effect on the participants and on us. The last few times we have taught the course, we have had so many students trying to get in (162 of them in 1995 and 199 this year) that we have had to draw names to decide which ones get to participate. In addition, we have had many members of the community in which we live who have asked to come and train with our group and we have received many requests for information on our course from faculty members of other universities and from people across the country, partly as a result of news coverage here in Iowa and partly because of an article describing our course that appeared in the October 1993 issue of *Runner's World* magazine.

One of the 1995 participants, Tanjala Kole, suggested that we find a way to make the course content accessible to more people. She was sure there would be lots of interest in it and she even volunteered to gather and edit the recollections and suggestions of a group of former participants. We agreed her idea was a good one and you are holding the resulting book in your hands. Over the years, we have modified the training program (it now requires just four days a week of running) as well as the class content somewhat as a result of what we have learned. We have put it all here for you. Because it has worked so well for so many people, we are certain that if you follow the program and do everything it tells you to do, you can and will complete a full 26.2 mile marathon and you will feel the same sense of accomplishment and personal satisfaction that we have seen on the faces of our students.

We have found that completing a marathon contributes a great deal to increasing one's self-esteem and self-confidence. When they cross that finish line, our students believe they can do ANYTHING. "Bring on the world," one of them said just after finishing, "because I can handle whatever life has in store for me." A great many of them have also found that training for a marathon provides a goal-oriented way for them to develop many of the exercise and eating habits that are part of a healthy life-style. Many of them have maintained those habits for years after the marathon.

If those sound like worthwhile benefits to you, please keep reading. If you need more convincing that training for a marathon is for you, go to the back of the book and read the articles we have included that describe our research. In the introductory chapter that follows, we will describe the entire training program for you and tell you how the book is layed out and what you will need to do to complete the marathon.

Acknowledgments

There are three authors of this book and each of them would like to offer acknowledgments individually.

David Whitsett wants to thank Scott Trappe for putting the authors in touch with the people at Masters Press. Scott's help was essential in connecting us with this fine publisher. Speaking of the publisher, Holly Kondras and Heather Lowhorn, both editors at Masters Press, provided us with invaluable help and support and were unfailingly pleasant to work with.

The organizers, officials and volunteers of the Drake Relays Marathon and later the Lincoln, Nebraska Marathon went far beyond the call of duty to support and accommodate our rookie marathoners and we appreciate their help. Finally, I want to thank my department head at the University of Northern Iowa, Dr. Julia Wallace, for her steadfast support and encouragement on this, as well as my other writing projects.

Forrest Dolgener wishes to thank Dr. Fred Kolkhorst for the many hours spent in the human performance laboratory testing and collecting the data on the students in the marathon classes. I also acknowledge the commitment and effort of all the students who willingly participated in the research conducted as part of the marathon class and for their unfaltering dedication to running that first marathon. You are all winners in my eyes.

Tanjala Kole wants to thank her parents, Bryce and Ruth Mabon, for their unending love and support that helped make her work on this book possible. You were always there when I needed an extra set of hands and you made it possible for me to write when there were many other things needing my attention. When I first told my children, Justin, Marshall and Grace, that I was going to write a book with Dave and Forrest, they said "All right! Way to go, Mom!" Thanks, guys, for believing in me right from the start and never wavering in your support. You always have been and still are my greatest inspiration. I love you more than you could ever know.

Thanks to all of the past participants who so graciously shared their thoughts and memories in order to help make this book possible. While the training program may be the heart of this book, you are its soul. A very special thank you to Kathy Schneider for her help in gathering and preparing the interview material. And though I list Him last, He is also first, for everything I do starts and ends with Him. Thank you, God, for these people in my life and the gift of this experience. I hope I have done you justice.

Dedications

To all the students whom I have been privileged to watch cross the finish lines of marathons with the light of achievement in their eyes. You have enriched my life. Thank you for the peak experiences. — DAW

This book is dedicated to my wife, Alice, and my daughters Jennifer and Amy. Without your support and love, many of my professional accomplishments would not have been realized. — FAD

To my parents, Bryce and Ruth Mabon and my children, Justin, Marshall and Grace Kole: This one's for you. — TMK

Introduction

Intent and Plan of the Book

This book is intended to be a complete manual to prepare you to finish a full 26.2-mile marathon. It contains everything you will need to know in order to do that. After this introduction, there are seventeen chapters. Each of the next sixteen chapters covers one week of the sixteen-week training program and each contains three sections. The first section focuses on the mental aspects of marathon training and each week's chapter offers you one or more mental techniques to use as you train for and run the marathon. One of the things that has become very clear to us is that the marathon is an event in which mental preparation is equal in importance to physical preparation. Consequently, we have included a wide variety of mental tools for you to practice and use. As you will see, these tools will become more and more important as the length of the training runs increases.

The second section gives you the training program for the week, as well as some information and advice on the physical aspects of training that are particularly relevant at that point in the program.

The third section contains recollections and suggestions from people who have taken our course and followed our training program. Remember, these are people just like many of you. They were not experienced runners either. They were beginners, but they got through the training and finished the marathon just like you will. Because you may be doing this training alone, or with others who are also training for their first marathon, we thought you would like to know what it has been like for other rookies, so we have included their thoughts here. They'll be with you all the way, just as we will be. If you would like to know who they are, you can turn to the end of this chapter where we have provided short bio sketches of each of them. You are almost sure to find one or more with whom you can identify.

The final chapter of the book tells you what to do during the weeks immediately following the marathon to make sure you recover well from the rigors of the event and get the full benefit of your achievement. At the back of the book we have included three appendices. The first appendix lists many of the marathons that are held in the world each year, and we have included it because one of the first things you will need to do is to choose which marathon you are going to run. More on that after we show you the training program. The second one contains a couple of articles we've written that explain the results of our research on this program. The third one offers you a list of other books and articles to read on some of the topics we discuss in the book, just in case you are interested.

The Training Program

Well, are you ready to see how much running you will need to do? Here's your sixteen-week training program.

MARATHON TRAINING PROGRAM				
WEEK	DAY 1	DAY 2	DAY 3	DAY 4	TOTAL FOR THE WEEK
1	3	4	3	5	15
2	3	4	3	6	16
3	3	4	3	7	17
4	3	5	3	8	19
5	3	5	3	10	21
6	4	5	4	11	24
7	4	6	4	12	26
8	4	6	4	14	28
9	4	7	4	16	31
10	5	8	5	16	34
11	5	8	5	16	34
12	5	8	5	18	36
13	5	8	5	18	36
14	5	8	5	9	27
15	3	5	3	8	19
16	3	3	walk 3	marathon	35.2

All values are in miles.
Try to do the long run on Saturday or Sunday and take the day before and the day after off.

In addition to the sixteen weeks of training outlined in the program, you will need another month or so to work up to the 3-mile distance you will start with in Week One. We'll tell you exactly how to do that a little later. But, for the moment, that means you should pick a marathon that will be held no less than five months from the time you expect to start getting ready. What you need to do right now is choose the marathon you want to run from the list given in the appendix of this book (or some other one you may know about) and then write or call the organizers and ask for an entry form to be sent to you as soon as they are available. Do it right now. Make the commitment. And start telling your family and friends that you are a marathoner and tell them which marathon you are going to run. (We'll tell you later on why that is so important.)

How We Know The Training Program Works

If you look carefully at the training program, you will notice that it requires you to run just four days a week and that the longest runs we want you to do are 18 miles. You may be wondering how you will be able to run 26.2 miles on just four days a week and no runs of over 18 miles. It will be enough. We are sure of that. Let us tell you how we know.

As we mentioned in the Foreword, we have taught our marathon class five times. Over 200 people have taken the course and used the training program and all of them but one have finished the marathon, so you will too. There was that one young man we mentioned in the Foreword who did not finish, but that had nothing to do with the how much running he had done during the training. He did all the training runs just fine. What he didn't do was to drink enough fluids during the marathon. As we will discuss later, hydration is one of the most important aspects of endurance training. He was fine after about a half-hour of rest, but of course he was very disappointed not to have achieved his goal. So, when we say we KNOW you can finish the marathon on this program, we mean it, but we mean if you do EVERYTHING we tell you to do, not just the running. (If you are interested in reading more about how we tested our training program, you may want to read those articles we have included at the back of the book.)

The amount of running required in our training program is modest compared to almost every other program you may have seen or heard about. That is because we have designed it for one purpose; to prepare first-time marathoners to finish. A great many people who decide to train for a marathon do a lot more training than they need to do and lots of them get what are referred to as overuse injuries while training that keep them from even starting the marathon, let alone finishing it. We have designed a program that will allow you to finish your first marathon by having you do enough training to do so while minimizing the chances that you will get injured in the process.

We want you to have a success experience, so that you will want to try it again. On your second or third marathon, you will have enough of what is called a "training base" that you will be able to train more miles per week and not risk injury and, as a result, do faster marathons. But this time, your first time, the goal is to get to the starting line in good shape and to finish, regardless of the amount of time it takes you. We cannot overemphasize the importance of maintaining this as your goal. Do not set a time goal for your first marathon! Your goal is to finish. Period. We will explain the psychological reasons for this in the next section. But, for now, we want you to believe that this training program IS enough to allow you to reach that goal. In fact, if you are a first-time marathoner, it is the PERFECT training program for you.

Choosing The Goal: Finishing

If this is your first marathon, you should have only one goal and that should be to complete it. One of the biggest mistakes you could make at this point would be to set a target time in which you want to finish. Why would that be a mistake? Here's why.

You have the opportunity in training for and completing this marathon to have a tremendously satisfying and motivating experience. But that will only occur if, after it is over, you feel you have succeeded. So, the definition of success that you adopt for this experience becomes very important. As we have said, if you do exactly what we tell you to do, you WILL finish this marathon. If that (finishing) is the goal you have set, you WILL have a success experience. However, if you set a target time and then miss it, even by a few minutes, you will have converted what could have been one of the greatest success experiences of your life into a failure! Please don't do that to yourself.

The goal should be to complete the marathon, regardless of the time it takes. If you set a target time in your first marathon, here is what can, and probably will, happen. Let's say you set a four-hour goal. First, setting a target time may make you train harder and faster than you should and you may become injured and not get to run the marathon at all. But let's suppose that doesn't happen. Let's suppose you get through the training and arrive at the starting line on marathon day ready to try to finish in four hours or better. You have figured out that this means you will need to average about a 9-minute-per-mile pace for the 26.2 miles. So you start out at that pace and try to keep it up for the whole distance. Maybe you even find that you can do that for 16, 17 or even 20 miles, but then you "hit the wall" (we'll talk more about that in Chapter 12) and slow WAY down and get really bummed out and decide the whole thing is a waste because you can tell you're not going to make the goal. Maybe you even get so down on yourself that you drop out and don't finish at all! But maybe you keep going and finish some time after the four-hour time and then feel that you have failed! Can you imagine? You have just gone 26.2 miles for the first time in your life and you feel you have failed. Now that WOULD be a waste!

Or maybe you know that the chances of maintaining a constant pace for the full distance are remote, so you figure you'll need to average about an 8-minute pace for the first 20 miles so that, when you are really tired in the last 6 miles, you'll be able to slow down and still make the goal. So you start out at an 8-minute pace and you keep it up for 16, 17 or even 20 miles and then you hit the wall even harder than you would have if you had been running at the 9-minute pace and you really crash and burn and end up staggering and walking and finally sitting down at the side of the road and crying and berating yourself for being a quitter! Don't think it could happen? Think again. It has and does to lots of people in every marathon. But it does not have to happen. And it won't happen to you if set your goal as finishing.

And another thing. Don't set the goal of "not walking." It's OK to walk. Almost all first-time marathoners do. It's not "cheating" to walk. It's even a good idea to walk some in the marathon BEFORE you feel you have to. (We'll explain some more about that in Chapter 10.) And when you do walk, it will be important to walk proudly with your head up. Your expression, (and your thoughts) should say, "I'm still moving toward that finish line and I'm doing just fine." If you've set the goal not to walk and then you do, you will feel, look and think of yourself as someone who has been defeated instead of as someone who is achieving something that most people will never even try.

So fix the goal as FINISHING. Tell yourself and all those other people who are important to you that your goal is to finish. That way you will feel terrific when you do finish and you will be anxious to see all those other people so that you can say when they ask, "How did it go?," (and they WILL ask), "It went great! I did it!"

Medical Clearance For Training

Before you begin the physical training programs, you should determine whether the physical training will be medically safe for you to undertake. As we mentioned briefly in the introduction, depending on your gender, age, health history, and cardiovascular risk factors, you may need to get your physician's approval to exercise in the way we will be recommending. These recommendations are made for your benefit and you are the only person who can insure they are appropriately followed. The recommendations come from the American College of Sports Medicine and are considered to be the best approach to risk classification.

The three definitions of the risk categories are as follows:

Apparently Healthy Individuals- those with none or only one risk factor for heart disease.

Individuals at Increased Risk of Disease- those with two or more risk factors for heart disease and /or one or more signs or symptoms of heart disease, pulmonary disease or metabolic disease. (The risk factors for heart disease are listed in Table 1 and the signs and symptoms of heart, pulmonary or metabolic disease are listed in Table 2.)

Individuals with Known Disease- those with cardiac, pulmonary or metabolic disease diagnosed by a physician.

Place yourself in one of the three risk categories based on the definitions above. Then go to Table 3 and follow the recommendations for yor risk category, age and symptoms. Following the recommendations in the table will help ensure that you will be able to complete the training and the marathon without any unnecessary risk to your health.

Table 1 Coronary Heart Disease Risk Factors*	
Risk factor	Definitions
Age	Men>45 years; Women>55 or premature menopause without estrogen replacement therapy
Family history	Heart attack or sudden death before 55 years of age in father or other male first-degree relative, or before 65 years of age in mother or other female first-degree relative
Current cigarette smoking	
Hypertension	Blood pressure >140/90 mmHg or on antihypertensive medication
High cholesterol	Total cholesterol>200 mg/dl or HDL<35mg/dl
Diabetes mellitus	
Sedentary lifestyle or physical inactivity	Having a sedentary job involving sitting for a large part of the day and no regular exercise or active recreational pursuits

*Adapted from ACSM's Guidelines for Exercise Testing and Prescription, 5th ed., Williams & Wilkins, 1995.

Table 2 Major Symptoms or Signs Suggestive of Cardiopulmonary Disease
1. Pain, discomfort, pressure or other abnormal feelings in the chest, neck, jaw, arms or back. The pain, discomfort or pressure typically occurs when doing some form of muscular effort and goes away when the effort is discontinued.
2. Shortness of breath at rest or with mild exertion.
3. Dizziness or fainting.
4. Labored breathing when lying down.
5. Heart palpitations or fast heart rates for no apparent reason.
6. Ankle swelling.
7. Intermittent pain in the calf muscle. This pain may feel like a cramp and occurs in response to walking or jogging. As the exercise level is increased, the pain increases. When the exercise is terminated, the pain stops.
8. Known heart murmur.
9. Unusual fatigue or shortness of breath with usual activities that have not caused fatigue or shortness of breath in the past.

Table 3 Recommendations for Medical Clearance Before Training

If You Are Classified As	And If You	Then
Apparently Healthy	Are male<40 yrs or Are female<50 yrs	You do not need medical clearance prior to beginning training.
Apparently Healthy	Are male<40 yrs or Are female>50 yrs	You should seek medical clearance from a physician prior to beginning training.
At Increased Risk	Do or do not have any of the symptoms in Table 2	You should seek medical clearance from a physician prior to beginning training.
Having Known Disease		You should seek medical clearance from a physician prior to beginning training.

Most people who would consider training for and running a marathon will be in the Apparently Healthy category. However, being in either the At Increased Risk or With Known Disease categories does not necessarily preclude you from training for and running the marathon. It just may be that medical clearance may be necessary to rule out any disease process that could affect your ability to train and run safely.

Getting Ready to Train

In the Introduction, we showed you the program you will be following, but in order to begin this formal training program, some preliminary training needs to be done in order to be able to do the formal training schedule. This may sound strange — Why not just incorporate this preliminary training into the formal training schedule? The answer to this is that everyone will be starting at a different initial level of fitness. Some will never have run in their lives. Some will have been recreational runners. Others may already be running 15-20 miles a week. The ability to jump right into the formal training program will be different for different individuals.

The general rule that needs to be followed, whatever your starting point, is to begin slowly and progress at a moderate rate during the early phases of the preliminary conditioning. The goal of this early phase of training is to condition the muscular and skeletal systems to be able to withstand the more severe demands that will be encountered in the formal training program. In our experience, the only reason that people are not able to complete a marathon is that they get injured during the training. The muscular and skeletal system gets injured because they are not adequately conditioned to withstand the strain of the 16-week training program. By gradually introducing more and more mileage at an increasing intensity of effort, the musculoskeletal system is able to adapt to the increasing demands placed on it. This progressive adaptation makes the muscular and skeletal systems stronger and able to withstand the stress that will be coming. During this preliminary training period, the primary objective is not to train the cardiovascular system, but to train the muscular and skeletal systems.

The training goal of this preliminary training is to be able to jog continuously for 30 minutes. There is no pace or speed goal, just keep moving for 30 minutes. In the several hundred people we have trained to run a marathon, we have never had someone who could not jog for 30 minutes after following this preliminary program. The length of the preliminary program will depend on where you are currently with regards to fitness and running history.

You should start this preliminary program at the level most similar to your current status. If you have no running history, you start at the beginning. If you currently walk or jog on a regular basis, you should start at the level represent-

Step	Walking/Jogging Pace	Training Days per Week	Total Time (minutes)	Number of Weeks
	Table 4 Preliminary Training Program			
1	Moderate walking pace (17-20 min./mile)	3	30	1
2	Moderate walking pace (17-20 min./mile)	4	30	1
3	Fast walking pace (13-16 min./mile)	3	30	1
4	Fast walking pace (13-16 min./mile)	4	45	1
5	Jog for 5 min. and then walk at fast pace for 5 min. Repeat 2 times.	3	30	1
6	Jog for 10 min. and then walk at fast pace for 5 min. Repeat once.	3	30	1
7	Jog for 15 min. and then walk at fast pace for 5 min. Repeat once.	4	40	1
8	Jog for 20 min. and then walk at fast pace for 5 min. Repeat once.	4	40	1
9	Jog for 25 min. and walk at fast pace for 5 min.	4	30	1
10	Jog for 30 min.	4	30	2

ing your current level for walking or jogging. It is important that the major concern is not whether you can cardiovascularly do a particular amount of walking or jogging. The important objective is that you have done enough of the activity that you have adequately conditioned the muscular and skeletal systems and will be less likely to have an injury later on.

Before moving on to Chapter One, we want to introduce to you a feature of this book that we think may be particularly valuable to you. While teaching our course, we learned that being part of a group that was training together was very important. We know that some of you will be doing that, but that for some of you it may not be possible. To give you some feeling of being a member of a group training together, we are going to include in each chapter some thoughts, recommendations and comments from people who have trained on this program in the past. In all of the chapters this third section has been written by the third author of this book, Tanjala Kole. As we mentioned in the Foreword, this book was her idea and she was a participant in our class in 1995. A good deal of what you will read comes directly from her, but she has included comments from a number of other participants as well. At the end of the chapter, we have included a list of short biographies of each of the people she quotes. If you didn't do so earlier, you might want to take a look at that list to see who they are.

Why a Marathon?

At some point, everyone who has ever trained for and run a marathon has asked him or herself that very question. The answers are as individual as the person asking the question. Each of us has a completely unique set of life experiences, yet as humans we share the desire to test our personal limits in search of how far we can go. The avenue of testing is limited only by one's imagination, fear threshold, and financial resources. Some people dive out of airplanes, others climb mountains, still others explore the depths of the sea. But for most of us, the arenas of challenge are less grandiose and a lot closer to home: how long can I work in the yard before having to go in and rest, or how far can I walk before turning for home, or how much longer can I tolerate this job before it drives me crazy?

Along with the need to grow by testing and expanding our personal limits, we humans desire and value what psychologists call "peak experiences." Peak experiences are positive happenings that have a profound and lasting impact. They are life-changing, and in retrospect are often considered the finest moments of our lives. They are experiences we value and memories we cherish. Some people actively seek peak experiences, but most of us rarely get beyond weddings, births, and the occasional vacation.

Running a marathon is a peak experience available to anyone that will take you to the brink of what you thought were your personal limits and beyond. It is easily accessible, relatively inexpensive, and is the single most physically and mentally challenging activity (equal only to childbirth) I have ever experienced.

"Well, if you've run a marathon you can't be anything like me," you say. Wrong. I would wager that we are more alike than we are different. On the brink of middle age and 80 pounds overweight, physically my best years are behind me. I used to be quite an athlete, but until the time I started the training program I hadn't run in 14 years! For me exercise consisted of trying to keep up with the demands of three budding adolescents as a single working mother while finishing the last semester of my undergraduate degree. (It had taken me 19 years to get through college! The only other things I've done that long are wear the same bathrobe and breathe! Marriage, children, divorce, and trying to make a living have a way of intervening, and two decades can pass before you know it.) I work too hard, and play too little. I'm so busy meeting everyone else's needs, I forget to consider my own. I would like to take better care of myself, but most of the time am just too tired to care. I have dreams, but little energy to make them happen. I usually just kind of take life as it comes, rather than going out after it. And I want more, but I don't make it happen. Sound like anyone you know?

Running a marathon was one of those dreams I had carried with me since I sat before the television and watched Bill Rodgers cross the finish line of the Boston Marathon — not once, but several times. Although I ran track in high school and beyond, the idea of running a marathon only flickered until the fall of November, 1994. It was a dream whose time had come...there I sat, fingers crossed, holding my breath, hoping that out of the 162 people who had attended the informational meeting for the "Marathon Class," mine would be one of the 50 names drawn from the bag. With my chances dwindling with the reading of each name, I struggled to make sense of it. Ever since returning to college two years before and hearing about the "Marathon Class" I had checked with Dr. Whitsett each semester since to see if it were going to be offered. How could it be that now in what would be my last semester, I wouldn't get in? Until now I had just taken for granted that I would be in the course if it were offered. Just like I had taken for granted that I would actually be able to run a marathon as a part of this class. Apparently, that was too much to assume. I started to feel very old, out of shape, and out of place in the company of so may young, hard-bodies. How could I honestly have thought that I could run a marathon!

So, with eight names left to be drawn, I prayed. "God, I have wanted to do this for so long. I don't know if I can do this, but I'm afraid if I don't do it now, I never will. If it's not going to kill me, please let me try. Amen." With a sigh, and a sense of peace, I opened my eyes — just as my name was being announced! You would've thought I was actually crossing the finish line the way my arms flew up and I shrieked a joyful, "YES!" As most stared, and some laughed, I beamed in the glow of answered prayer. I had my chance — and I knew I would live to tell about it!

One month later I was literally flat on my back. I had (once again) injured my lower back and as I lay on an ice pack I again found myself searching to make sense of the situation. Why did this have to happen now? I was already supposed to have started the preliminary training, and it was all I could do to walk from the couch to the freezer to change ice packs! Maybe my mother was right. When I'd told her I was going to run a marathon her response was, "Don't you have enough going on already?" My own kids hadn't been much more supportive...only recently had their initial, "Yeah, right!" wilted into a weak, "Oh, whatever."

I guess I could understand their skepticism. After all, this certainly wasn't the first time I had come up with a big idea only to have something unexpected "keep" me from going through with it. I hated that tendency about myself. Despite all my noble intentions, there always seemed to be an excuse handy for not starting or for stopping shortly after I'd just begun.

As I lay there with my back going numb and my mood growing dark sorting through all the possible culprits to blame for my current situation, the only deserving person I could come up with was me. But I refused to believe that my getting into the class had been an accident. I had asked God to let me in the class, and He had. I was supposed to be there; I was supposed to run this marathon. My family's lack of initial support had nothing to do with my current situation. I had done it to myself, and I had to accept that and take responsibility for getting myself out of it. In that mental moment, I started my training. I vowed that I was not going to let anyone or anything keep me from doing this — including me. I got off the couch. I went outside and hobbled one block. One block — that's where I started! Nineteen weeks later I ran 26.2 miles!

Moral of the story: If I can do it, anyone can do it! I don't believe it was an accident that you picked up this book, and have read this far. You can do this, if you want to. The only prerequisite is that you really want to. You don't have to be in shape — you don't even have to like to run. You only have to be willing to make yourself a priority equal to all the others in your life for 16-20 weeks. If you follow the training program as outlined in this book you will finish a marathon! And it will be an experience that will change you forever.

But don't take my word for it. Let me introduce you to some other past participants and their reasons for wanting to run a marathon. At the time she started the program, Chris Henle was a 21-year-old who had never run more than two miles. In fact, she hated to run! Why would someone who hated to run even contemplate running a marathon! Here's what she said:

I guess it was the challenge that intrigued me. I hated to run, and had never run more than two miles in my life. Because of that, running a marathon was so unlikely for me that the class seemed like a good way to try it. When I first started the pretraining in December, I had friends who smoked and still ran better than I did! That was really frustrating, but I stuck with it.

Chris wasn't the only one who hated to run. During the informational meeting Patti Hasty Rust bravely asked the very question that many others were probably thinking. She remembers that she asked:

Has anybody ever taken the class and finished the marathon who did not like to run? And everybody just kind of laughed. I don't think Dave or Forrest really knew how to answer the question — evidently no one had or had ever admitted it.

During the meeting, different people had talked about what a neat experience it was, and how afterward they felt that they could do anything. Hearing stuff like that gets you excited about doing this, but you also think, "Oh come on, could it really have that big an impact on your whole outlook?"

But the thought of running a marathon intrigued me, and the prospect that these two men could take someone who didn't even like to run and train that person to run a 26.2 marathon was enticing. Even though I was 31 years old, really out of shape, had a one-year-old son, had a million other things going on in my life, and hated to run, I put my name in the bag. And it got drawn! I felt like it was meant to be.

I used the pretraining schedule they gave us. I basically started from ground zero...alternating five minutes of jogging with five minutes of walking, and gradually building up from there. By the time class started, I was running for 30 minutes straight, but it wasn't anywhere near five miles — maybe half of that because I was so slow. But Forrest said not to worry about it, so I didn't. I thought, "Hey, if the expert's not concerned, why should I be?"

Another non-runner, 22-year-old Keith Wendl's initial reasons for running a marathon were much more tangible:

To attract girls! I had my sights on one in particular; she had participated in the 1993 Marathon Class. But along with that, I had always been impressed by the people who came out of that class. They seemed to be the leaders on campus or in organizations; they were always so posi-tive. I wanted to be a part of that.

Even though the class wasn't going to be offered until after I graduated, I attended the informational meeting. As I sat there and listened, I knew that this was going to be a turning point in my life. I was either going to get picked and stay for the class, or I would leave campus after gradua-tion and get a job. My name got picked! There hasn't been a day since that I haven't been grateful because the experience of that class has forever changed my life.

Jill Miller, a 23-year-old participant in the 1993 class remembers it this way:

It was November. I was sitting in Dr. Whitsett's psychology class when he told us about a class he and another instructor were offering the following semester known as the "Marathon Class." I had never been an avid runner; in fact, I had never run more than two miles at one time in my life. Until that moment, I never would have dreamed that I could run a marathon. But as he talked about the students in the past who had taken the class and finished and about how it had changed their lives, I knew this was something I wanted to do. And he was right — the techniques I learned in preparation for running a marathon have changed my life. I now apply them to everything I do. It was the most positive experience of my life. I learned to believe in myself, push my limits, and turn my dreams into reality.

Jennifer Dykes enjoyed the unique position of serving as a research assis-tant during the 1995 Class. She not only participated as a class member, but helped to gather and record the psychological data being investigated during that semester. This 20-year-old was already running three miles per day prior to the start of the class and had this to say about the experience:

Looking back, it was definitely one of the best experiences I've had. I made a lot of friends along the way, but became especially close to one woman in particular. We have committed to run at least one race per year together. I can still remember the feeling crossing the finish line. It was awesome!

Many people ask, "How did you manage to do all the training and even-tually run the marathon?" For me, I just ran. I don't know any other way to get through it...you just run until it's time to stop. The next time

you run for a little bit longer until it's time to stop. And after the run,
you look back and wonder, just like everyone else, how you ever did it.

Jane Mortenson was one of several members from the community who were not officially in the class, but followed the training program and ran with the class during the long runs and the marathon. A non-runner until in her 40s who started running with her teenage sons, Jane had a long-standing desire to know what it felt like to cross that finish line:

I had watched people run long distances before and wanted to just be
one of them for a while and see what it was like; experience it for myself.
It's nothing that anyone can tell you how it feels. It's something you've
got to experience for yourself. Having had a bout with breast cancer, I
definitely wanted to experience everything I could. That doesn't mean
just reading books about it — you have to do it yourself. The cancer
taught me that you have to experience anything and everything you
can. Running a marathon gives you the confidence to do other things.
For example, now that I am faced with a recurrence of the cancer and
have a lot of challenges ahead of me, I find myself thinking, "If I can do
that marathon, I can do this." It's a good thing to have in your personal
blueprint. Running a marathon is not easy, but it is definitely worth-
while.

Originally from Warrensburg, Missouri, 25-year-old Elizabeth Kilgore reports, "This program works. After I did it, I trained two of my friends to run long distances with these same techniques. They said they couldn't have done it without the tools I taught them."

The accounts could go on and on...in fact, if I included one from each of the participants who have officially gone through this training program as a class member or unofficially on their own, there would be well over 300 reports here...each different, yet all the same in the fact that this experience has profoundly affected their lives. As we mentioned earlier, out of the five classes of participants, only one person has failed to finish the marathon (his story will come later). That is a success ratio that few researchers or trainers can claim. As Elizabeth Kilgore said, this program works. All you have to do is follow it without allowing your own self-doubt to get in the way.

Do something for me, for yourself, that might help you decide. Go for a walk — by yourself. Leave the walkman at home. Leave the day behind and as you walk, listen. Listen to what you're normally too busy to hear. Nature. Your body. Your heart. The Higher Power at work in your life, if that is your belief. Listen to the "yeah, buts..." and ask yourself if you are going to continue to let them control you, or if it's time that you took control of them. Granted, running a marathon is certainly not the only way to exercise control over your life. But it is one way. And it could be your way. We will lead you through it, and if you follow our instructions, you will finish. And it will change your life. That's a promise.

The Marathoners

Here is a list of all the runners we have quoted in this book. By giving you some information about each of them, we hope to illustrate the wide range of experience, size, age and weight of the people who have become marathoners by following the training program outlined here. There are 10 men and 16 women described below. They range in age from 19 to 55, in height from 5'0" to 6'2", and in weight from 100 lbs. to 230 lbs. Most had little or no running experience before beginning to train on our program. A few had done a fair amount of running before. All of them completed the marathon, and so will you.

Mark Block: Age 22, 6'2", 160 lbs. Had been a high school miler and 2 mile runner and a collegiate cross country runner before breaking his neck in an auto accident. The accident occurred in August of 1986. He did the marathon in May of 1988. (See his story in Chapter 9.)

Heidi Brandt: Age 21, 5'10", 138 lbs. Ran for exercise several times a week, but had never run in a race or for more than 45 minutes at a time before starting to train for the marathon.

Jennifer Dykes: Age 20, 5'4", 120 lbs. Had been running up to 3 miles a day for 2 years before beginning marathon training, but said she "never liked to do it."

Don Greene: Age 37, 5'6", 175 lbs. Had been a high school athlete, but had been inactive for many years before beginning marathon training.

Jason Haglund: Age 21, 6'2", 165 lbs. Had been a 400 and 800 meter runner in high school, but had not run at all for 3 years before starting to train for the marathon.

Jennifer Haglund: Age 21, 5'3", 114 lbs. Had been a high school miler and 2 miler, but had not run for 3 years before beginning marathon training.

Geraldine Zapf Hall: Age 55, 5'6", 130 lbs. Had done some jogging up to 3 miles and had run "a few 5 kilometer races and one 10 kilometer race but I walked some of the way in those."

Scott Hazleton: Age 20, 5'10", 175 lbs. No prior running experience. "Absolutely none," he said.

Chris Henle: Age 21, 5'7", 118 lbs. She had occasionally jogged up to 2 or 3 miles prior to starting marathon training.

Todd Hixson: Age 20, 6'1", 180 lbs. No running experience as such, but had played high school football and basketball.

Eric Johnson: Age 20, 6'1", 210 lbs. Had done some light jogging up to 3 miles but "not on any regular basis."

Amy Kepler: Age 20, 5'8", 135 lbs. Had done some running before, including some distances over 10 miles.

Elizabeth Kilgore: Age 25, 5'4", 130 lbs. No prior running experience.

Tanjala Kole: Age 37, 5'6", 215 lbs. Had been a track athlete in high school, but had not done any running for many years.

Jeri Kurtzleben: Age 23, 5'7", 135 lbs. She had run occasionally but never on a regular basis and never over 3 miles. She told us, "Before starting to train for the marathon, I thought you had to be a world class runner to exceed 3 miles on a regular basis."

Bob Leslie: Age 22, 5'11", 160 lbs. Had been a cross-country and track runner in high school, but had not run for over a year before beginning marathon training.

Jill Miller: Age 23, 5'7", 123 lbs. Had done some light jogging up to 1 or 2 miles before beginning marathon training.

Jane Mortensen: Age 44, 5'8", 149 lbs. Had been an occasional jogger and had run a couple of 5 kilometer races ("slowly," she told us) before starting to train with our group. Jane decided to train for the marathon "to see what it would feel like to cross the finish line" and because she was dealing with the pain of cancer and its treatment and thought the "endorphins that come with heavy exercise might help."

Michelle Roland: Age 23, 5'4", 120 lbs. Had been running about 30 miles a week before she started training with our group (even though she was not enrolled in our class.)

Patti Hasty Rust: Age 31, 5'5", 145 lbs. Had tried jogging a couple of times but said she "didn't like it at all." Decided to take our course and train with us anyway.

Kathy Schneider: Age 19, 5'0", 100 lbs. No prior running experience.

Ron Steele: Age 37, 5'9", 170 lbs. Had run 6 previous marathons. Was a local news anchor who became interested in our class and our approach to marathon training.

Julie Stone: Age 22, 5'8", 126 lbs. Had done some running up to 6 or 7 miles before beginning marathon training.

Eric Stoneman: Age 21, 6'2", 230 lbs. His running experience was limited to "one 600-yard run in the Presidential fitness test in school and few laps here and there when I goofed off during high school football practice and the coach made me run."

Tricia Tuttle: Age 22, 5'7", 140 lbs. Had done a little running but said she "didn't like it because I thought you had to be fast to enjoy running."

Keith Wendl: Age 22, 6'0", 175 lbs. Participated in track in high school, but had run only occasionally since then...("only when I was interested in a woman who was a runner.")

Chapter 1:

Week One

Beginning the Training Program

 PART 1 Making Your Own Reality

We human beings have a unique capacity to make our own reality. We are pretty sure that all the other creatures are stuck with reality as it is, but we have the ability to imagine things as we wish them to be and, by a fascinating psychological twist, we then begin to behave as if that is really how things are. Sometimes that ability works to our advantage and sometimes it doesn't, but even that is within our power to determine.

Here is how it works. In the frontal lobes of your brain, (the part that fills your forehead), you have the ability to make visual and auditory images of things that you want to happen in the future, or of things that you hope will not happen in the future, or even interpretations of things that are going on right now. If, when you make these images, you develop the belief that they will come to pass or are taking place the way you have imagined them, they influence your present and future behavior through creating expectations.

For example, if your head is full of images of yourself running easily and effortlessly on your long training run of the week and you are telling yourself that you feel strong and powerful and can run forever, you will have a more enjoyable run than if your head is full of images of yourself suffering and straining and if you are saying to yourself, "I am exhausted. I am dying. I can't keep this up." And this will be true whether your body would have been feeling strong that day or not! That is, your state of mind creates a bodily reality!

Now of course there are limits to this, but what we are telling you is that your mind does influence your experience in profound ways and it does so all day, every day. If you allow your brain to be full of negative images, your experiences will be mostly negative. If, on the other hand, you become skilled at creating positive images, your experiences will be mostly positive. That is what it means to create your own reality. We will be returning to this idea often in this book, but for the moment we want to discuss a particularly important aspect of this reality.

Locus of Control

Psychologists have been studying people's concepts of what is called locus of control for many years. The word locus means "place" and what the psychologists are interested in is what effect it has on people if they believe the place of control in their lives is somewhere inside them as compared to the effect it has on them if they believe their lives are controlled by forces outside themselves.

Before reading on, stop and think about this for a few moments. What do you believe? Are you mostly in control of the events in your life? Do you hold yourself responsible for how things go for you? Or do you tend to assign the credit (or blame) to others or to luck, fate or some other force outside your own influence? If you believe that you are mostly in control of the events in your life, you tend toward what psychologists call an internal locus of control. If you believe that your life is mostly controlled by forces outside you, you lean toward having an external locus of control.

No matter which of these two points of view sounds more like you, we are not talking about reality here. That is, for our purposes in this discussion, it doesn't matter whether the events in your life are REALLY in your control or not; it only matters whether you THINK they are. If people believe they are in control of events in their own lives, they usually try to exercise that control, whereas if they feel what they do or don't do makes little or no difference in how things turn out, they usually don't even try to influence events. When it comes to training for a marathon, it helps a lot to adopt an internal locus of control because you are going to need a lot of determination and motivation to get this done. We are going to be giving you a lot of help with developing that internal locus of control as we go along, but for the moment it will be a good idea to begin working on convincing yourself that you can do anything you set out to do. Believing that is a very important part of developing an internal locus of control. If this subject interests you and you want to know more about it, check the article by Julian Rotter that is included in the readings list at the back of this book.

Beginning Your Training

The Training Program at a Glance

You are now ready to begin the more structured training program. As we showed you in the introduction to this book, this program lasts 16 weeks and if you are able to complete the entire program, you will be able to complete the marathon. This is a program that prepares you to finish your first marathon. It is not a program that will necessarily allow you to run a marathon in the best time you could possibly run it. It will allow you to have a successful first effort and will lay the groundwork for future marathons if you so desire. Sixteen weeks of training is the shortest program that will consistently allow success. The program is also a four-day-per-week training program. We have experimented with training programs of four to six days per week and have found that four-days-per-week programs are just as successful as programs involving more than four-days-per-week. We conducted an experimental study of just this issue and found no difference in the four-day-per week program and a six-day-per-week program. (See the article describing this study at the back of the book.) The runners in the study liked having three days of recovery each week as opposed to just one day. After you get a marathon or two under your running shoes, you may want to experiment with more frequent training sessions per week, but for this first marathon, we have full confidence that four-days-per-week is the appropriate frequency of training.

The four-day-per-week training program includes two "short" days, one "medium" day and one "long" day each week. This program is built on the principle that the most crucial element of training for your first marathon is to get in one "long" run each week. Initially this long run is not so long, but is long relative to the distance you will be running on the other days of the week. As the program progresses, the long runs become longer and longer compared to the other three days of the week. The longest single run is 18 miles during weeks 12 and 13. Trust us, if you can go 18 miles in training, you can go 26.2 miles during the marathon.

A second general principle that is adhered to in this program is that once you begin the structured training program, the training mileage should not increase more than 10% per week. Increasing training mileage too quickly will increase the chance for injury, the number one enemy of any marathoner. Each time mileage is increased, the body needs a week to adapt to the increase. If the increase is too great, the body does not completely adapt and after several weeks the tissues begin to break down and become injured. Also, it is a big mistake for "average" runners to try to mimic the training programs of high-ability runners. To think that the average runner could run 80-100 miles per week without suffering injury or overtraining syndrome is nonsense. High ability runners can train 80-100 miles per week because they have a genetic ability that allows them to train at these high miles. Even if she or he could run 80-100 miles per week or more it would not permit the average runner to run a marathon in under two and a half hours as high ability runners do. This high level ability is primarily due to genetics and only a very small percentage of the population is born with this kind of ability. We can all get better by running more marathons and by improving our training, but it is unreasonable to try to do what elite runners do.

A third aspect of the training program is that the recovery days should be spread out over the week and not bunched together. You should not run four days in succession and recover three days in succession. If at all possible, one recovery day should precede the long run and one recovery day should follow the long run. The long run should be sandwiched between two recovery days. The recovery day prior to the long run helps ensure adequate muscle fuel to be able to do the long run and the recovery day following the long run helps ensure that the desired training adaptations will occur and injury risks will be reduced. The third recovery day should be used at some point during the remaining three training days. This pattern for the recovery days becomes more important as the long runs become longer. For the first several weeks of the program it will not be as crucial, but establishing an early general pattern of training/recovery will he helpful as you progress in your training.

Beginning now with the formal training program, the training will be described in terms of mileage, not time as it has been in the preliminary training program. Although exact and precise distances are not imperative, you should have a pretty good estimate of your mileage. Go out in your car or bicycle and measure off several running routes of 3-8 miles. Variety in running routes is useful for motivational purposes. Running the same route every day can become very boring for some people. Also, running on soft ground as opposed to asphalt or concrete will be helpful in decreasing the risk for injury. It may not always be possible to run on soft ground, but take advantage of the opportunity when you can. One last suggestion regarding running surfaces is in order. Running next to the curb on most roads is not recommended. The problem is that most roads are sloped toward the curb and when you run next to the curb facing traffic, your right leg is always running on a higher surface than your left leg. If this becomes a habit, it can cause enough biomechanical alteration in your normal running gait that injury is more likely to occur. If you can't run on a running trail or level ground, it is better to run on a sidewalk than next to the curb because sidewalks are normally level side to side. If you must run on a road, move out from the curb as far as possible but be cautious and watchful for oncoming traffic.

Week 1 Training
Day 1: 3 miles
Day 2: 4 miles
Day 3: 3 miles
Day 4: 5 miles
Total for Week: 15 miles

You should be at a point in your preliminary training that allows you to jog 30 minutes continuously. The mileage for the first week of the training program is going to be increased to a total of 15 miles. The two short days are 3 miles each, the medium day is 4 miles, and the long day is 5 miles.

How Fast Should You Run?

Your pace each day should be one that is "cardiovascularly comfortable" for you especially during the first 15 minutes of the run. Starting out a run at too fast a pace can be devastating. Starting out at a pace that is slower than your normal pace allows for proper warm-up and will enhance your ability to finish the run. At no point during the run should you feel it is difficult to breathe in a rhythmical fashion. If you do, you should slow down. Your legs may become fatigued, but this is normal and expected. The major objective of the first several weeks of training is to just get some mileage in. However, pacing is important and we have included a section in Part Two of Chapter 9 called "Determining your Appropriate Training Intensity." You should skip ahead and read that section right now before continuing this chapter.

Now that you have read the material in Chapter 9 about using the RPE as an indication of how hard you are working when you run (you DID go and read that, didn't you? If not, do it now or the next paragraph won't make complete sense to you) we want to introduce to you an important feature of the book that will appear in each chapter from now on.

It is a training log and it will appear as the last page of each chapter. What we want you to do is fill it in as you go. As you will see, we have provided a space for each training day and within that space there are places for you to enter the number of miles called for in the training program for each day, the number of miles you actually ran (we hope these two numbers are the same for most, if not all, of the days), your RPE (rate of perceived exertion) and then a comments space where we suggest you write things like what the route was that you ran, who was with you, what the weather was like, how you felt mentally and physically during and after the run, any injuries you may experience and what you are doing about them, etc. When you get farther into the training period, this will become a very valuable tool, both physically and psychologically, to use as a review of what you have accomplished. Try to establish the habit of filling it in right after each run when everything about the run is fresh in your mind.

Running Shoes

Good running shoes are a marathoner's best friend and you should not underestimate the value of appropriate running shoes. If you do not have or cannot afford a pair of good running shoes, don't train for a marathon. Invariably you will get injured and wind up spending far more on treatment of the injury than you would have on a pair of running shoes.

Shoes act as shock absorbers for the forces that are developed during running. Running is classified as a "traumatic" type of exercise because of the constant pounding that occurs. The bigger you are and the more and faster you run, the more important shoes become. It is the constant pounding and the forces that are developed each time the foot strikes the ground that eventually causes most running injuries. At best, good running shoes can eliminate injuries and at worst they can reduce the chances of serious running injuries.

Fortunately the runner has a wide selection of good running shoes from which to choose. However, there are some important distinctions between types of running shoes that should be understood in order to select the most appropriate type for your foot and running biomechanics.

Types of Running Shoes

There are four primary types of running shoes produced by most manufacturers and made for training on roadways, sidewalks and smooth tracks and trails. The four types are motion-control shoes, stability shoes, cushioned shoes, and lightweight training shoes. Because shoe types have some overlapping characteristics, several shoe types may be appropriate for any given runner. Experience and a little "trial and error" will help you to eventually select the best shoe type for you. Lightweight running shoes will not be discussed since they are primarily for high-ability runners.

Motion-control shoes are designed to control excessive or uncontrolled movement in the joints of the foot. These shoes are constructed to be relatively rigid, and offer stability and maximum support along the inside border of the shoe. These shoes are particularly appropriate for heavy runners with flat feet in need of extra durability and control of foot movement.

Stability shoes are characterized by a good blend of cushioning, support along the inside border of the shoe and durability. They are made for normal-sized runners who do not need a lot of motion control.

Cushioned shoes have the most cushioned mid-soles and the least support

along the inside border of the shoe. They are for runners who hav
feet who underpronate. (See definition of pronation below.) They are g
for runners with high arches who do not overpronate.

What is Your Foot Type?

In order to know which of the three categories of shoes would be best for you,
you should determine your basic foot type. Foot types fall into three categories,
normal, flat, and high-arched. To understand the relationship of the various
foot types and the appropriate type of shoe for each, a brief description of foot
mechanics during running would be helpful. Part of the role of the foot in running is to act as a shock absorber to the tremendous forces developed as each
foot strikes the ground. In order for the foot to be a good shock absorber, there
must be some movement in the foot as it strikes the ground. Normally, the foot
should strike the ground at the heel or mid-foot and then roll inward toward
the inside margin of the foot. This is called pronation and the movement helps
to distribute the landing forces over more of the foot's surface area. If the foot
does not pronate sufficiently (called a supinated foot), the forces are focused on
a smaller area of the outside portion of the foot. In some cases, the foot
overpronates, rolling inward too much. This puts strain on the muscles, joints,
and tendons of the lower leg.

Normal feet have a normal-sized arch. When a normal foot lands on the
ground, the foot rolls inward (pronates) in order to absorb and distribute the
landing forces over more of the foot. Normal-weighted runners with a normal
foot usually do best in a stability shoe with moderate control features. Runners
with normal feet and biomechanics usually show shoe wear on the outer edge of
the heel, under the ball of the foot, and at the front of the sole.

The flat foot is characterized by a low arch which causes over-pronation when
the foot lands on the ground. This excessive motion can lead to various overuse
injuries and one should attempt to control the motion by wearing motion-control
or stability shoes with firm mid-soles and control features. Do not wear highly
cushioned shoes with little stability and control. Runners with over-pronation
problems show shoe wear along the inside edge to the heel and forefoot.

The high-arched foot doesn't pronate enough when it strikes the ground resulting in poor shock-absorption characteristics. The best type of shoe for the
runner with a high arch is a cushioned shoe. The idea is to encourage more foot
motion so this runner should stay away from motion-control or stability shoes.
Runners with high-arched feet show shoe wear along the outer portion of the
heel and forefoot.

How to Tell Which Type of Foot You Have

There is an easy way to get a pretty good idea what kind of foot you have.

Normal Arch. *Feet with a normal arch leave an imprint that has a relatively wide band connecting the forefoot with the heel. The band is usually about a third to half the width of the fore-foot.*	***Flat Foot.*** *The flat foot has a wide band connecting the forefoot and the heel. The band is almost as wide as the forefoot.*	***High-Arched Foot.*** *The high-arched foot does not have a con-necting band between the forefoot and the heel. Also, some of the inside portions of the forefoot and heel do not make an im-print giving the characteristic highly-curved imprint.*

Moisten the bottom of your feet and step on a piece of dark paper (so the foot imprint shows). Compare your imprint to the three diagrams in Figure 1.1.

Replacing Running Shoes

Running shoes are very much like the tires on your car — they both wear out after they have accumulated enough mileage. The need to replace running shoes should be determined primarily by the accumulated mileage. Most good running shoes will last about 500 miles. This will vary somewhat according to your size and running mechanics, with smaller, efficient runners getting more mileage out of their shoes. Unfortunately, it is difficult to tell by looking at a running shoe if it is time to replace it. Running shoes can look pretty good in outward appearance but their shock absorbing qualities may be all used up. Wearing running shoes too long increases the chance of injury. Runners should regularly replace their running shoes after they have accumulated sufficient mileage.

Which Brand is Best?

There is no one best brand of running shoe. All major manufacturers (Nike, Saucony, Reebok, Adidas, Avia, Mizuno, Etonic, Brooks, and Asics) make excellent running shoes in all the shoe types discussed above. A good shoe will usually have a retail price of $60-$200. The $200 shoe is not necessarily better than the $60 shoe, but it usually has more bells and whistles. Most runners can get along just fine with $60-$80 shoes. The major criterion should be how the shoes fit your feet. Running shoes should feel comfortable when you first put them on. Running shoes should also be slightly larger (1/2 size) than normal shoes because the foot swells about half a size when running. Some space should be left between the longest toe and the front of the shoe. The heel should fit snugly into the heel counter. The shoe should be wide enough to allow the foot to move upwards. Some experimentation with different types of running shoes may be necessary before you find the one just right for you. However, too frequent experimentation can be expensive. Once you have found a shoe that feels comfortable and hasn't caused any significant discomfort or injuries, stick with it. Don't be overly swayed by the tremendous amount of advertising for running shoes. You are the only one that knows what shoe feels the best.

Twice each year in October and April, the running magazine *Runner's World* publishes an excellent buyers' guide to the newest and latest running shoes. This is an excellent resource of the current trends in the running shoe industry and should be an indispensable resource for runners.

Running Clothing

The importance of appropriate running clothing varies with the seasonal changes in temperature and humidity. During neutral to hot weather, the major concern is getting rid of the enormous amounts of body heat that can be produced by running and the general rule is that less clothing and loose clothing is better. The more the skin surface is exposed, the easier it is to get rid of the heat produced by muscular contractions. Loose clothing allows more optimal heat removal because it is easier for air currents to reach the skin and for sweat to evaporate.

High humidity compounds the problem of getting rid of body heat. When you exercise on a hot day, most of your body heat is eliminated through a process called evaporation. This is the process where you sweat and then the sweat is evaporated from the skin. It is the evaporation of the sweat that actually produces the majority of the heat loss. If the air already has a high content of water in it (i.e., high humidity) it becomes more difficult and sometimes impossible to evaporate the sweat. If the sweat doesn't evaporate, heat loss is negligible. Think of a time you exercised on a warm and humid day. Remember how the sweat seemed to just roll off you. It really was rolling off because it was not evaporating due to the humidity. On warm days with higher humidity, you need to cut back on the pace you run and make sure you drink a lot of fluids as explained in Chapter 5. Don't feel bad about running at a slower pace on warm and humid days.

In cold weather, the problem is to keep too much heat from escaping to the environment. The goal is to provide adequate insulation while avoiding accumulation of sweat in the clothing. Multiple layers of clothing are ideal because air is trapped between layers and acts as insulation. The innermost layer should be made of a moisture-wicking material like polypropylene, so that moisture is carried away from the skin. You want the layer of clothing next to the skin to remain as dry as possible because this reduces heat loss. In windy and rainy weather, the outer layer should be water and wind resistant.

The tendency for the novice runner is to overdress for the cold weather. If you dress so that you are comfortable while you are not running, you will overheat when you start to run. Theoretically, you should be cool at the beginning of the run but as you begin to produce more and more heat, you warm up and remain comfortable for the remainder of the run. Perhaps a better way to allow for this warm-up effect is to wear an outer layer that can be easily removed when you get warmed up and reapplied should it be necessary.

Another factor that can dramatically affect the type and amount of clothing that should be worn is the wind. When you run an out-and-back course, the wind may be in your face for half the distance and at your back for the other half. More clothing may be necessary when the wind is in your face than when it is at your back. The ability to remove and add a layer of clothing will easily solve this problem. Some runners prefer to run out with the wind at their backs and return with the wind in their faces once they are producing maximal heat. This would be more a matter of preference since adding and removing clothing would have the same effect.

There are two conditions related to running clothing which might impair training but are easily solved. The first, referred to as "runner's nipple," is irritation of the nipples (in both males and females) due to the friction of the clothing and often complicated by sweating. This tends to occur more often as the runs get longer and longer. As the clothing next to the skin absorbs sweat, the clothing becomes more gritty and increases the friction against the nipples. It can become so severe in some runners that the nipples actually begin to bleed.

There is no reason to suffer painful or bleeding nipples. There are several solutions and it is recommended that you select the one that works best for you. One solution is to put band-aids over the nipples. A second solution is use some type of lubricant, like Vaseline, to reduce the friction. A third solution is to make sure that the clothing next to the skin is the type of material that transports the sweat to the outside layers and does not itself become saturated with moisture. In females, this will obviously apply to the bra.

The second condition that can cause some inconvenience is chaffing of the skin on the inner thighs caused from the exposed thighs rubbing together. Again, this is more likely to occur as the running distances get longer and longer. This can easily alleviated by wearing longer shorts, like biking shorts, or by using a lubricant on the thighs, like Vaseline.

For either runner's nipples or thigh chaffing, an ounce of prevention is worth a pound of cure. If you know you are susceptible to either of these conditions, or just want to play it safe, use the preventive solutions described above before the problem develops. Although neither of these conditions should prevent you from training, training will be more comfortable if the conditions are prevented from developing.

How to Construct Your Own Reality

As we said earlier, reality is not a "once and for all" thing. It's something that we constantly recreate through our beliefs and behaviors. Change your thoughts or actions and you change your reality. Think what that means...you are the architect of your life. You are the one who takes the raw materials and experiences and constructs the structure that is your life. Think of the power and responsibility associated with being designer, contractor, and resident all in one. Then realize that most of us do this without knowing what we're doing. That's like building a house blindfolded. Awesome and scary at the same time!

So how does one, especially a non-runner, construct his or her own reality when it comes to doing a marathon? That's what the rest of this book is about. Dave and Forrest have already given you a few of the pieces. In the rest of this chapter, I and other past participants are going to talk more about those and add a couple more. Throughout each week of training you will be given additional pieces of information that will be crucial to your successful completion of the marathon — like pieces of a puzzle being handed to you just when you need them.

But if you're like me, it's easy to get impatient and anxious when it feels like there is a lot at stake and someone else is in control. So let's start with an issue that I think is basic to this whole program and your level of success in it. Trust. I know the subject crossed my mind at this point in the training, and I had even known Dave for a couple years before that. I knew that he was a person who genuinely cared for people and took seriously his professional responsibility to his students. I trusted him with my mind. But now we were talking about my body. I don't know why that should feel any different to me, but it did. For the next sixteen weeks it felt like I was essentially turning over my body (and mind) to these two professors knowing that they were going to physically and mentally lead me somewhere I'd never been before. It felt scary, and I wondered if I could — or should — trust them. Maybe you're feeling the same way. If so, get in the "skeptic" line behind me. If trust isn't an issue for you, great! You may want to skip the next section.

My job in this book is to give it to you straight. Now, that's not to say that Dave and Forrest aren't, because I know that what they're telling you is true and works. But you don't know that yet. This undertaking may be the most monumental physical and mental task that you have ever undertaken. Second-guessing the validity of the program will only work against you. So I'm going to do that for you. I'm a great skeptic. I'm also a very poor liar, so what you get from me (and the other participants) will be straight from the hip. That way you can relax.

So, can you trust these guys and what they're saying? Yes. Every single person who has ever gone through this program would say the same thing -- especially the one and only guy who didn't finish! Whether or not to trust is a decision we make...it's part of the reality we create. I and the others you are about to meet know you can trust Dave and Forrest, but you must be the one to decide if you will.

Rob Leslie had run cross-country in high school, but never more than ten miles at one time. Initially, that turned out to be more of a disadvantage than an advantage:

I didn't know what to expect, because I was with a lot of people who hadn't run before. How were they expected to run a marathon! In less than four months time, Whitsett and Dolgener were going to train these people who had never run before to run a marathon. It didn't seem right to me. I was kind of worried.

They started us out really easy, like three miles and I wanted to go more but they discouraged me from doing so. It was hard to stay in that short amount of distance because of my previous running experience, but I followed the schedule. After a while I could see why it made sense, but at first it was hard.

Another skeptic was Eric Johnson, a 20-year-old from Vinton, Iowa who had never run more than three miles before:

At first I was skeptical because I didn't know how Whitsett could change me into a marathon runner. I have the body of a football player, not a marathoner. Because I thought I was in pretty good shape physically, I didn't prepare for the first long run. I thought I had it in the bag. When we actually did it the thought of five miles made me cry. I was hurting and didn't think I would be able to do it. I was scared. That was the last time I failed to take them seriously.

Ron Steele, managing editor of news operations for local television channel KWWL, audited the 1988 class and ran with them in the Drake Relays Marathon that spring. Although he had run other marathons prior to that one, still the issue of trust crossed his mind:

> *I already knew Forrest through my wife, and had high regard for him. I hadn't met Dave prior to the class, but it didn't take long for me to develop tremendous respect for him. I definitely wanted to believe what Forrest and Dave were saying. No doubt about that. They give you this nice training schedule that you are to follow, and to do that is certainly a form of trust. Even though I had trained for and run six other marathons, I had never seen anything like their training program. It seemed laid out perfectly. It was just fantastic! They give you the expectations and the tools you need to meet them. They make it easy for you. It's basically a no-brainer. You just cross off the days. I never doubted I was in good hands.*

Jane Mortenson had run a few 5K's (3.1 miles) before starting to train for the marathon at age 44. For her, trust really wasn't an issue:

> *I didn't worry too much about trust. I knew Dave had run so many marathons before and that Forrest was an expert in his field, so I just trusted that they knew what they were doing. I was really impressed by the level of concern they seemed to have for everyone. It didn't seem to matter if you were or were not a member of the class — everyone got equal attention, advice, help, and support.*

As I see it, there are really only two things that could keep you from achieving this goal. The first is if you get injured during training. The second is your attitude.

Before the training even began, I remember asking Forrest if he thought I was being realistic about thinking I could run a marathon. At 5'7" and 215 pounds, I was 80 pounds over my ideal weight. Walking up two flights of stairs was enough to wind me. I had a bad back. The only fruit to pass over my lips were the apples in the McDonalds apple pies I routinely ate with my Quarter-Pounder value meal. I felt like a hippo who was trying to run with the cheetahs. As he handed me the pretraining schedule, Forrest said, "Tange, the only thing that will keep you from doing this is if you get injured. Because of your weight, you're going to have to take it slower than the others, but that's no reason why you can't do this." I suppose he could have said I should just forget it, but he didn't. Bless his soul!

Throughout the training I was extra careful when it came to anything that might result in injury. I took seriously everything that Forrest said, and followed his recommendations as closely as possible. And I stayed injury-free.

The other potentially lethal issue is attitude. Trying to do this with a negative attitude is like trying to run in a lead coat with shackles on your feet. Odds are you won't make it...and if you do you will be so exhausted from the effort that it won't have been worth it. For this to be a successful experience, you must have a positive attitude. Attitude has nothing to do with facts and everything to do with perspective. Attitude doesn't change the fact that a glass is filled with fluid to its midpoint, but it determines whether you see the glass as half full or half empty. To run a marathon and feel good while doing it, you have to see things from a "half full" perspective.

For most of us, our normal perspective is just a matter of habit which we usually don't think much about. This would be a good time to think about it, because our usual perspective reflects our general attitude which becomes a part of our daily reality. So how does one change his or her attitude? By changing your perspective and the meanings you attach to situations. The fancy name for this is cognitive reframing. The simple explanation is that you make a point to see things in a different, more positive, way than you might otherwise have done. As a result, often you discover new meanings and different feelings associated with those same events, and it changes your reality.

Let me give you an example by repeating a journal entry I made a few weeks into the training:

> *Today there were times during the run when I started to hurt and waves of discouragement would hit me. When that happened I did what Dave said to do. Instead of whipping myself with a "Buck up you weeny" mental tongue lashing, I said, "Oh, there you are, pain; I've been waiting for you. Come run with me." The wash of relief I felt was immediate, profound, and invigorating. All the tension left my shoulders and gut. The ache in my knees and hips changed from one of external painful assault to one of internal friendly companion. My knees still ached, but it was OK. I watched my feet and enjoyed the sensation of flexing the joint in order to propel each foot forward. The sensation of movement was compelling and motivating.*

During the first few weeks of training when my knees would start to ache I would interpret that as "evidence" of how out of shape I was, how weak my knees were, and my fear of getting hurt escalated in correlation to the pain. Later in the training, although my knees still hurt, I made a conscious effort to interpret that ache as a sign of strength — a sign that the muscles and ligaments were getting stronger so that they could do what I was asking of them. The pain was the same. The difference was in how I was interpreting it, and how I felt as a result. Whereas before I was discouraged, fearful, and would use it as an excuse to stop, now I am encouraged, and wouldn't think of stopping because that would only weaken them. Everything is the same, except my thinking. Oh, the difference a mind can make.

I'm not the only one who used Dave's "Come run with me" technique. Eric Johnson reported, "I hated running hills at first, but I learned to think of it differently. I started greeting the hills by saying, 'Hello hills. Come on and run with me.' It changed the way I felt about hill running completely."

The feeling of being overwhelmed depends on whether your perspective is panoramic or more narrow. In this case, blinders are definitely recommended:

Patti Hasty Rust:

The first day of class when we got the running schedule I had a sudden attack of panic. I sat there looking at all those miles and thought, "Oh, my gosh! How am I ever going to do this?!? What am I doing here?" Thank goodness it was temporary. I still knew I wanted to do this, but just how many miles we were going to have to run didn't really hit me until I saw the schedule. It would be easy to get psyched out. So I tried to just focus on what I had to do that day.

Ron Steele:

Trying to get control of your vision, or how you see things, helps you as far as your perspective on everything that's going on around you. If you look at something and it's overwhelming, you need to break it down so that it's not so overwhelming.

Jane Mortenson:

It seemed overwhelming, but doable as long as I stayed focused on the small increments. It's just like life — you don't think you can get it all done, but if you break it down into little pieces then you can get through anything. So it was just a matter of staying focused on what to train for that day and not to think of the 26.2 miles.

Trusting yourself, adopting a more positive perspective overall, and accepting responsibility for the power you have to create your own reality through the choices you make are all components of developing an internal locus of control

(ILOC). There are some other things you can do that will help an ILOC to take root and blossom. But first, let's spend a minute on what ILOC isn't. It doesn't mean that you take a "looking out for number one and all others be damned" viewpoint. It doesn't mean that you suddenly have supernatural powers to do things that aren't humanly possible just because you think you can. Nor does it mean that you have to deny the fact that you need and want the love, support, and guidance of others.

Having an ILOC means that while you may not be able to control everything that happens to you, you are in control of how you react to those things through your thoughts and actions. Being aware of this and making conscious choices is how you exercise an ILOC. Choosing to train for and run a marathon is evidence of ILOC. By doing that you have chosen to experience something that most people probably would not choose. You are definitely not sitting back and waiting for life to come looking for you...you are out there chasing it!

There are some things that you can do to help your ILOC to take root. One is to tell others what you are doing. The reason for this is not to take a poll to see if in fact you should be doing this, nor are you seeking permission or validation for your decision. Rather, by identifying yourself to others as a person who is training for and intends to run a marathon, you are helping to create that identity for yourself to yourself. By telling others that you are going to run a marathon, you start to believe it yourself. So start telling others, but beware...you may not get the response you expected. But that's OK:

Chris Henle remembers, "When I told my family and friends that I was going to run a marthon I got quite an interesting mix of responses. Most were shocked, a few were impressed, and some even thought it was a form of torture!".

Given that she had run long distances previously, 20-year-old Amy Kepler was a bit surprised by her parent's reaction..."I don't think my parents understood what this marathon was all about. But while they may not have understood, they didn't try to stop me and in the end became one of my main sources of support."

Patti Hasty Rust, the devout non-runner, had this to say:

One thing that really stays in my mind is the different reactions I got from people as I told them what I was going to do. Most people just looked at me like, "You're crazy and I can't understand at all why on earth you would want to do something like that," and some people actually said exactly that. But a couple of people at work were impressed, which was encouraging and nice. Most of my family members were supportive, although my mother was just really surprised that I would even attempt anything like this. But I said, "Well, if Oprah can do it, I can do it!" And she said, "But Oprah doesn't have a one-year-old son." I think she was worried about the time factor. The way I looked at it, I had been taking one class a semester for a while in pursuit of my MBA, and I didn't see this taking any more time than any other class. It was just going to delay me a semester in graduating. To me, it was worth it.

Tricia Tuttle, another person who had never done much running because she basically hated to run, had similar feelings, "It was a unique experience. I knew it would require a lot of dedication. The more I told people about it the more I had to do it."

Even though she had previously run a few 10K's (6.2 miles), Geraldine Zapf Hall encountered skepticism from others when she announced her intentions regarding the marathon:

When I started telling people, the reactions were mixed. Some people would say, "Why are you doing that?" But it never bothered me. It just made me want to do it even more. I would just ask them back, "Why not? I always wanted to do this, and so why shouldn't I try?" There wasn't much they could say to that. The further I got in the training the more excited everyone got about it — even the skeptics!

So does operating from an ILOC mean that you have to go through this training entirely on your own? Heavens, no! Remember that this program has been offered in the context of a class, where participants not only share class time, but also do the weekly long run as a group. But that's not to say that success can only be realized if this is done with a group, because several people have taken this program and successfully completed it on their own or in the company of one or two others. How you do this is up to you. Here are a few ideas of what has worked for others:

Ron Steele:

The training is definitely something that somebody could do on his or her own outside of a group. I did! And I have used this same training program since to train for other marathons. The schedule is really easy to follow. It's still a challenge, but definitely doable.

Jane Mortenson:

I was already walking three days/week for 30 minutes at a time when I got the preliminary training information. From there I just went out and ran as far as I could, and then walked until I felt like I could run again. In a really short time I was running more than I was walking. Our first long run was five miles, and I actually made it! I was stunned! I had no idea that I could do that.

I must confess that initally I didn't think this was something I could do on my own. I ran with another student half of the time during the week-day runs, and that did help keep me on task. Just having one other person to run with and be accountable to really seemed to help me stick to it — especially at first. As you soon find out, though, especially when it comes to the long runs, you don't always end up staying together be-cause of your different paces. But just having someone to stretch with, start together with, and have those first few minutes with was a big help for me.

Keith Wendl:

Running with family or friends helps keep you committed. You know you have to do it or you're going to have to answer to others. Plus it helps make it a lot more fun. Being with those people became the best part of my day.

Jennifer and Jason Haglund offer a beautiful example of the good things that can come out of this experience — not only in the area of locus of control, but in other areas as well. They met and married as a result of this experience:

Jennifer Haglund:

One of the greatest impacts this experience had on me was that I be-came more of an internal person. I was able to succeed and improve through this experience like never before. As a result, I came to believe more each day that I had the power to make my own successes and control my own life.

Jason Haglund:

The greatest thing I gained from this experience is that I am a better person today because of it. It challenged me to make the most of myself and gave me the tools I needed to do just that. It wasn't just about run-ning a marathon — it was about learning about myself and how to create my own reality. Now I feel more confident about everything. Both

Jennifer and I credit the marathon class for giving us the confidence we need in order to venture into new and unknown areas and experience the world we live in.

General Tips from the Marathoners — Week One:

• I have terrible bunions. I kept trying different shoes, going back to the shoe stores asking for their advice and nothing seemed to help. Then Forrest recommended cutting holes in the shoes right where the bunions were. I took a knife and cut a hole through my new hundred dollar shoes right where the bunions were and then made the hole bigger with my finger. When I wore the shoes the bunions just popped through the hole and never bothered me at all after that. It was a lot cheaper than bunion surgery!

• Get your shoes as soon as possible. Once I had spent the money on the shoes I was mentally committed. I had never had shoes that expensive or that fit so well. Just wearing the shoes was enough to make me feel different about myself. Not to mention that once I started wearing those shoes my back stopped giving me problems! I think it had to do with the fact that for the first time in my life I was wearing shoes that gave me the support I needed and held my feet in alignment with the rest of my skeleton. It was amazing! I've worn the shoes ever since and have not been back to the chiropractor in over two years! That's what I call a miracle. And another thing, buy some good quality running socks to wear. Between the good fitting shoes and the cushy socks, you'll feel like you're walking on air. Plus, you'll feel like a marathoner.

	Scheduled Distance	Actual Distance	RPE

Day 1

3		

Comments:

Day 2

4		

Comments:

Day 3

3		

Comments:

Day 4

5		

Comments:

Total Miles This Week_____Cumulative Total_____

Chapter 2:

W e e k   T w o

Developing Your Training Base

Focusing On The Positive; "…But It Doesn't Matter."

As you begin developing your training base, one of the most important features of your mental preparation will be an ability to maintain a positive attitude. One of the things that has become clear to us through working with people training for the marathon is that in order to maintain a positive attitude about training and running, it is necessary to develop a positive attitude about life in general. It is almost impossible to be positive about training while being negative about most other aspects of your life.

To develop this kind of attitude, if you don't have it already, it will be important that you begin using a particular phrase whenever you catch yourself saying or thinking something negative. The phrase is, "..but it doesn't matter." We know how difficult it is, especially early in your marathon training, to avoid saying or thinking things like, "I am really tired today," or "My legs are sore today," or "The weather is really rotten today," and then to use these factors as reasons not to run that day. So, what we want you to do is this. Whenever one of these negative phrases comes into your mind or out of your mouth, we want you to add "but it doesn't matter" to the end of the sentence. Why? Because it really DOESN'T matter unless you believe it does. You can, and will, run anyway. And you will be really glad you did when you are finished.

Keep in mind that we want you to do this with regard to everything in your life, not just running. As we said above, it is very difficult to develop this attitude about training if you don't develop it about other aspects of your life. So, we want you thinking "..but it doesn't matter" if you happen to slip and think or say something like "My boss is really getting on my nerves today," or "This driver in front of me is a real jerk."

The general idea here is that if we can develop a view of ourselves that includes the idea that we routinely overcome WHATEVER obstacles we face, we will, in fact, overcome most if not all of them. During our marathon class, we work hard on developing this point of view, so our students are often heard to say during training runs, "There are a lot of hills in this run, but it doesn't matter." Or, "The wind is really strong today, but it doesn't matter." Later, when your mental discipline becomes even stronger, you will be saying things like "I love these hills and I love running into the wind," but for now, just work on adding "..but it doesn't matter" to any negative ideas you may have.

PART 2 | Physical Preparation

The first week of the training program is over and you can probably look back and say "That wasn't too bad." Because you are in the early stages of training, you are mentally and physically fresh and the amount of training you have done up to this point has not really taxed your mental and physical capabilities. Remember that one of the primary objectives of this early phase of training is to gradually allow the muscular and skeletal system to adapt to the trauma of running so you will not have an injury later on. You may not have many, or any, aches and pains from the first week of training and that is good. However, don't get overzealous and think you can go out and dramatically increase your mileage this second week because the first week was a piece of cake. This gradual progression is for a purpose — to be able to complete a marathon at the end of week 16.

> ### Week 2 Training
> Day 1: 3 miles
> Day 2: 4 miles
> Day 3: 3 miles
> Day 4: 6 miles
> ### Total for Week: 16 miles

The mileage for week two stays the same as week one except the long day is increased by one mile from five to six miles. The total mileage for the week will be 16 miles, with more than a third of the mileage occurring on the long run of the week. As these long runs get longer and longer, it will be increasingly more important that you try to take a day off running before and after the long run. In a few more weeks you will be doing enough mileage on the long run to really deplete your energy stores so you want to start paying close attention to your diet as well as having a recovery day following the long run.

Running Form

Have you ever watched someone else run and said to yourself "Wow, he runs funny," or "Wow, she runs so smoothly?" People do vary in how they run, and there is a correct way to run. Your running form can have a tremendous impact on your risk for injury and on how you perform at marathon time. Depending on what your running experience has been and what type of running you have done in the past, you may need to change your running form.

The running form that is best for marathon running is different than the running form that is best for sprinting a 100-yard dash. These two distances epitomize the two ends of the spectrum of running form. The individuals that usually have to make the most change in running form are those that have been competitive sprinters in high school or college or who have played sports requiring short bursts of speed, like football and basketball.

Does it really make a difference what your running form is like? It really does, for two primary reasons. First, running form is related to injuries. Incorrect running form, particularly in the lower body, increases the likelihood of injury. This is especially true when training for and running the marathon. The longer the distance you train, the more likely running form will have an impact on injury. When you train for the marathon and you spend hours running each week, small deviations from correct running form can become major problems when multiplied by the number of times your feet strike the ground during a week of training.

The second reason your form is important is because the amount of energy you have to expend to run is related to your form. If your form is very inefficient, you will have to expend more energy to cover the same distance at a particular pace and this will contribute to greater fatigue and poorer performance. Given any level of cardiovascular capacity, the more efficient you are in your running form, the easier it will be to run a given distance at a given pace.

Lower Body Running Form. The major issues in the lower body are the footstrike and the amount of vertical bounce you have. The footstrike refers to what kind of position the foot is in when it strikes the ground with each stride. For marathon training, the correct footstrike position is the heel-first or the flat-foot position. Either your heel should strike the ground first, like it does in walking, or your foot should land with the heel and forefoot contacting the ground at the same time. The wrong foot position is an initial forefoot strike, sometimes referred to as running on your toes. You run on your toes when you run at fast speeds for shorter distances. For slower speeds and longer distances like the marathon, running on your toes increases the likelihood of injury because it causes much more stress on the supporting structures of the foot. Each time the foot strikes the ground it absorbs tremendous forces and if these forces are not evenly distributed over the entire foot surface, the foot may not be able to tolerate the trauma.

The second factor regarding lower body form is the amount of vertical bounce. The more excessive the movement of the body in a vertical plane, the less efficient you are. It takes energy to displace the body vertically, and if this displacement is excessive, the energy is wasted. You want most of your energy to go toward propelling you forward, not upward. So how do you know if you have too much vertical displacement or bounce? Sometimes it is as easy as noticing how you feel. If you feel like you are bouncing up and down each time you take a stride, you are probably excessive. A second way to know is to focus your eyes on an object in front of you and if that object appears to be moving up and down each time you take a step, then your movement is probably excessive. A third thing that provides some clues is the degree of heel kick you have. If your heels elevate more than 12 inches off the ground as the foot strikes and moves toward the rear as contact with the ground is lost, then you are probably excessive in your vertical movement.

Upper Body Form. The correct upper body form for distance running is to have a slight forward-lean of your trunk at the waist. The arms should swing in a relatively short arc that moves slightly across the body as opposed to directly forward and backward. This slight movement across the body helps to maintain the correct alignment of the trunk each time you stride forward. However, if the arm swing is too aggressive and moves too far across the body, it tends to cause excessive upper body rotation which may cause an inefficient running style. The forearms should be held relaxed at between 90 and 120 degrees of bend at the elbow. Pick the position that feels most comfortable to you. The fingers should the slightly flexed and relaxed, not clenched. Maintaining a slight contact between the thumb and the forefinger will usually be a comfortable position.

A big mistake that a lot of runners make is to try to carry the arms too high. This forces the muscle in the shoulder and neck to work harder and causes a tenseness in the upper body. It is very important to run with a relaxed shoulder and neck region because this is one of the first areas that fatigues. More about eliminating this excessive tension is covered in Chapter Four. The upper body should feel relaxed, not tight. Too much muscular tension increases fatigue during long runs.

Breathing

Throughout most of your daily activities you don't have to think about your breathing. It is pretty much automatic. Your brain controls your breathing in response to the need of the body to bring oxygen into the lungs and get carbon dioxide out of the lungs. Even though breathing seems to be automatic, you can voluntarily change your breathing pattern at any time. When you run, you usually become more aware of your breathing because of increases in the rate and depth of breathing.

Although you could probably get by in your running without consciously altering your breathing pattern, it may be beneficial to pay more attention to your breathing in order for it to be as effective and efficient as possible. Most runners prefer to breathe with what is called a 2:2 breathing pattern. A 2:2 pattern is when you breathe in for two strides and you breathe out for two strides. Every two strides coincide with a full inspiration or an expiration. For the type of running you will be doing, a 2:2 pattern is an efficient breathing pattern.

Initially, if you are not used to this pattern, you will have to focus on your breathing and think about breathing in for two strides and breathing out for two strides. It is probably helpful to even breathe in two stages, corresponding to each single stride, and then breath out in two stages, again corresponding to each single stride. The two stages refers to simply breaking up your total inspiration or expiration breath into two discrete stages, each about half of the total inspiration or expiration. This really gets you in tune to how your body is functioning and it develops a rhythm to your running. The pattern is "In, In, Out, Out, In, In, Out, Out,........" You begin to function almost like a machine, with your breathing in perfect coordination with your running stride.

Many novice runners think they should breathe only through their noses. This is absolutely not true. You should breathe through both your mouth and your nose. Unless you were running extremely slow, you could not get enough air through just your nose. You should run with your mouth open and just breathe normally and air will enter your lungs through both the nose and the mouth.

PART 3 | What Matters/What Doesn't

When it comes to training for and running a marathon, a few things do matter and a lot of things don't. I and other past participants would like to share with you some of those things that at first we thought did matter but found out through the course of training really did not matter.

Age

Geraldine Zapf Hall didn't start running until 1986 when she was 46 years old. Until the spring of 1995, the longest distance she had ever run was 6.2 miles. Several times she contemplated running longer distances, but thought she was just too old for that to be a realistic goal:

Whenever I watched others run long distances, which to me was any-thing beyond a 5K, I would find myself thinking, "Wouldn't it be won-derful to be able to say that I did that." But I never really thought that I could do it. Still, that feeling of wanting to was always in the back of my mind. Somehow I found out about the "Marathon Class" and I called one of the professors, Dave Whitsett, to find out more about it. At some point in the conversation my age came up. I said, "I'm 55." He said, "So what." I'll never forget that! It's like he didn't say, "Yeah, well, why don't you try something else." Instead, he said that the class was already full, but that I was welcome to run with them during the long runs and the marathon. That's how I got started.

Now 47 years old, Ron Steele was 37 in 1988 when he participated in the class and ran what was then his seventh marathon. On the subject of age, Ron had this to say:

Age is only an issue if you make it one. I was definitely the "old man" of the class in 1988, but so what. In some ways I think some of my younger classmates kind of looked up to me because I was out there with them going through the training just like they were. And I certainly enjoyed being around them; they were so fresh and optimistic that just being around them was very uplifting for me. I've never had as much fun training for a marathon as I did that one. Age just kind of disappeared because everyone was in the same boat, and we had fun.

Time
Patti Hasty Rust:

When I started this I was worried about how much time it was going to take. In addition to my regular duties as an information systems ana-lyst, I was working on a major work-related project and had taken on some supervisory duties, plus I was serving on some time-consuming church committees. Then, in addition to getting the runs in, there was my son, husband, and taking graduate classes toward an MBA. I prob-ably had more stress on me at that time than at any other time I can think of. It's amazing to me, but I really think that training for that marathon helped me to get through that time. I don't know how to ex-plain it exactly, but I think it gave me a better mindset toward every-thing I was doing at the time, and helped me manage and deal with the stress better than I would have if I hadn't been in the marathon class.

Jane Mortenson was also concerned about the amount of time involved in training. As an administrative law judge for the State of Iowa and single mother of two teenage boys, extra time was one thing that was in short supply in her life. She says:

Training for a marathon does take time. It just comes down to deciding what to cut out to make the time. It's certainly not wasted time. Mentally you can use that time for constructive things like prayer, personal reflection, personal planning, etc. My sons supported me 100% and didn't mind if dinner was late or I was gone more. They proudly kept track of the miles I ran.

Eric Johnson remembers it this way:

My time management was great. I didn't waste my time playing video games or anything. I was taking 19 credit hours, was a dormitory resident assistant, and had a job. I could do it all! I want that semester back!

Weather

More from Eric Johnson:

My routine would start at 10 p.m. when everyone else on my floor would be getting ready to settle down. I'd put on all my layers of clothing and then do my stretches. I'd parade around the hall like a rooster; everyone knew when they saw me that I was ready to run. I was on cloud nine. They'd say, "How many tonight?" "Eight miles (or whatever it was)," I'd reply. Then they'd say, "But it's 10 degrees outside!" And I'd say, "I know, you want to come?" Coming back in I'd go through the long hallway on purpose so everyone would see me. I'd then cool down, stretch, shower, eat some simple carbos, and sleep like a baby. I'd go to bed smiling. I love to run in the cold now.

What Others Think

Patti Hasty Rust:

When I would tell people about the training and get negative reactions, my thought was that they just didn't understand. They didn't know what I knew about this class. They hadn't read the newspaper article, or heard the past participants talk about it. It really didn't matter to me if someone else thought it was a crazy idea. Well, except for my mom...that one bothered me a little bit because I was really feeling like I wanted her support on this. (By the time we got to the marathon, she was my biggest supporter!) But when it came to everyone else, I just ignored the negative comments and concentrated on the positive ones. I was doing this for me, and it didn't matter what they thought.

Jane Mortenson:

I didn't tell many people for a while, because I didn't want to set myself up for failure and then have to explain why I wasn't following through if something happened. I did tell a few really close friends. They thought I was nuts and shouldn't do it because of my health. But I told them that's why I should do it now, because I was in good health at the time.

Which Marathon

Past marathoner, Ron Steele offered this insight:

Of all the marathons I've done, it's funny that I still don't have a favorite. They're all about even; they were all neat. Which one you run really doesn't matter. The experience will be awesome regardless.

Speed/Pace

More from Ron Steele:

One thing I learned from this class that I've never heard anywhere else is to stop using a watch. I used to run with a watch. I was one of those guys during the marathon who would be saying, "Oh, my goodness I'm a one and a half seconds off my pace!" After this class, I stopped doing that. In fact, I haven't worn a watch since!

Kathy Schneider, a 19-year-old with no prior running experience, had this to say:

Many people thought that because I was training for a marathon that I ran fast and lots of long distances. But really we only had one long run a week. I never was a fast runner and I still don't run fast. It doesn't matter how fast you run, or even if you walk every now and then, just as long as you finish.

During the marathon, I took Dave's advice and didn't use my watch. My brother ran with me and he kept track of his time. He couldn't believe I didn't want to know the time. He thought we were raised in a cult all semester!

Jeri Kurtzleben had never run more than three miles before starting this training. This 23-year-old non-runner from Wesley, Iowa, shared this observation:

I'm glad this book is focused on AMATEUR runners. I would have loved a book like this. When I was training for the marathon I looked for them and there weren't any out there. There was one book, though, that had a training schedule for the marathon. They had three categories: amateur, medium, and professional. And each had a time limit! It was really discouraging. I felt like I was nothing because I wasn't running at their pace. So, I put that book away. It didn't matter that I wasn't running a 9-minute mile or an 11-minute mile. I didn't need that. What mattered was that I was doing it!!

Following is a journal entry I made at this point in the training. Perhaps you will find it helpful:

In the long run this week, I let everyone else go out ahead of me, so that I started at the end of the pack. This felt better to me than last week when I started at the front of the group and was quickly passed by everyone. I was surprised by how upsetting that was to me. As I ran I tried to sort out my feelings and realized that I am used to being in front — regardless of the arena. Probably sounds egotistical but when you're used to being a leader among your peers, the front position is what feels normal and becomes your expectation for yourself. After a while, that position is something you just take for granted.

It may sound like I am discouraged. Actually, it's just the opposite. If I know that a situation will most probably be upsetting to me, than why should I subject myself to it when I don't have to? So what if I go out last, if that's where I'm going to end up anyway? What's more important to me is that at least I am out there! Just having the ability to do something doesn't count half as much as having the gumption to actually do it. I think of all those years when I did have the physical ability but no desire, and I feel sorry for myself — sorry for all the discarded opportunity and experiences I cheated myself out of.

With this group I run at the end of the pack, and that's OK. Considering all the factors, it's an appropriate position for me. Until now I've never had any real sympathy for the turtle in the story The Tortoise and the Hare. It is hard to imagine the turtle's position if you've never been in it. Well, I'm wearing his shoes now, and seeing things from a whole new perspective. There are lessons to learn and value to be gained from all positions. It's not important where you finish...only that you do.

Pain

It would be callous and irresponsible to say that pain does not matter. When it comes to the body, pain serves a purpose. In Section Two of the next chapter, Forrest will be addressing the subject of running injuries, signs and symptoms commonly associated with each, and what you can or should do in response. While pain is something that you should pay attention to, it does not always need to stop you. It is something that you should react to intelligently, rather than emotionally, and rationally evaluate what an appropriate response would be.

Likewise, past injuries or medical problems do not necessarily mean that you will not be able to successfully complete the training. Remember my recurring back problem I spoke of in the introduction? It never bothered me during the training. If anything, going through the training helped strengthen my back and has been paying me dividends ever since. Several other past participants have stories and thoughts to share on this subject.

Twenty-two-year-old Tricia Tuttle reported:

> I had a stress fracture three months before I started training for the marathon. I always worried that it would give me trouble during the training. I had never before done anything so physically demanding. But I just kept training according to the schedule, and it never gave me any problems.

Chris Henle remembers:

> In the beginning of training, I had tendinitis. I worked with Forrest and the trainer who was helping with the class, and ran through it. Midway through the training, the pain got better. It really didn't matter, just like Dave said.

At age 19, Kathy Schneider was one of the youngest members of the 1995 class. Only 5 feet tall and weighing barely 100 pounds, she was also one of the most petite. What Kathy may have lacked in stature she made up for in personality. She always had a smile on her face regardless of the distance, and she was constantly encouraging fellow classmates. Several months after completing the marathon, my respect and admiration for Kathy deepened even more when she shared the following story with me:

> I have scoliosis. Every night from the time I was two years old until I was seventeen I wore a back brace that ran from my neck to my hips. At

my last doctor's appointment, I was told that the best treatment for my back was to stay fit. I had never run in my life, but became very interested in trying the marathon because of the excitement on Dr. Whitsett's face when he talked about the class at the informational meeting. At the time, I didn't think about what my doctor had advised, and it wasn't until later in training that I realized the connection. I didn't have any difficulty with my scoliosis throughout training.

Also, I have only one adrenal gland and one kidney. When I was one year old I had cancer, and the adrenal gland was removed along with the tumor. Six years later, I had the kidney removed due to the damage caused by the radiation. Usually, I never give it any thought. I've always been an active person and started training for the marathon without any thought to my adrenal gland.

I never mentioned my scoliosis or adrenal gland to anyone in class. I wanted to run "myself" without the influence of my body, if that makes sense. I wanted to run the marathon more than anything that semester. I never had any problems other than what I thought were normal aches and pains associated with doing something as physically demanding as this training. So no matter what hurt I just kept going, because like Dave said, it doesn't matter.

Jane Mortenson is another past participant with a significant medical history. A survivor of breast cancer that surfaced nearly a decade before, this 44-year-old was one of a handful of older adults to participate with the 1995 group. Her effervescent enthusiasm for the training and life in general was contagious; anyone running with her couldn't help but be "infected" by her positiveness. At the time, most of us did not know all of Jane's story. I wish we had. She would have been even more of an inspiration to us. She remembers:

When I was diagnosed with breast cancer in 1987 it came as a total surprise. There was no history of it in my family and I was just 35 at the time. I had a mastectomy, but unfortunately the cancer had spread to my lymph nodes so I had to take 13 months of chemotherapy. That experience taught me that we all need to do what we want to do in life, because you never know when your number is going to be up. Running a marathon was one thing I had always wanted to experience. I found out about the class through an old high school friend whose daughter was planning to take it. I was in good health at the time; didn't have any recurrences or major problems. So I felt now was the time. My doctors were aware of what I was doing, but I don't think they thought I would really do it so they didn't discourage me.

I was battling a lot of chronic pain from a car accident that had happened years before. I tried everything and nothing seemed to help. I was used to living with pain, but I thought maybe the exercise would help. And it did! When the endorphins kicked in during the long runs that alone made it worthwhile. I was in heaven...I would have relief from the pain for a while.

The Saturday morning long runs turned out to be the highlight of my week. As crazy as it may sound, that was my fun time. I had some friends who would go to an aerobics class on Saturday mornings, and after all of us were done with our activities we would meet at my house and have a "tea party" of fruit, muffins, coffee, and Gatorade. It became a little ritual for us. Having that to look forward to was really good. It made the training fun! I really looked forward to those times sitting with my friends on my patio guzzling Gatorade and giggling as the endorphins floated through my system. And then afterwards taking those luxurious bubble baths! It was the best part of my week!

I never worried about the exercise exacerbating my condition. On the contrary, I thought it was a step in the right direction. In fact, I probably took better care of myself than I have at any other time. I was eating right, exercising routinely, feeling good about myself. You can't put your whole life on hold and wonder and worry about what might happen. Look in the obituaries. Every day people die ahead of their time from car accidents, aneurysms, and heart attacks. You can't sit around and worry about what might happen. If something happens, then you deal with it. You can't not live. Otherwise, what's the point. There are so many people who are just existing and not living. You have to take chances. A marathon may be a pretty extreme thing to do, but on the other hand it's something I always wanted to do. I'm not going to let the fact that I had cancer stop me from doing anything.

Jane's story illustrates how focusing on the positive helps one to develop an internal locus of control. As we said earlier, this is important all the time — not just when you're doing your training runs. In fourteen weeks, this training program will be over and you will run a marathon, but the skills you learn during that process can have lifelong consequences if you continue to apply them. One of the most important involves adopting a habit of seeing the positive instead of the negative. Initially if you have trouble identifying the positives associated with the training, create some. Jane's Saturday morning "tea parties" immediately following the longest, hardest run of the week are a perfect example. I doubt if she was thinking anything but positively as she basked in the warmth of late morning sun in the company of good friends. Use the training as an opportunity to initiate some self-promoting rituals for yourself. This is a great time to be good to yourself.

Prior to starting the training, 21-year-old Heidi Brandt had never run more than six miles at one time even though she loved to run. Morning became her special time:

> *I'd always run in the morning, no matter what. If I didn't I'd be out of sorts for the rest of the day. It's peaceful in the morning, too. It became the best part of my day.*

Nights worked better for Patti Hasty Rust due to her hectic schedule, and she had this to say:

> *No matter how I felt before, I always felt better after I ran. It seemed like I had to do most of my running after work, sometimes as late as 9:00 p.m. There were so many times when I really didn't feel like running because I was totally exhausted from my day. But I would make myself go, and I always felt better afterward.*

Ron Steele had this insight:

> *The most challenging aspect of doing something like this is learning more about yourself. Running, for me, opens up my mind and allows me to think. I think you find another side of yourself when you actually put your heart into something. That is one of the things that makes marathoning special. It is maybe one of the few times you truly approach your potential.*

Jeri Kurtzleben admitted:

> *I was scared to death for the first few runs; didn't even think I could run five miles. But every time I finished a Saturday morning run it felt like another feather in my cap. It's too easy to get negative with yourself. I don't think that way anymore. Now it's more like, "OK, what did I do wrong; what could I do to fix it?" I'm a more positive person than I was before I trained for the marathon.*

Julie Stone, a 21-year-old from Ankeny, Iowa. who had never run more than five miles before she took the class summed it up when she said:

Once the training started, I had mixed feelings about the whole thing. I wasn't sure what I had gotten myself into, but I was excited. Looking back, I don't know how I did it all, but it did put things into perspective. Now I have a more positive outlook in general; a higher operating threshold. If I can run a marathon, I can....

General Tips From the Marathoners — Week Two:

- Carbohydrates really do make a difference. I don't think that was emphasized enough from the start. Once I increased my intake of carbos I really noticed a difference in how I felt, especially after the long runs.
- I drank more water. I ate more veggies and low-fat foods.
- During the training, we were advised not to use our head phones. I haven't used them since. They are still in my closet.
- When you are running, drop your arms. Dropping your arms at your elbow so that they gently swing no higher than 45 degrees will relax your shoulders and neck and help you to conserve energy. Plus, your arms will be mirroring the motion of your legs and your overall body movement feels more in synch and fluid.

	Scheduled Distance	Actual Distance	RPE	
Day 1	3			
	Comments:			
Day 2	4			
	Comments:			
Day 3	3			
	Comments:			
Day 4	6			
	Comments:			

Total Miles This Week_____Cumulative Total_____

Chapter 3:
Week Three
Building on the Base

 PART 1 | **Performance and Arousal**

What is the relationship between performance and arousal? That is, do we generally perform at our best when we are very aroused and excited or do we do perform at our best when we are not at all aroused and excited? The answer is neither one. We usually perform at our best when we are moderately aroused, that is, sort of in between caring too much and not caring enough. This is an issue that has received a great deal of attention over the years from psychologists interested in human performance. It has been studied a lot and, although there are some situations in which it seems best to be very aroused, an endurance activity like training for and running a marathon is not one of them. It has been fairly well established that we do our best at endurance activities under conditions of rather low arousal. What this means is that it will be in your best interests to avoid getting very worked up for your training runs and, as we will discuss in detail in Chapter 16, especially important to remain calm on marathon day.

The reason this is important is that when you get highly aroused, your sympathetic nervous system becomes activated and this results in all sorts of unhelpful (for marathoning) physiological changes in your body. Examples include increases in heart rate, blood pressure, oxygen consumption and loss of body fluids through excessive sweating and urination and none of these will help you perform well in training for and running the marathon, although they are great if you need a burst of strength for a very short period of time. So what we want is for you to become good at maintaining a relaxed, confident approach to your training. On most days, this will be reasonably easy to do, but you may find yourself having trouble staying calm as you get ready for the long run of the week, particularly when we get to Week 10 and beyond. For that reason, we are going to work more with relaxation techniques in Chapter 10 and, if maintaining a low level of arousal is already becoming a problem for you, you may want to look ahead at Part One of that chapter now. There is also some help for you in Part One of Chapter 6, where we discuss using Self-Talk. You may want to use some particular self-talk phrases to help you maintain the low level of anxiety you are shooting for.

 Physical Preparation

> ### Week 3 Training
> Day 1: 3 miles
> Day 2: 4 miles
> Day 3: 3 miles
> Day 4: 7 miles
> ### Total for Week: 17 miles

This week you progress from 16 to 17 total miles. The short days remain the same at three, four and three miles, but the long day is increased by one mile to seven miles. You are still in that early stage of training where the muscular and skeletal systems are adapting to the trauma of running and you don't want to increase the trauma too much. As described later in this chapter, the result of increasing mileage too quickly is injury. Your cardiovascular system could probably tolerate more running but it would be adding to that accumulated trauma which you want to keep at a minimum until all the systems affected get better conditioned. Be patient, larger increases in training will be occurring in future weeks.

Running Injuries

Most runners unable to complete a training program for running a marathon are unable to do so not because they can't do the cardiovascular work, but because they get injured. Injury is the number one enemy of both the novice and experienced runner, especially when training for a marathon. Most injuries are not from pulled or strained muscles or ankle sprains. They are not injuries that the runner says "Oops, I just injured myself." They are injuries that creep up on you and appear almost out of nowhere. They are called overuse injuries and they result from the accumulation of training you have been doing in combination with your running form that may predispose to injury.

Certain individuals are going to be more susceptible to injuries than others.

Unfortunately, it is difficult to determine who the most susceptible will be. Some structural factors that may make it more likely an injury will occur are body weight, hip width, the angle of the lower leg at the knee, and the mobility of your feet. The only one of these you can directly affect is the body weight. The others you just have to live with, but you can do things that will indirectly affect these characteristics. These preventive factors are discussed in more detail throughout this section.

Prevention is the best way to deal with overuse injuries and suggestions on how to prevent them are included at the end of this section. But, when injury strikes, early detection and treatment is extremely important in resolving the injury with minimal down time from training.

Most overuse injuries begin with minor, annoying symptoms, most commonly some degree of pain. The pain is rarely described as a sharp pain, but is most often a dull, aching pain. Initially the pain may only be evident at the beginning of a run or just when getting out of bed in the mornings. If running is continued, the pain often progresses and becomes more intense and lasts for longer periods of time. Most running injuries are self-limiting in that eventually they will either go away or become so painful that you will have to discontinue or limit your running. However, Achilles tendinitis and stress fractures are injuries that can lead to severe consequences if not properly diagnosed and treated.

One thing that is known about running injuries is that you are more likely to get them the longer and harder you train. Training at a slower pace will decrease the chances of running injuries. A certain amount of training has to be done in order to run the marathon, but running more than is necessary will increase your chances of injury. So don't get overzealous in your training. Stick to the recommended schedule and you will reduce your chances of getting a running injury and still be able to complete the marathon.

The best approach to running injuries is to try to prevent them in the first place, but, if you do begin to have symptoms, treat them early. There are specific treatments for the specific injuries, but there is a general protocol that can be followed to decrease symptoms and start the healing process for just about any injury. Sometimes, this general protocol will be all that is necessary to solve the problem. In other cases, you need to determine and eliminate the cause of the injury.

The following are suggestions for preventing running injuries. If you utilize these suggestions as much as possible, you may never have a running injury.

- Stretch on a regular basis. For details, see Chapter 4.
- Start your training program slowly and progress slowly, as indicated in our introduction.
- When possible, run on soft surfaces like grass or dirt trails. If you have to run on concrete or pavement, stay out of the gutter as much as pos-

sible and run on a level surface.

- Wear good shoes that are made for your type of foot. For details, see Chapter 1.

At the first sign of an impending injury, begin the following treatment. Continue until the symptoms have resolved or until additional medical advice is sought.

- Apply ice to the affected area after the run and 3-4 times throughout the day. The best way to do this is to use an ice massage. Fill a paper cup with water and freeze it. After it is frozen, tear or cut away the upper part of the cup to expose the ice. Rub the ice on the affected area for about 10-15 minutes, constantly moving the ice around. If you want to use an ice pack and just leave it on the area, put a towel or washcloth between the skin and the ice pack. This will prevent the possibility of damaging the area with too much cold.

- Take over-the-counter anti-inflammatory drugs like ibuprofen. Over-the-counter ibuprofen is Advil, Motrin, and Nuprin. Ibuprofen should be taken with food because it can be hard on the stomach in some individuals and it should not be taken for longer than 1 week without consulting a physician. Appropriate dosage for treating overuse injuries is 1200-1600 mg per 24 hours. If you cannot tolerate ibuprofen, you can utilize other anti-inflammatory drugs like naproxen (Aleve) or asprin. When in doubt, consult your physician.

- Try to determine what the cause of the injury may be. Try running on softer surfaces, make sure you are using correct running form, check your shoes for wear, and reduce your intensity and duration of running.

Common Running Injuries

The following section describes the most common running injuries. Most of these injuries, if recognized and treated early will not force you to discontinue training but you may need to decrease your training depending on what you are doing. In any case, the most important aspect is early recognition and treatment. In general, you should be alert to any pain that appears while running. The sooner you treat it, the more likely you can eliminate it quickly.

Patellofemoral Pain Syndrome. Patellofemoral pain syndrome is usually first noticed as pain localized just behind the kneecap (patella). It usually develops as a non-descript ache which you start noticing during a run. It often becomes more painful when running uphill or climbing stairs due to the added stresses on the kneecap. There are several potential causes of patellofemoral pain syndrome and when caught early, it usually responds to treatment quickly. In some cases, the problem is due to abnormal movement of the kneecap across the knee joint. Strengthening the quadriceps muscle (the large muscle in the front of the thigh) by performing knee extension exercises will force the kneecap to move with better alignment across the knee joint. While working on strengthening the quadriceps, wearing an elastic knee brace with a hole where the kneecap is will provide additional tracking assistance for the kneecap when running. Runners suffering from patellofemoral pain tend to be overpronators, meaning that when their feet strike the ground they roll hard onto the inside border of the foot. Wearing running shoes with good support on the inside border can help prevent overpronation. These types of running shoes, called stability shoes, were discussed in more detail in Chapter 1.

Iliotibial Band Syndrome (ITBS). Iliotibial Band Syndrome usually presents as pain over the outside of the knee. There is usually general tenderness along the outside of the knee with spot tenderness located just above the joint line. If allowed to progress, the pain can become so severe as to prevent any running. Walking usually lessens or alleviates symptoms while climbing or descending stairs and hill running usually aggravates the pain. The pain is occurring in the iliotibial band, a thick band of connecting tissue that begins at the hip joint and runs down the outer portion of the thigh until it crosses and joins the outside of the fibula, the non-weight-bearing bone on the outside of the lower leg. Just above the knee joint the iliotibial band lies next to the outside surface of the part of the femur that forms the knee joint. Each time the knee is flexed and extended the iliotibial band rubs across this outside portion of the knee joint and in some runners, results in iliotibial band syndrome.

The most important treatment for ITBS is stretching of the iliotibial band. Lengthening the iliotibial band by stretching will reduce the friction as it rubs across the outside of the knee. Specific exercises for stretching the iliotibial band are presented in Chapter 4. As with the patellofemoral syndrome, overpronation of the foot can also cause ITBS. Motion-control shoes can be very useful in reducing and preventing ITBS. A third cause of ITBS can be leg length discrepancies. Depending of the degree of discrepancy, foot orthotics (devices made for you by a medical specialist) may be necessary. If you run, on a paved road, try to stay out of the gutter because this causes constant poor alignment of the foot when it strikes the ground.

Shin Splints. Shin splints, sometimes called medial tibial stress syndrome, present as pain and tenderness along the inside border of the tibia, the large bone in the lower leg. The pain is most commonly present in the lower 2/3 of the inside of the lower leg and is due to inflammation of the muscle-tendon-bone junction of several muscles located in the lower leg. Infrequently, the pain is present in the upper 1/3 of the outside of the lower leg, just below the knee, involving a different group of muscles than ordinary.

In the early phase of this injury, pain is usually present at the beginning of a run, but may disappear after running 5-10 minutes, only to reappear an hour or two after the workout. Commonly, the pain will be present in the morning after getting out of bed. As the injury progresses, the pain may be present throughout a run.

Specific treatment for shin splints is similar to treatment for the other common running injuries. Overpronation of the foot when it strikes the ground can cause shin splints. Motion control shoes can prevent or reduce overpronation of the foot. Running on hard, unyielding surfaces may be part of the cause. Try to run on grass or soft trails as opposed to pavement or concrete. Running consistently on the same side of a paved road in the gutter can cause shin splints. When possible, move out of the gutter area or stay on the sidewalk when you have to run on hard surfaces. Lastly, stretching the muscles that flex and extend the foot can help with shin splints.

Plantar Fasciitis. Plantar fasciitis is characterized by pain located along on the bottom of the foot, from just in front of the heel to the midfoot region. The injury is caused by the repetitive stress of running leading to microtears and inflammation of the plantar fascia, a thick connective tissue band going from the heel to the toes. In the early stages of the injury, pain may be evident during the early portion of a run but may go away after several miles. As the injury progresses, the pain may be present throughout the run and even when walking.

Treatment for plantar fasciitis includes running on soft surfaces and wearing shoes with adequate cushioning and a shock-absorbent heel cup. Depending on the structure of your feet, more permanent orthotics may be necessary to relieve the stress on the plantar fascia. Stretching and strengthening the Achilles tendon and the muscles of the calf may also be beneficial.

Achilles Tendinitis. The Achilles tendon is the tendon connecting the calf muscles (gastrocnemius and soleus) to the back of the heel. It is the large cordlike structure you can pinch just behind and above your heel. The calf muscles and Achilles tendon are probably the most important muscles in running because they are responsible for plantar flexion of the foot which provides the forces for running (and walking and jumping). Tendinitis is inflammation of a tendon, in this case the Achilles tendon.

Achilles tendinitis usually causes pain in one of two distinct areas, and sometimes in both. The pain may be located just above where the tendon inserts into the back of the heel or it may be at the point of insertion, which is the bony projection forming the back of the heel. The pain is primarily evident when the foot is plantar flexed, as when lifting your heels off the floor and coming up on your toes. As with other types of soft tissue injuries, during the early stage the pain may be noticeable in the beginning stages of a run but as you warm up the pain may disappear. The pain is often noticeable as you first get out of bed in the mornings. As the injury progresses, the pain becomes more intense and may be noticeable throughout a run. If the initial perception of pain in the Achilles becomes worse and progressive, running should be discontinued until the problem is resolved. Continued trauma to the Achilles and advanced tendinitis can progress to macroscopic tears and partial disruption of the tendon.

In the early phase, Achilles tendinitis usually responds to rest, anti-inflammatory drugs, a slight heel lift in the shoe, and Achilles stretching. However, the root cause of the problem needs to be determined or it will just come back when running is resumed. Common causes include overworn shoes, running in the gutter of the road, overpronation of the foot, and running on hard surfaces. As indicated earlier, overpronation of the foot can be helped with motion control shoes. If there are more serious biomechanical problems with the foot, a permanent orthotic may be beneficial.

Stress Fractures. A stress fracture is a thin crack or partial break of a bone resulting from too much stress on the bone. Although stress fractures can occur almost anywhere in the lower extremities, there are three common sites in runners. These are the lower 1/3 of the tibia, the lower 1/3 of the fibula, and the metatarsals of the foot (where the toes connect to the forefoot. Pain usually appears gradually over a 2-3 week period of time and gets progressively worse if training in continued. Stress fractures commonly cause local tenderness or spot tenderness in the affected bone, as opposed to the more diffuse tenderness of shin splints.

The only way a stress fracture can be diagnosed is to see it on X-ray, bone scan or other imaging technique. Unfortunately, the early phase of a stress fracture does not usually show up on an X-ray and a bone scan is usually necessary to make a diagnosis. Early diagnosis is important because continuing to run on a stress fracture may cause more severe injury. If the stress fracture is caught early, treatment usually consists of not running until the injury is healed, usually 4-8 weeks. Often, some form of cross-training can be performed during this time so as not to lose all the conditioning already attained. Depending on the degree of injury and site of injury, more problematic stress fractures may require immobilization of the affected part.

Like the other injuries mentioned, stress fractures are caused by the repetitive trauma associated with running. Some obvious preventive actions include running on soft surfaces and wearing good, cushioned shoes. Depending on the individual, biomechanical instability of the foot on making contact with the ground can lead to stress fractures. Runners who over-pronate should wear a motion-control shoe to help with this problem.

Cross-Training

As mentioned earlier in this section, running injuries may require you to either decease your training mileage or perhaps to stop running entirely. This may be more damaging mentally than physically. Depending on the length of time you have to decrease or quit running, you can do some things that will limit the loss of conditioning.

Cross-training is training that uses a different mode of activity to train the same body system. For example, running and bicycling are both excellent cardiovascular activities and they both train the heart. If the objective of a training program were to improve cardiovascular conditioning, it would not matter whether you ran or biked. Both would train the heart in a similar fashion.

However, in training for a specific activity like running a marathon, your objectives are to train the cardiovascular system and the specific muscles used in running. While biking would do a good job of training the cardiovascular system, it uses mostly different muscles than running, so you would not be training the muscles used in running. You could retain and even improve your cardiovascular conditioning, but training would not be optimal because of the use of different muscles.

The objective of cross-training when used in an injury situation is to utilize a mode of training that will train the cardiovascular system and come as close as you can to using similar muscles as in running. Two of the best activities for doing this are water running and using a stepping machine. With most types of running injuries, water running and stepping could likely be done because they are much less traumatic than running. They also use some of the same muscles as running, so they would give you the specific muscle training as well as cardiovascular training. Other modes of exercise which would offer some benefit for runners would be cross-country skiing and roller blading. Bicycling would not be as good a choice as the others, but if it were the only alternative, it would be much better than doing nothing.

If you do have to do cross-training during an injury, how much should you do and at what intensity should you do it? There is a general rule that applies in this situation. Different modes of cardiovascular exercise can be equated based on the duration of effort and the training heart rate. For example, week 3 of your marathon training schedule has you running 3, 4, 3, and 7 miles. If you were doing cross-training, you would train for the same time (not distance) it would normally take you to run the distances in your marathon training schedule. Additionally, you would train at an exercise heart rate equivalent to your heart rate while running. If you can, you should cross train for the same total duration and at the same heart rate as you would have been doing running.

Depending on the type and severity of the injury, you would likely have to cut back on only some of your running. Maybe you would be able to run two days of the week but not all four days or you might be able to run two miles but not four. In these situations, run when you can, and then substitute the cross-training for the running you cannot do.

One word of caution regarding cross-training. If you use cross-training in the later stages of your training program, you may find that it is much more difficult to maintain the desired heart rate for the necessary duration with the cross training compared with running. You may not be able to cross-train at the same heart rate and duration that you were able to do running. The reason for this is that the muscles that you use for running have become so trained that they are able to work harder and longer than the muscles used in the cross training. As you continue to use the cross-training, you will be able to do it for longer periods of time and at higher intensities. Until you are able to maintain the same heart rate and duration with the cross-training that you were able to do with the running, use rest periods in between bouts of cross-training.

For example, if you are supposed to train for 40 minutes, but you cannot do 40 minutes of continuous cross-training, do two 20-minute bouts with a 5 or 10 minute rest between each bout. The next training session, do an initial 25-minute bout, rest for 5 or 10 minutes and then do a 15-minute bout. Increase your duration each time until you can train the total time continuously.

PART 3 | Hidden Agendas

If you are having difficulty maintaining the low level of arousal that was discussed in the first part of this chapter, ask yourself just what it is that you are getting anxious about. When you think about the program or the runs, what comes to mind and how are you feeling? If you are concerned about the distance involved, go back and reread the introduction where Dave and Forrest talk about how they know this program works and double check that your goal is to finish — nothing more. If you are afraid of getting injured, reread Forrest's sections (section 2) in Chapters 2 and 3 where he talks about how to avoid them. If you find that you are having trouble constructing a reality from a positive internal locus of control, realize that that is more habit than anything and may take a while to change. Just keep plugging away at it and over time you will notice an overall shift in your general perspective.

Perhaps your concerns are centered in areas other than the actual running. Perhaps you came into this program with some peripheral goals and expectations for yourself, and those are the things that are bothering you.

I did that. And it was at about this point in the training that I showed up at Dave's office nearly in tears from disappointment. The conversation went something like this:

"I'm having a problem with the training and I wondered if I could talk to you about it," I started.

"What's going on?" Dave asked.

"I'm just feeling so disappointed with myself. Things aren't going like I'd planned," I answered.

"But you looked great when you finished Saturday's long run. You were beaming as you told me that you had just run further than you ever had before in your life! What isn't going as you'd planned?" Dave asked.

After hesitating I admitted, "Well...I had hoped that I would lose some weight as a result of all this running, and so far I don't think I've lost any."

Dave leaned forward in his chair and rested his elbows on his desk. "Wait a minute, this is about weight — not the running?"

As I nodded my head, he shook his and said, "Tange, don't do this to yourself. Don't take what can be one of the best experiences of your life and turn it into a disappointing failure by attaching inappropriate expectations onto it. This is not a weight loss class — it's about preparing yourself to successfully finish a marathon. As a consequence of the training, you very well may lose some weight and it sounds like you would like it if that happened, but the goal here is not about losing weight."

As I sat there quietly processing my thoughts, he continued, "It's quite possible that your weight may not change that much for two reasons. First, muscle weighs more than fat. As you shift your ratio of body fat and muscle, you may not see much change in weight. What you are more likely to notice is a change in inches and how clothes fit. Second, you are going to have to eat if you expect to do the runs. Food is fuel and without fuel your body won't be able to deliver what you are asking of it."

He was right. I knew that. I was doing it to myself again...starting out with one thing and attaching covert agendas to it until eventually the whole thing became unrealistic, overwhelming, and undoable.

As I walked to my car replaying our conversation in my head, I realized that while what Dave had said didn't change the fact that I needed to lose weight and was disappointed that it had not automatically started to fall off as a result of the exercise, his comments had helped me to see that adding weight loss onto the training program as an additional requirement was only setting myself up for failure. I sure didn't want to run 26.2 miles and feel like a failure. That would be masochistic! So mentally I shelved the issue of weight loss for a more appropriate time. This was not it.

By the way, over the course of training I did end up losing about 20 pounds. The weight just kind of came off on its own as a result of increased intake of carbohydrates, conscientious reduction of dietary fat, and all the calories I was burning due to the running.

I'm not the only one who approached the training with hidden agendas. In fact, I suspect that in one way or another most people do that. Perhaps the difference is more an issue of level of awareness regarding the presence of peripheral expectations, and not whether there are any. Ultimately, what really matters is how compatible the additional expectation is with the original goal. Does it subvert or promote the primary goal?

Keep this in mind as you read the following reflections offered by past participants. Perhaps you will find a little bit of yourself between the lines as you contemplate what your hidden agendas might be:

Keith Wendl:

I started out being really competitive. But then Dave advised us not to do that because we would just set ourselves up for failure, even if we did finish. So I relaxed and started to have fun with it.

Patti Hasty Rust:

It took me a couple of weeks to realize that I was not going to be 31 years old and out of shape and go out there and train for a marathon and be competitive. That was hard for me because I have always been competitive; liked challenge. The first two Saturday morning runs I ran too fast and was in bad shape by the end. I couldn't figure it out; the runs weren't even that long and I felt like I was going to die. After listening to Dave and Forrest I realized I was probably going at a pace that was too fast for me. So I slowed down, forced myself to stop seeing it as a competition, and just tried to focus on enjoying myself. I found a pace where I could feel good all the way through and finish feeling good. That's the pace that I stayed at — even though it was slow. Once I made these changes I started to really enjoy the whole process...that's pretty amazing for someone who started off not liking to run!

Another thing...don't say to yourself that you're never going to miss a run. All you're doing is setting yourself up for failure. If you look at the whole scheme of things, things are going to come up and you're going to miss a run or two. I had to miss a Saturday run once because our whole family was sick with the flu; another time I was down with a sinus infection. If you stop to realize that we're talking about several months of training, missing one or two runs out of that is nothing. Once I felt better, I just ran a little extra to make up for it. There's some room to play as far as the training schedule to make it work within the rest of your life. Missing some runs is no reason to quit.

Jane Mortenson:

Don't fall apart if you can't make the whole run one day. Just pick up the pieces and go on. Walk if you have to. You are just doing this for yourself. Once you've done it, it doesn't matter how fast you went. What does matter is the fact that you stuck with it and finished. It's worth it in the end when you cross that finish line and know you did it.

Tanjala Kole: *This week's long run was seven miles. I have never run seven miles in my life! My knees ached, my hips were sore, the muscles in my butt were tender, but I did it and it felt great! As I was running back, I thought about the crows that had circled me last week like prairie buzzards waiting for me to drop. Today they were nowhere in sight. Hah! Fooled them! They'll have to look for some other road-kill to scavenge.*

Seven miles is a long way! Whenever I became aware of the presence of the blocks ahead and felt the weight of the their distance, I looked at my feet. I blurred everything else out except them, and I watched them run. Even though my pace is still incredibly slow, when I focused on my feet and the street passing beneath them it was easy to imagine that I was running. I mean like really running! It was motivating. Soothing. Inspiring. Hypnotic. Enough to keep me going. With what I was trying to do, that's the name of the game. So I watched my feet, and teased myself into a jogging mindset...and did seven miles!

Ron Steele:

So many people choose to quit. Choose to stop living. They're really cheating themselves, you know. I think people don't really understand what they can accomplish if they want to. They have no idea how talented they are. I think you find another side of yourself when you actually put your heart into something. That's one of the things that makes marathoning special...it's one of the few times when you actually meet the challenge of doing something that is probably the most physically and mentally difficult thing you've ever done. For me, I can't recall anything more difficult than finishing a marathon. Maybe that's why I've done so many of them. It's one of the few times in my life when I've felt completely self-fulfilled.

General Tips From The Marathoners — Week Three

- Eating lots of carbos and drinking more fluids helped. Taking ibuprofen before and after the long runs really helped. But I think what helped most of all was icing anything that ached — especially my knees. If I iced right after the long runs, I wouldn't have any pain at all. That really made a difference and helped me get through it.

- The ibuprofen really helped. I got to the point where I took it before and after the longer runs to help reduce the muscle aches, joint tenderness, and swelling. I used ice, too. At first I had shin splints. Stretching before and after the runs seemed to help, along with the ibuprofen and ice. About the fourth week of training, they just disappeared.

Here's how Forrest recommended we handle blisters:

- Pop it with a sterile needle to allow the fluid to drain out, but do not cut away the skin.
- Keep it clean and whenever possible allow air to get to it.
- Unless you are running, keep it as dry as possible. Do not apply ointments. Cover with a loose band-aid if it helps reduce irritation while wearing shoes.
- When running, plaster with Preparation H (yes, you heard right) and cover with a band-aid. The same ingredients that help heal hemorrhoids, promote healing of the skin around a blister. As soon as you are done running, clean well and keep as dry as possible.

	Scheduled Distance	Actual Distance	RPE
Day 1	3		
Comments:			
Day 2	4		
Comments:			
Day 3	3		
Comments:			
Day 4	7		
Comments:			

Total Miles This Week_____Cumulative Total_____

Chapter 4:

Week Four
You're 25% There!

 Behavior & Attitude: Acting "As If..."

What do you think the relationship is between changes in behavior and changes in attitude? That is, which do you think leads to the other? It probably seems like attitudes are the causes of behavior, so it would seem as though attitude change would come first. Have you ever been told you had an "attitude problem?" How do you suppose anyone can tell what another person's attitude is? Can we see attitudes? No. What CAN we see? Behavior. So, when we say someone has an attitude problem, we are really saying we see behavior we dislike and we are assuming that a bad attitude is the cause of the behavior.

This is another area in which lots of psychological research has been done. That research shows that as a rule, attitudes are justifiers of behavior rather than causes of it. That is, most of the time we develop attitudes in order to explain our behavior to ourselves and/or others. This is important to know when it comes to training for a marathon for the following reason. You are going to need a lot of confidence and optimism to keep going on the training in the next several weeks and to keep going in the marathon. Maybe you already have that confidence and optimism. Maybe you are already convinced that there is no way you are going to quit on the long runs or in the marathon either. Maybe you are already sure that you are going to cross that finish line with your arms raised in triumph. If so, that is terrific, because that is exactly what is going to happen. But maybe you are not yet so confident of that. Maybe on some days you think that and, on other days, when you are not feeling very strong, you wonder if you'll be able to do it. So, if you think you need to develop that attitude, how are you going to do it?

Here's how. By acting as if it were already true. And how do people who are confident and optimistic about things act? They walk around with their heads up and with a steady, confident look in their eyes. When asked how their training is going, they say it is going great and that they have no doubt they are going to do well. When asked how they feel, they respond that they feel terrific. Sometimes they even volunteer (without being asked) that they are really enjoying the training and that they feel strong and confident. When they run, they smile and look like they are enjoying it. You may be thinking that this description sounds like that of people who are conceited and arrogant and who bore others with endless talk about their training. That's not what we are recommending. Confidence is quiet and understated, but it is very clear. It has more to do with how you carry and present yourself than with how loud you are. The point is that if you act as if you are confident and optimistic, you will begin to feel confident and optimistic. And that is a lot more fun than feeling pessimistic and unsure of oneself.

Another example of the relationship between behavior and attitudes is the relationship between achievement and motivation. Which comes first? Again, it seems like motivation (the attitude) must come first, but it doesn't. The most motivating thing to most of us is to do well (achieve). It feels so good that we want to make it happen again. That is one reason the training program you are following is constructed in the way it is. Every week you run farther than you ever have before in your life! What an achievement! And you have come to believe that you can do it again next week. And you will. Each week's achievement serves to motivate the next week's behavior. We know that sometimes (especially during the long runs) you feel as though you can't go on, but every time you do, you increase the chances that will do so again the next week and the next and so on. And when the moment comes in the marathon when you feel you can't go on, (and for most of you, that moment WILL come) you will go on anyway because you have done it so many times in the past and because of that, you will believe that you can do it again.

In the next part of this chapter, we are going to be discussing stretching. Many people find it difficult to get motivated to stretch in the way we will recommend. It seems to them to be a waste of time. If you find that you are one of those people, try using the idea described above to develop a different attitude toward stretching. That is, try acting as if you like stretching, as if it is a very relaxing and satisfying way to spend a few minutes now and then. You may find that it becomes exactly that.

Physical Preparation

> ## Week 4 Training
> Day 1: 3 miles
> Day 2: 5 miles
> Day 3: 3 miles
> Day 4: 8 miles
> ## Total for Week: 19 miles

This week you increase your mileage by two miles for the week. The mileage goes up from four to five miles on Day 2, and from seven to eight miles for the long run. You are just consistently and conservatively increasing your total mileage. Remember, consistency is key. The shorter days are increasing total mileage and the long day is building up your long-duration endurance. Adequate recovery remains important and will become more important as the mileage increases.

Be tuned in to how you are feeling on your runs. Listen for any consistent aches and pains, especially those that persist after the run. At the first sign of persistent pain, start a preventive treatment program as detailed in Chapter 3.

Stretching

Stretching is one of those things that we know we should do but it is usually no fun to do it. When we are pinched for time, stretching often is the thing that gets shortchanged. Unfortunately, stretching is one of the most important things runners can do, especially marathoners. So just get used to it. It can save you a lot of suffering later on.

There are two reasons to stretch. The first reason is to prevent an immediate injury resulting from performing forceful muscular contraction with muscles that are insufficiently warmed up and stretched. Whenever muscles are going to be vigorously and forcefully contracted, they need to be warmed up and stretched first. Not doing so significantly increases the risk for a muscle pull or strain. For example, if you were going to be running 100-yard sprints, playing basketball, or softball, it would be imperative to warm up and stretch the muscles beforehand. The warm-up and stretching makes the muscle more pliable and allows the fibers to stretch and be more elastic so that when the muscles are vigorously contracted and stretched during the activity, injury is less likely. Since you are not going to be doing the type of running that requires forceful contractions, stretching before you run is not as important as stretching after you run.

The second reason to stretch is to prevent overuse injuries, the number one enemy of marathoners. As explained in Chapter 3, overuse injuries do not occur as the result of something you just did. They occur as a result of accumulated trauma that may have been occurring for weeks. Regular stretching of the muscles reduces this accumulated trauma and the potential for overuse injuries. You may be able to get by with little or no stretching for several weeks or even months but suddenly, out of nowhere, just when everything seems to be going so well, injury strikes. Stretching does not guarantee that you will not get injured, but it certainly decreases the chances of debilitating injury.

How to Stretch

There are several types of stretches, but the most effective and time-efficient stretch is a static stretch. A static stretch is one in which the muscle is put on a stretch and held in the stretched position for a length of time. The key is holding the stretched position for an extended length of time. The length of time can be as short as 10 seconds or as long as several minutes, with the longer the better. The adaptation that the muscle goes through occurs during the holding of the stretched position.

When you are first beginning to stretch, holding the stretch for 10 seconds is adequate. But you should increase the holding time progressively until the stretch is held for at least 60 seconds. Research tells us that the benefits from stretching continue to increase up to at least 3 minutes of holding time. However, if you are stretching 4 or 5 muscle groups, with two or three of those requiring both sides of the body to be stretched, you could be spending 15-20 minutes stretching. High-ability runners often spend this length of time because, to them, staying injury free is extremely important. It basically gets down to how much time you are willing to invest in an activity that may make the difference in becoming injured or not.

The muscles should be stretched enough to feel it but not so much that it is painful. Just put enough stretch on the muscle so it feels tight. As you maintain this amount of stretch, it may become more painful. At the point at which it becomes painful, decrease the stretch a bit and continue holding for the designated period of time. As you spend more time stretching, the same degree of stretching becomes easier.

When To Stretch

Any time you are going to be using forceful muscular contraction in activities such as sprinting, jumping, or fast changes of direction, you need to stretch the muscles involved before you do the activity. This will decrease the likelihood of injury. However, before you do this stretching, it is best to warm up the muscles by doing some easy jogging for 5-10 minutes. This prewarm-up will significantly improve the effectiveness of the stretch.

Regular stretching to prevent overuse injuries is a bit different from stretching to prevent acute injuries. Because most marathon training, especially for beginners, is done at a slow to moderate pace, you don't have the same potential problem with muscle pulls and strains from forceful contractions that you have in sprinting. Therefore, the best time to stretch to prevent overuse injuries is usually after the training run, not before. This is because the muscles will be very warmed up following the training run and they will respond to the stretching optimally at this time. The training run itself serves as a warm-up for the muscles for the purpose of stretching. If you can and are willing to invest the time, it would be optimal to stretch both before and after the run. However, if you are able to stretch only once, stretching after the run will be more beneficial.

Stretching is a lot like training the cardiovascular system. The more you stretch, to a point, the greater the improvement in flexibility. You should probably gear your stretching program to your running program. Stretch each time you run. Flexibility can be improved by stretching as few as 2 times a week but greater injury prevention will be evident with more frequent stretching. Just make your stretching a regular part of your overall training program. When you run, you stretch.

What to Stretch

Which muscles need to be stretched? First and foremost, the muscles used directly in running need to be stretched. These include the calf muscle (gastrocnemius and soleus), the front (quadriceps), the back (hamstrings), and the outside (iliotibial band) of the thigh, and the front of the lower leg (tibialis anterior). In addition, several other muscle groups are important. The low back is an area that needs attention because of its role in maintaining a good running posture and the high likelihood of low back problems in runners. The shoulder and neck area needs to be stretched because it is one of the first areas to become fatigued and tight on a long run.

Figures 4.1 through 4.8 illustrate some good stretches for the muscle groups mentioned above. Other stretches will work and if you have a favorite stretch for a particular muscle group, use it. The only thing that is important is that the muscle is put on a stretch and held for an extended length of time.

Figure 4.1 Calf stretch (gastrocnemius and soleus)

a) *Lean against a wall with the right foot about 6 inches from the wall and the right knee slightly bent. Place the left foot 18-24 inches from the wall with the leg straight. Force the heel of the left foot against the floor and lean into the wall at your hips. This stretches primarily the gastrocnemius. Repeat with opposite leg.*

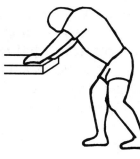

b) *Assume a similar position as in 4.1a except bend at both knees, keeping the heel of the left foot flat against the floor. This stretches primarily the soleus. Repeat with the opposite limb.*

c) *Stand on a step or a curb with the ball of the right foot on the step and the right heel hanging off the step. Let the right heel drop as far down as you can. This can be done one foot at a time as illustrated or both feet at the same time.*

Figure 4.2 Quadriceps stretch

Stand on left foot with the right hand on a wall for support. Bring the right heel up close to the buttocks. Grab the right foot with the left hand and pull the entire leg up and back toward the left shoulder. Don't just press the heel into the buttocks, but lift the entire foot as if you were going to touch your left shoulder blade with your heel. This stretch may also be performed by lying on your side on the ground.

Figure 4.3 Hamstring and low back stretch

a) Sit on the ground with the left leg straight out in front and the right leg flexed with the bottom of the foot touching the inner thigh of the right leg. Bend at the waist as to touch your nose with the right knee. Repeat with opposite limb.

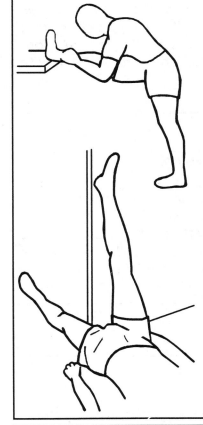

b) While standing, place the right straightened leg on a table or other supportive structure. Bend at the waist as to touch your nose to the right knee. Repeat with opposite limb.

c) Lay on the floor next to a door opening or wall with your left leg through the opening. Slide your hips next to the opening and raise the right leg and place the foot against the door opening or wall. To put more stretch on the hamstrings, slide your buttocks as close to the wall as you can (this stretch is only for the hamstrings). Repeat with opposite limb.

Figure 4.4 Inner thigh stretch

Sit on the ground and place the bottoms of both feet against each other. Place your elbows on your leg and force your knees down toward the ground.

Figure 4.5 Outer thigh (iliotibial band) and low back stretch

a) Sit on the ground with left leg straight out in front. Place the right foot next to the outside of the right knee. Place the elbow of the left arm on the flexed knee and twist the torso as if you were looking over the right shoulder. Repeat with opposite limbs.

b) While lying on your back on the ground, place the left leg over the right knee as illustrated. Use the left leg to press the right knee toward the ground allowing the right hip to rotate toward the left. Repeat with the opposite legs.

Figure 4.6 Hip flexor stretch

Position right foot in front and left foot behind as illustrated. Keeping the right knee directly over the right foot, lower your left thigh and knee as close to the ground as you can. Repeat with opposite legs.

Figure 4.7 Low back and gluteal stretch

a) Lying on your back, grasp the left knee and pull it up to the chest. Repeat with opposite leg.

b) Lying on your back, grasp both knees and pull them to the chest while tucking the chin to the knees.

Figure 4.8 Arm and shoulder stretch

a) Raise the right arm directly over the head and grasp the right elbow with the left hand. Hold the right elbow and bend sideways toward your left.

b) With the arms in the same position as in a), pull the elbow back toward the left shoulder blade.

c) Bring the right arm directly under the chin while grasping the right elbow with the left hand. Pull the right elbow toward the right shoulder.

d) Position the right arm behind your back and grasp the right arm with your left hand. Pull the right arm toward the left hip and attempt to touch your left ear to your left shoulder.

e) With your right hand, grasp the wall or a structure behind you, keeping your right arm straight. Turn your chin toward the left shoulder.

f) Interlock your fingers and turn your palms up and lift them as high above your heads as you can. Repeat stretches a) through e) with the opposite arms.

PART 3 | Are You a Marathoner? YES, I AM!

After this week's long run, you will have one-quarter of the 16 weeks of physical training behind you. Think of all those miles you've already run that you probably never would have believed you could. Think of how much you have already accomplished and how much better physically you are feeling because of it. Any initial aches and pains you had have probably subsided by now, and you're feeling stronger and more comfortable during the runs.

Likewise, you are probably feeling more positive about the runs and your ability to complete them. If you have been practicing our suggestion to follow any negative thoughts with "but it doesn't matter," you have probably noticed an increase in your general level of positivism — and perhaps others have, too! Here is how some past participants found themselves feeling at this point in the training:

Kathy Schneider reflected:

> By the third week, I already felt as if I could run forever! I look back now and laugh because at the time I still didn't know what I was doing. It just felt so good to be out there doing this.

Elizabeth Kilgore reported:

> The runs were hard, most of them, but I remember feeling like the queen of the earth when I finished them. I particularly remember eight miles kicking my butt. The route that particular day doubled back and then added several hilly streets in order to achieve eight miles. I was the most negative that I ever was on that day — I think I let the hills psyche me out. Now when I run, I purposely hit the hills just because I can. The demon is conquered!

Not only do you feel more positive, you actually are becoming more positive. The results of research conducted during the 1995 class support this. Jennifer Dykes, a class participant who assisted with the research, explained:

> My experience with the marathon included a different dimension than most since I was helping with the research involved at the time. The research we were conducting involved measuring six components of mood state: anger, tension, depression, vigor, confusion, and fatigue. Of course, vigor was the only positive one, and for the group, vigor shot way up and

all the others sank way down over the duration of the course. It was hard to listen to everyone be so enthusiastic, not only about the upcoming marathon, but about how participating in the course had changed every facet of their lives. I wanted to say, "I know, I've seen the data!" But, I managed to keep my mouth shut until the whole thing was over. It was amazing to watch the entire class get into a healthier frame of mind.

But even with all this success, it is quite possible that you still may not feel much like a marathoner or totally believe that you will actually be able to run the marathon when the time comes. If this is true for you, don't worry. Over the next several weeks you will be learning specific techniques and engaging in activities which will help accelerate the development of positive feelings and beliefs. Many of these techniques are based on the "acting as if" principle described in Section One of this chapter. By replacing your mental "what if" with the action of "as if," it becomes your "it is" reality. Behavior exerts tremendous power over cognition. If you want to change the beliefs, change the behavior. One of my journal entries offers a good example of how simple this can be and how quickly thoughts and feelings can change as a result:

This week I noticed an interesting change in self-perception. Dave told us to start identifying ourselves as marathoners to others. Whenever I considered doing this, the words stuck in my throat as my mind battled over the believability of it. At this point, I don't feel like a marathoner. I feel more like a walrus waddling down the street in running shoes! Frankly, I'm not 100% sure I want to commit to being a marathoner in the eyes of others. What if something happens and I can't or don't actually run it. What if I give them this expectation of me and then I don't live up to it? What if...?

As we headed out on this week's long run, I remember thinking, "Gosh, I hope nobody asks me if I am a marathoner" because I wasn't sure that I could lie convincingly enough. But one of the disadvantages/advantages of running last, is that you get met by everyone else as they are on the way back. As others passed me they would say, "You must be a marathoner," to which I would (have to) respond, "Yes, I am!" Before too long, I was actually looking forward to saying it, and by the time I finished the run I was starting to see myself that way.

When I got home, I took a shower and hunted for some dry clothes to put on. I had to dig some clean socks out of the laundry basket, and I purposely hunted for my other pair of "marathon" socks. The idea of putting on "regular" socks just wouldn't do, because after all, I am a marathoner.

Likewise, running was not something Keith Wendl normally did, as the following confession revealed:

During my college days, the only time I ran was when I was interested in a woman who was a runner! In fact, that's what got me interested in the "Marathon Class" in the first place. But once I was in the class, I was totally committed. I took the training literally and worried I wouldn't be able to finish the marathon if I didn't make every single mile. I remember there was a bad snow storm in December when we were still in the pretraining phase, but I bundled up and ran. I hated it, but I still went. One time it was pouring rain and I ran anyway; I hated it. I ran during spring break in South Padre; it was so hot and I hated it. I hated running alone and in bad weather the most. But I still went. The further into the program we got, the more excited I became. By the time we hit the marathon, I was going NUTS! Now I love to run! Going through this experience has totally changed the way I feel about running.

As these accounts illustrate, what you do is often more important that what you believe. Actions will initiate corresponding beliefs and feelings. Behaving "as if" is just one more way to influence your reality by exerting an internal locus of control.

The connection between achievement and motivation that was described earlier is yet another example of the power of behavior to influence cognition. In this particular relationship, achievement is behavior in action, increased motivation is the cognitive consequence, which in turn inspires more behavior. And the positive cycle repeats itself.

Following are examples offered by myself and others who have experienced this for themselves:

An interesting change has happened regarding the concept of distance. Initially, every run was considered long. It was hard to get going because of how far the miles seemed. Five, seven and eight are BIG numbers when you are talking miles! I was intimidated by the distance. But as the mileage increased on the Saturday runs, only those distances not yet run continued to be considered "far." Any mileage that had already been accomplished and surpassed no longer qualified.

Now only the first couple of miles (especially in the Saturday runs) seem long, tough, a real effort; once I'm by those it's like I get into a groove and start to relax. I think about other things, or I focus on my feet, my breathing, my arms moving, the act of running...anything except the number of miles. And the miles just slip away under my feet. It's like I'm not even aware of them.

Often, it isn't until I near the end of the run that I find myself thinking in terms of distance, and then it is to report to myself how much is left. But instead of saying, "I've still got a mile to go," I find myself thinking, "Only one to go." Only. There was a time when I couldn't have imagined doing one mile; now I'm saying, "ONLY one mile." It's shocking to hear yourself define as "only" what you used to think would kill you, but once you've gone further than that it impacts how everything else is interpreted.

Kathy Schneider:

Physically, I feel so much better, and it feels good knowing that I am active. What I didn't expect was how everything seems to be going better — my classes, my studying, even my moods!

Jane Mortenson offered a tip that has already been mentioned in an earlier chapter, but bears repeating here:

I am a very visual person. It really helped me to chart my progress by marking the completed runs on my training schedule with a yellow highlighter. I posted this on my refrigerator and looked at it frequently. It helped keep me focused and motivated. By the end of our training, the whole sheet was yellow. I loved being able to "see" my accomplishments.

Is this mental stuff important? YES! The mental messages we tell ourselves are what often keep us from even trying. The irony is that by doing whatever it is you think you can't, you dispel the power of the mental myth that you can't. The hardest part of running a marathon (or anything, for that matter) is starting — taking that first step.

The power of inertia is in our perception. If we think we have yet to begin, the power of perceived inactivity can become a slow-setting concrete that keeps us from starting. If instead we perceive that the journey has already begun, and contemplate the successes already registered (however small), inertia becomes an illusion and loses its relevance to a process that is already underway.

Initially in undertaking a challenge such as this, one's tendency is to focus on the physical aspects and ignore the mental components. Until this point in the training, doing that probably hasn't seriously inhibited your ability to finish the runs. But from here on, the mental elements become increasingly critical to your successful completion of the marathon. You must take them seriously. You must practice them with the same diligence as the physical components. Because if you don't, you will not finish the marathon. As a non-runner who in twelve weeks will run 26.2 miles, you will need to utilize every bit of training available to you in order to make that an enjoyable, peak experience.

But don't just take my word for it. Here's what others had to say regarding the importance of the mental component:

Julie Stone:

If I had to decide which had more of an impact, mental or physical, I'd definitely have to say mental.

Eric Johnson:

I did some of the mental techniques, but not all of them. I got scared when Whitsett told us that if we didn't use them during the marathon we may not be able to make it. After that, I worked harder at using the mental stuff.

Patti Hasty Rust:

For me, it was really more mental than physical. One of the reasons I had never liked running before taking this class was that when I ran I would hear myself breathing hard and think about how tired I was or focus on whatever part of my body was in pain. It was such a negative experience that it was hard to keep going.

The whole focus of the mental aspect of this class was concentrated on the positive and the techniques we could use to develop positive mental conditioning that would help us get through the tough parts. The mental elements of the class really were what got me through the training and the marathon.

One of the few participants with any prior long-distance running experience, 20-year-old Amy Kepler had this to say:

As a result of going through this training, my thinking is more positive. I now know without a doubt that you can do anything if you work for it. Those times when I do get down I ask myself if I am preparing to quit or am I preparing to keep going? I think one of the best things about running is that it makes you stronger mentally.

This week, test the power of the "as if" and the importance of the mental components of class by repeating the phrase, "I am a marathoner" in time with your steps. As you run, say it over and over. Also, start telling people about what you're doing. Each day tell one new person that you are a marathoner — not that you are trying to run a marathon, but that you are a marathoner. Instruct your family and friends to routinely ask you, "Are you a marathoner?" to which you answer, "Yes, I am!" And by the end of the week you will feel differently about yourself. Any uncertainty you might have had about your ability to complete the rest of the training and successfully finish the marathon will be gone. Because, after all, you are a marathoner!

General Tips From the Marathoners — Week Four:

• I didn't stretch as much or as well as I should have. I didn't get hurt because of it, but I could have. I always felt that maybe I was cheating myself out of the benefit I could have had if I had made more time for stretching.

	Scheduled Distance	Actual Distance	RPE	
Day 1	3			

Comments:

Day 2	5			

Comments:

Day 3	3			

Comments:

Day 4	8			

Comments:

Total Miles This Week_____Cumulative Total_____

Chapter 5:

Week Five
Your First 10-Miler

 PART 1 Visualization: Making Videos in Your Head

One of the most powerful techniques for increasing your mental toughness is called visualization. That just means making pictures in your head. You do it all the time. You imagine things almost constantly. Some of what you imagine helps you perform well and some of it doesn't. You are going to need some powerful tools in order to do well in your training and in the marathon and visualization is one of the best. This week you will be doing your first ten-mile run and this is a wonderful opportunity to work on visualization.

What we want you to do is to construct two short "mental video tapes." Each should be about one to one and a half minutes in length. The first one should be about the best training run you have ever had. Here is how to construct it. First choose the run you are going to use in the "tape." Now think hard about that run. Where did you run? What did you see? What smells can you remember? What was the weather like? What did you wear? Who else was with you? How did you feel? You should write down the answers to those questions as well as any other details you can remember about the run. Now use those details to construct a short "mental highlights" tape of the run. Write down each scene that is going to be in the tape. Then practice imagining the scenes in the order you wrote them down. Practice it over and over and over again until it becomes so clear that you can "run the tape" in your head at will.

Your second mental highlights tape should be of what you imagine it will be like to finish the marathon. Again, it should be short. Imagine what you will look like, what the weather will be like, who will be there, what you will say to them, what they will say to you, what you will be wearing, how you will feel, etc. Write all of this down and then construct the tape the same way as you did the first one. Once again, practice running the tape in your head (exactly the same way each time) until you can do it effortlessly.

There are two ways in which we want you to use these tapes. First, whenever you find negative images coming into your mind, imagine that there is a video tape slot in the side of your head and that someone has inserted the wrong tape! Imagine removing the negative tape, tossing it away and inserting one of your two positive tapes. Play one of your positive tapes. Play it several times. Do this while you are running if you start to feel fatigued and start thinking about how tired you are. Do it anytime you find yourself thinking anything negative about training for or running the marathon. Remember, this will take practice, just as the physical part of your training does, so if you have trouble doing it at first, just keep at it and you will get better and better at it in the same way as the running is making you stronger and stronger. Some of your practice should come during the long run each week, because that is when you are simulating the marathon experience. So, construct the tapes and start using them in your first 10 mile run this week.

In addition, you will start to feel another benefit of playing these tapes. Your brain cannot tell the difference between imagining having a great run or finishing the marathon and actually doing it! So, as far as your brain is concerned, you will be creating achievement experiences every time you play the tapes and, as we described in the last chapter, achievement leads to motivation, so you will feel your motivation level go up as well! So every time you play your tapes you increase the probability of having a great experience on marathon day!

The second way we want you to use the tapes is during the marathon itself. There will almost certainly be times in the marathon when you will feel negative thoughts creeping into your mind. When that happens, remove that negative tape, symbolically throw it away (imagine throwing it in a trash can), replace it with your marathon finishing tape and play it! You will be amazed at the instant energy it gives you. We'll remind you of this in Chapter 14 when we review all the mental preparation strategies.

There is another form of visualization that may be of use to you as well. One of your authors has been a distance runner for 25 years and has run at least 1500 miles in each of those years, including 10 marathons, many half-marathons and four 23.5-mile Grand Canyon crossing runs. He has, in all those thousands of miles and hours of running, developed many specific visualizations that have helped him when he has felt fatigued. Perhaps you will find that you want to develop some of your own. In Section Three of this chapter, we will offer you some examples of visualizations that have helped some of the people who have taken our course. But here is one that has been of great value to your author. When he feels fatigued in very long events, he imagines that he has many thousands of tiny muscle fibers in his legs which have been held in reserve and are waiting to be called upon. He imagines that he sends out the call. They receive the message and pass it on down the line. They call out, "Let's go. He needs us now!" And he imagines them streaming into his legs and helping him to go on. In his mind they look like little soldiers in blue helmets who are very energized and eager to join the battle. We know, we know. It all sounds very weird. But it works. He goes on. Often, he even speeds up! And so will you.

 Physical Preparation

> ## Week 5 Training
> Day 1: 3 miles
> Day 2: 5 miles
> Day 3: 3 miles
> Day 4: 10 miles
> ## Total for Week: 21 miles

Congratulations! You will be breaking two psychological barriers this week, the 10 mile barrier for a single run and the 20-mile-per week barrier. Your total mileage this week is 21 miles with the jump being in the 10-miler on the long day. All other days are the same as the previous week.

Imagine, 10 miles in one crack. To run 10 miles you are probably going to be running for 1.5-2 hours. The long runs are now becoming more dependent on adequate fluid and carbohydrates. Learning to drink adequate fluids during the run as well as being optimally hydrated before the run are critical. The remainder of the chapter discusses fluid consumption and details the specifics of what you need to be doing. Please read carefully because it will be some of the most important information you will be getting.

Fluid Consumption. The human body is approximately 60-70% water. Water is the environment in which the cells live and function. In order for the cells, including muscle cells, to function normally, the watery environment must remain fairly consistent. When the body is asked to function at optimal levels, as in running a marathon, it is critical that the fluid content of the body be maintained. The fluid level of the body is not only important for running the marathon, but also for all the training runs. In short, it is important to keep the fluid levels optimal all the time, both during training and during the marathon.

Adequate body water is important for two primary reasons. The first reason is simply because the cells function in a watery environment and adequate water is necessary for normal function. The watery environment of the cell maintains the integrity of the cell structures, the many chemical reactions that occur in the cell, and the very life of the cell.

The second reason is that water plays a central role in getting rid of body heat generated by muscular activity. When we exercise for extended periods in warm weather, the body produces tremendous quantities of heat which must be gotten rid of. The rate of heat production by active muscles can be as much as 100 times that of inactive muscles. If the body stored this heat instead of dissipating it, the internal temperature would rise at a rate of 1.8 ° F every five to eight minutes during moderate exercise, resulting in overheating (hyperthermia) and collapse within 15 to 20 minutes. The primary way we get rid of heat when exercising in the heat is referred to as evaporative cooling or, in common terms, sweating. In order to be able to sweat adequately, you need adequate body water because sweat is mainly water. If you lose the ability to sweat adequately because of low body water, you run the risk of heat illness which, in extreme circumstances, can lead to death.

The Best Drink. If maintaining body water is so important, what is the best way to do it? The answer is to drink enough of the right kind of fluid at the right time. The type of fluid, the amount of fluid, and when you drink the fluid influence the beneficial effect the fluid will have on water replacement.

There are two reasonable possibilities concerning the right type of fluid, plain water and specially formulated and relatively expensive fluid replacement drinks such as Gatorade. Do these special drinks do a better job than just plain water? Are they worth the added expense? The answer to these questions is, "It depends."

It depends on how rapidly you need the fluid replaced and whether you need energy and electrolytes in addition to the fluid. As a routine fluid to drink throughout the day and with meals water is a pretty good fluid to drink. Most experts say we should drink at least 8 glasses of water a day under normal circumstances. This requirement for water may increase to 12-16 glasses per day in warm weather or if we are active and sweat quite a bit. It is difficult to make a general recommendation regarding how much water is necessary for a particular individual due to the variation in weather and activity level. Suffice it to say that it is almost impossible to get too much fluid. So when in doubt, drink more, not less. Although water is a sufficient beverage to consume routinely throughout the day, water is not the best drink in some circumstances. These specific circumstances are discussed in detail below.

In certain circumstances, the specially formulated fluid replacement drinks have several distinct advantages over plain water for the runner training for a marathon. Fluid replacement drinks are better than plain water for consuming within two hours before a run, during a run, and for three hours following a run. Even though fluid replacement drinks could be consumed instead of water at times other than these specific times, it is not as necessary. Certainly plain water is more convenient and cheaper.

Fluid replacement drinks are better than plain water in the circumstances mentioned above because, in addition to the fluid, these beverages contain some carbohydrates (usually less than 10% carbohydrates) and electrolytes, primarily sodium chloride. The carbohydrates can provide energy during the run and are most useful in runs longer than one hour when there is an increased chance you may run out of energy. For example, drinking a fluid replacement drink during a marathon may provide enough additional carbohydrates so you don't run out of carbohydrates near the end of the run (generally referred to as "hitting the wall"). Could you get these extra carbohydrates by eating something during the run instead of drinking a fluid replacement drink? Yes, but in order for the carbohydrates to be readily available to the body, they need to be simple carbohydrates like glucose or fructose. The nice thing about the fluid replacement drinks is that the carbohydrates are easily absorbed into the blood and made available to the body rather quickly. Also, most runners' digestive systems tolerate a fluid source of carbohydrates better than a solid source during a run. Beverages with a carbohydrate content of greater than 10%, such as fruit juices and pop, are not recommended for fluid replacement. Too much carbohydrate in the fluid will slow down absorption and rehydration.

The addition of sodium to the beverage has several distinct advantages over plain water. The sodium enhances the taste of the fluid and makes it easier to drink. This may not seem too important at first glance, but many studies have shown that athletes drink more fluid when the drink tastes better. In addition to palatability, the sodium promotes fluid retention in the body resulting in a faster return to normal body water levels. This is especially important when training on warm days because the quicker you can replace the fluid lost in sweat, the less likely you are to lose enough body water to cause a problem.

When and How Much Fluid? In order to train for and run the marathon with the least difficulty, you want to go into each training run (and most especially the marathon) having optimal amounts of body water. Starting off the run with optimal body water simply makes it less likely you will run short of water during the run. Once you have started the run, you should drink at every water stop to maintain adequate body water throughout the run. Once you have completed the run, drink enough fluid throughout the rest of the day so that when you run the next day, you are at optimal levels again. In general, you want to maintain optimal or near optimal levels of body water all the time so that when you need the water for your runs, it is already there.

When making decisions regarding when to drink fluid and how much to drink, four time periods are important. The time periods are within two hours of the run, during the run, immediately after the run and throughout the remainder of day and night before the next run. The following recommendations cover these four periods.

1. <u>Within Two Hours of the Run</u>: Drink about 2 cups (16 fluid ounces) of fluid about 2 hours before your training run to promote adequate hydration and allow time for excretion of excess fluid. This will help ensure that you are optimally hydrated during the run. A fluid replacement drink is the drink of choice for this situation.

2. <u>During the Run</u>: For runs lasting less than 30 minutes, there is no need to drink, as long as you were hydrated at the start of the run. For runs lasting 30-60 minutes, the need to drink fluid during the run depends on numerous factors, most notably the environmental conditions. Especially if it is warm and humid, sufficient water can be lost after 45-60 minutes of running to cause a decrement in performance. The wise thing to do on 30-60 minute runs is to drink 1 cup of fluid every 15-20 minutes if it is available. If nothing else, it will be good practice for the longer runs. However, for the 30-60 minute time frame, a fluid replacement drink is not absolutely necessary if you were well stocked with carbohydrates at the start of the run.

During training runs lasting for longer than 60 minutes, fluid replacement is essential and the recommended rate is 6-8 fluid ounces (about 1 cup) every 15-20 minutes or approximately every two miles, whichever comes first. Drink a fluid replacement drink to get the carbohydrates. It is important to start drinking early in the run and not wait until you become thirsty. Drink throughout the entire run. Because the exact amount you need to drink depends on how big you are, how fast you are running, and the environmental conditions, you may need a little more or less than the recommended amount. This is an area that you need to do some experimenting with. In your training runs you need to practice drinking fluids and matching the fluid consumed with the fluid lost. You also need to adjust your fluid consumption according to the temperature and humidity. Always err on the high side, not the low side. A fluid replacement drink is the drink of choice for this situation.

3. <u>Immediately After the Run</u>: Following the run, you should continue drinking a fluid replacement drink for at least a couple of hours. Drink at least 2 cups of fluid for each pound lost during the run. This will help ensure a rapid return to normal body water status and the carbohydrate in the drink will begin the process of replacing the glycogen you lost during the run. As mentioned in the section on nutrition, this is an important time to begin to consume some additional carbohydrates, so drinks with a higher carbohydrate content, like fruit juices, can be consumed during the time period immediately following the run.

4. <u>Throughout the Day</u>: For general consumption of fluid throughout the day,

plain water is usually adequate. There is no particular advantage of drinking fluid replacement drinks as a general source of fluid throughout the day as long as you drink sufficient water and consume sufficient sodium at your meals. Just make sure you drink adequate amounts of whatever fluid you drink throughout the day. Carry fluid with you throughout the day and drink it on a regular basis. Studies have shown that you need to drink 1.5 times as much fluid as you have lost in order to replace all the lost fluid. This is because you will naturally get rid of some of the fluid you are drinking through urination and other normal routes of water loss.

Are You Drinking Enough?

There are several ways to determine how much fluid you should be drinking. First, it is important to note that thirst is not a very good guide to your need for fluid. Your thirst drive is controlled by both fluid level and electrolytes in the body. Drinking plain water without electrolytes can actually fool the thirst drive into thinking that body water is adequate when in fact it is low. That is why you should not rely on your thirst drive to determine when and how much fluid you drink.

More reliable ways to determine the need for fluid are body weight and the color of your urine. Track your body weight day to day. It is not uncommon to lose several pounds of weight as a result of a training run. Runners commonly lose two to four pounds per hour when exercising in the heat. This weight change is water loss, not fat loss. When you consider that running a marathon requires less than 1 pound of fat energy, you can easily see that losing two to four pounds following a training run has to be primarily water loss. You should be drinking enough fluid throughout the day to bring you back to within a half a pound of your weight before the run. The best way to do this is to weigh at the same time of the day, preferably in the morning following urination. Each morning, your weight should be within a half pound of your weight the preceding day. The half pound margin allows for some fat weight reduction that may occur with training, but this weight reduction should not be more than two pounds a week assuming that you are drinking adequate fluid. Most experts recommend drinking one and a half times the amount of fluid loss. So if you lose two pounds of body weight, you need to drink at least three pounds of fluid. One pound of fluid is equivalent to about 16 fluid ounces or two cups. So if you need to replace three pounds of fluid, then you need to drink at least six cups (48 fluid ounces) of water. Remember, this is six cups in addition to what you would normally drink throughout the day. If you normally drink eight cups a day, you should drink a total of 14 cups, spread throughout the day.

The second way of tracking your fluid levels and a good method to use in conjunction with weight loss is the color and quantity of your urine. When you are adequately hydrated, your urine will be clear to pale yellow in color. The darker yellow the urine and the smaller the quantity , the more fluid you need. Dark yellow urine is a sign of inadequate body water which causes the urine to become more concentrated. It may sound strange, but smart runners should constantly evaluate the color of their urine and adjust their fluid intake accordingly.

Bad Brew. It is well known that both alcohol and caffeine cause fluid loss. Even though the effects of alcohol and caffeine consumption on fluid loss during exercise really have not been well studied, logic would suggest that when fluid replacement is a priority, caffeine and alcohol should not be consumed. This is not to say that runners should never drink alcohol or caffeine, but rather you should think about the timing of drinking such beverages. You certainly would not want to drink caffeine or alcohol during a training run nor would you want to consume large amounts the night before a training run or the marathon. Moderate consumption of alcohol or caffeine the night before can probably be offset by adequate fluid consumption as recommended above. However, the regular use of caffeinated beverages as your primary source of fluid throughout the day is definitely not recommended.

Heat Acclimatization

Have you ever gone out to exercise on that first really warm day of spring, after you had been exercising in the cooler (or cold) weather for several months, only to find that it was really difficult to exercise at the same distance and intensity that you had normally been able to do? There is a simple physiological explanation for this. You were not acclimatized to exercising in the heat. Perhaps the worst environmental event that could happen on marathon day is for it to be hot when you have been training for months in neutral or cool weather. If the body is not used to exercising in the heat, it is not very efficient the first couple of weeks that you have to exercise in such conditions. The result is that the body heats up more and faster, more fluids are lost, and work capacity decreases. In short, you simply cannot do as much muscular work.

Obviously, you can't control the weather, but you can do something to prepare for the possibility of running the marathon in the heat. The only way the body will adapt is to exercise in the heat. We naturally make this adaptation when it gradually warms up during the spring. But, depending on where you live, you may face the possibility of running the marathon without having had the opportunity to acclimatize to the heat. Here is a recommendation that may be very beneficial should you face this situation. Remember, this applies only if you would normally be training in cooler weather but face a chance of having to run the marathon in hot weather. Three weeks before your marathon date, begin overdressing for your runs on your short and medium days. Wear more clothing than you would normally be comfortable in so that you create an artificially hot environment. Also, you will need to increase your fluid intake to cover the excess loss of fluids that will result. You will also need to decrease your training intensity a bit during the first week or so of trying this to allow your body to adapt gradually. If it does turn out to be hot on marathon day, you will be much more prepared.

One more comment on this point. If you have chosen a marathon that is in a location far from where you are training, make sure you know what the weather is likely to be on marathon day. If it is likely to be very different than the weather in which you will be training, you need to be especially careful to go into the marathon prepared for that.

PART 3 | Monkey See, Monkey Do...

Part of a popular current TV commercial claims that "Image is Nothing," and we would agree regarding some things. But when it comes to the images we carry in our heads that is not true. These pictures (or visualizations) have a way of becoming self-fulfilling prophecies, and because of that, they have tremendous power. If you think of the brain as a computer, visualizations are the pictures that appear on the monitor. Just as with any computer, someone has to enter the data and, if the monitor is on, it displays whatever is entered. What the monitor reflects is reality as the computer knows it in that moment. Ultimate power and control to control reality are in the hands of the computer programmer.

The brain is constantly on. The computer is continuously accepting information. Whoever controls the keyboard, dictates reality. Who is at your keyboard? Having an internal locus of control means that you control your keyboard and what becomes your reality. You are doing the data entry - not someone or something else.

Visualizations paint a picture of reality which the "operating system" (your body) goes to great lengths to enact, because when it doesn't, the mind and the body are inconsistent (or dissonant). That's similar to trying to print something and getting an error message instead of the product. There is nothing more frustrating! When this happens, it is as if thousands of warning signals go off throughout your whole system alerting it to the fact that there is a malfunction. Until an adjustment is made either in input or output, the system experiences the stress of the dissonance. As humans our systems require a homeostatic state to survive, and we have become extremely adept at making any adjustments necessary to maintain this. We do not like dissonance — we prefer resonance.

This is why visualization works. Your body will work to enact the reality it sees on our mental monitor. As was said in Section One of this chapter, we do this all the time...it's just that most of the time it happens without our thinking much about it. Until the day we talked about this in class, I wasn't aware of using visualizations in my running, even though I was doing so. Once the concept was explained, I started using the technique intentionally and it made a huge difference in my running.

Following are examples of the types of visualizations described earlier. These visualizations are what past participants found helped them to successfully complete the long runs and the marathon and actually enjoy the process! Feel free to adopt any that you think may be helpful for you...or better yet, use them as mental springboards from which to create your own.

As the star in your "best run" video, not only will you see yourself having a great run but will relive the emotions and experiences associated with it. 21-year-old Jason Haglund found this to be true:

> *According to Dave's instructions to make a short video of your best run so far, I took pieces of my 12-mile run complete with sights, sounds, and smells of that morning, including the exhaust of a passing laundry truck with the morning sun rising in the background. I now use that video every time I run; just playing it is enough to bring the entire semester back to mind.*

Jeri Kurtzleben took a slightly different approach:

> *I imagined running a race in my home town with all my relatives and friends cheering me on. I was at the head of the pack. It really helped me because it was a positive feeling and it showed in my running times. I was more positive about the whole thing.*

While it is certainly preferable to be the star of your own video, there are situations when it might be advantageous to utilize the image of someone else. Elizabeth Kilgore offered this tip:

> *I watched the scene in the movie* Wildcats *where Goldie Hawn outruns the football team. For me it was a big motivator!*

I, too, got better results by using someone other than myself in my "best run" video. Some history is needed to help explain why. As a kid, I loved to run. I would pretend that my legs were those of a horse and I "galloped" everywhere I went — why walk when I could ride in my mind?

In high school, I was a sprinter. I set a school record in the 220-yard dash that stood for years. All my mental pictures of running were as a sprinter. I had both internal and external "videos" of myself running. I could be a spectator watching myself run, or I could relive the experience complete with bodily sensations, hear my breathing, feel my heart pounding as my arms and legs flew in perfect rhythm.

Now, 20+ years later, I have a different body with different capabilities. Sprinting is not one of them. So when I started training for the marathon, it was as if I were running "blind." I had no memories or mental pictures to plug into of how to run as a 36-year-old, overweight woman. What was I supposed to look like? How was this supposed to feel? What kind of gait should I have? I couldn't "see" myself running because I had no memories of myself doing it in my current condition.

In order to compensate for my lack of personal experience, I searched for images of others to substitute. I started with the image of a power walker since that is what I thought I looked most like in the beginning. A powerful, purposeful walking machine — like the wheels of a locomotive being turned by the connecting arm. But you can only walk so fast. Even after my gait had changed into a fluid jog, I continued to hang onto the walker image and my speed was slow.

So, in search of a marathon runner image I went to a local video store to see if they had anything that would help. The clerks looked at me strangely when I asked if they had any sports videos on marathon/distance running. The only thing they could suggest was the 1980's movie *Chariots of Fire*, which I did rent and watch, but since this movie is about sprinters it really didn't help me.

That same weekend, I happened to catch a television commercial for a shoe company that featured a marathoner in training. It showed him running - long, relaxed, fluid strides. The caption said: 80 miles/week — 10 marathons/year. Although I saw it only twice, it was enough — I had it in my mind. The next time I ran I replaced the power walker image with the marathoner "video." As I ran I kept seeing his legs taking those long, fluid easy strides and over the course of that run my legs adopted that same stride without any conscious intervention or effort on my part. They just unconsciously matched what my mind was seeing. The effect this had was immediate and dramatic. My speed/mile dropped by about 15% overnight!!! And I was able to maintain that pace the entire run — which happened to be 12 miles that day!

This experience converted me into a believer in the power of cognitive resonance. In my case, it didn't seem to matter to my brain that the person it was watching on the monitor was not me. The same message went out for the operating system to adapt accordingly. The results were so dramatic I wouldn't have believed it if they hadn't been happening to me. Not only did my body movements change, but so did my emotions. I felt much less anxious, more relaxed and confident. It was as if I was that marathoner. And it felt great!

The second video you are to construct is of yourself finishing the marathon. This will be entirely your own creation since your marathon finish will be unique to you, but here are a couple from past participants:
Elizabeth Kilgore:

Dave told us to make those mental tapes of ourselves finishing the marathon. In mine, my mom was waiting for me at the finish line and told me that she loved me and was so very proud of me. I told her about my tape.

Like a lot of moms, my mom came to see the marathon. We waved goodbye to each other at the start and I headed out with the others. Throughout the marathon, she was looking for me but could not find me anywhere. Frantic that she might miss seeing me finish, she went early to the finish line and stood there for two hours! I had been looking for her during the marathon, and was kind of disappointed that I had not seen her. When I finally ran into the stadium and rounded the last curve toward the finish line, there she was - just like in my video! She told me she loved me and how very proud of me she was. I cried for the next 30 minutes! It was the most emotionally intense experience I have ever had.

Twenty-two-year-old Rob Leslie had this to say about visualizations he actually used during the marathon:

It amazed me how they put that psych part into it. I pictured myself in a little bubble still full of energy and that helped me in mile twenty. Also, I pictured that I was running with my best friend from college; we were always pushing each other. Near the end I imagined him saying, "Come on, Bob, let's finish this thing." At the end of the marathon when I was turning onto the track for some reason the 1984 Olympics came to mind and I finished feeling like a champion! Wow!

A third type of visualization is those that will help you relax and reenergize during long runs and the marathon. Let your imagination run wild and see what you can come up with that will be helpful to you when you start to feel fatigued or have negative thoughts. Here is a sampling of what has worked for others:
Tanjala Kole:

As I grow tired, I imagine the fatigue that has formed in my body as a thin layer of skin that is slowing me down. Starting at the top of my head, I mentally begin peeling this skin off. I peel it off my forehead, over my ears, nose, and chin. I feel it come off my neck and slough off my shoulders. It dissolves off my torso. I pull it off my arms in long strips and off my hips in big pieces. I can feel my thighs breaking through it, and it starts falling off my legs in sections. It is as if I am running right out of the fatigue that encases me. I "see" big sections of dry skin laying on the ground behind me or blowing away in the wind as I emerge smooth, fresh, new, unhampered. I don't feel tired. I can keep going. I go through this process several times during a run, and it is just as effective the tenth time as it was the first.

Julie Stone:

I had some knee problems. As I ran I would imagine each step as a color in how my knee felt. There would be a whole spectrum, red would be the best and blue the worst. I was saving red for the marathon. Each time my foot would hit the ground the color would change. I could modify the color with other mental aspects such as repeating over and over in my mind like, "I can, I can, I can...she can, she can...we can, we can...you can, you can. You really have to focus and keep your mind and body in synch — when your body gets tired, then your mind gets tired unless you take charge and change it.

Another technique I used was pretending to run with my shadow. It sounds crazy but it made me feel like I wasn't running alone, especially during the weekday runs.

Patti Hasty Rust:

I would imagine different people who had really made an impact on my life running next to me. So one time it might be my dad, another time my mom, a friend, or a co-worker. Even my one-year-old son. It helped to keep me going.

Jane Mortenson:

I sometimes pretended I was a lawn mower or a treadle sewing machine which took a while to start. The first three miles were the toughest before I got into a smooth rhythm. Once I got into the rhythm I could keep going and going...it became automatic and magical. I just followed the rhythm of my own machine.

Another visualization I used was when I noticed someone running at my pace but several feet ahead of me, was to pretend the runner ahead of me and I were encircled by a great big rubber band. I imagined myself being pulled along at their pace. Unfortunately, the rubber band sometimes snapped if I couldn't maintain their pace and they would leave me. Nonetheless, it had helped for a while and I could just pick out another runner to "attach" to.

Something else I found helpful when I thought I could go no further was to pop a candy Life Saver in my mouth and believe that I had truly given myself something substantial to help me get through this difficult time — a true life saver! Those wonderful little candies and their name became a big help for me.

Ron Steele:

I can't remember if Dave gave me the idea but when I was tired I would think about being on a big, tall sailboat, the old kind with the oarsmen in the bottom, and my oarsmen would be sleeping. And I'd say (to myself), "OK, guys, I'm getting a little tired. It's time for you to wake up and start rowing this boat." And one by one each guy would start to row. My legs were their oars.

Also, I remember Dave telling us to think of our feet as feathers. Whenever I would do that, my feet would start to feel much lighter.

General Tips From the Marathoners — Week Five:

• Take hydration seriously! If you don't you will get yourself in trouble. If you've ever been dehydrated you know what I'm talking about. If this has never happened to you, this is what you have to look forward to if you don't keep drinking: stomach cramps, nausea, headache, diarrhea, light-headedness, dizziness, muscle weakness, extreme fatigue. It's no fun. It feels like the flu — only worse. Even after you start drinking again, it can take 24-48 hours before you feel back to normal. Take the advice of someone who didn't take Forrest's warnings about hydration seriously enough and had to learn the hard way — don't wait until you feel thirsty before you drink. Anticipate your body's need for fluid and drink as much as possible before, during, and after the longer runs. For me, that was anything over eight miles. At this point, if you have any doubt about the importance of hydration or have any questions about what, when, and how much to drink, go back and reread the second section of this chapter where Forrest talks about it.

	Scheduled Distance	Actual Distance	RPE
Day 1	3		
Comments:			
Day 2	5		
Comments:			
Day 3	3		
Comments:			
Day 4	10		
Comments:			

Total Miles This Week_____Cumulative Total_____

Chapter 6:

W e e k S i x

Getting Close to 25 Miles per Week

 PART 1 | **Using Self-Talk to Remain Positive**

Back in Chapter 2 we talked about focusing on the positive. In that chapter we suggested adding the phrase "..but it doesn't matter" to the end of any negative thoughts or statements that might slip into your mind or out of your mouth. We hope you have been doing that. In this chapter we are going to offer you some additional techniques for remaining positive and optimistic.

These techniques are based on what has been called "self-talk." Just as we are almost constantly making pictures in our heads, we are also almost constantly talking to ourselves in our heads. (Some of us do it out loud.) What you may not realize is that these things we say to ourselves influence our behavior and attitudes a great deal. And when you speak to yourself about yourself, it is particularly significant because whatever you say becomes part of your perception of yourself. These self-descriptions then become reality, because they are a form of what we might call self-programming. For example, suppose you often say to yourself something like "I'm just no good at remembering names." Do you realize that operates as a self-instruction? That is, each time you say that to yourself (or out loud to someone else about yourself), your brain receives it like a computer receives a line of programming. Your brain hears it as "Do not be good at remembering names" and your brain will follow instructions and you will get worse at remembering names. The good news is that the same thing will happen if you constantly say good things about yourself to yourself. So, believe it or not (We hope you do.), if you keep saying to yourself "I'm really good at remembering names" you will actually get better at it! And this will happen whether you actually believe it while you are saying it or not.

The power of this technique as a part of marathon training is almost unlimited. Your self-talk with respect to marathon training should include such phrases as the following:

- I am a marathoner. (If you're doing what we asked you to do, you've been saying this one since you read the introductory chapter.)
- I never get tired.
- I never quit on a run.
- I love to run.
- I run four times a week and I never miss a training run.
- I love to run hills.
- I run no matter what the weather is like.

What we want you to do now is to construct a "self-talk paragraph" for use during the rest of your training for the marathon. It should be a brief (4 or 5 lines) paragraph that is made up of sentences like those above. Here is an example.

I am a marathoner. I love to run and I do it four times a week. I am in great shape and I look and feel like it. I never get tired when I run and I never quit before I finish my runs. I always feel strong when I run and I feel terrific after I get finished. I love the feeling of accomplishment and the anticipation of my next run. I am a marathoner.

When you have finished composing your paragraph, make at least two copies of it. Put one of them right next to your bed and read it over out loud as soon as you wake up. We want you to do this every day from now until the marathon. Keep the other one with you all the time and read it over (out loud whenever reasonable or to yourself if you feel you need to) several times a day until it becomes easy to repeat it verbatim without looking at the written copy. After you have it memorized, continue saying it several times a day whenever you have an opportunity, but especially whenever you feel doubts creeping into your mind or whenever you feel fatigued or a little down. You should also use the paragraph just before all of your runs and several times during each run, particularly when you feel fatigued or are in some discomfort.

In addition to your "self-talk paragraph," you should be using positive self-talk in all aspects of your life, not just with respect to running. This is important because we have found that it is very difficult to be positive about running if you are negative in other areas of your life. So, here are some phrases that you need to banish from your vocabulary.

- I can't......(you fill in the blank). Try "I can..." or, " I choose not to....."
- I'm no good at......(you fill in the blank again).
- With MY luck....(for example, "With my luck, if I wash my car, it will rain today). This one is particularly bad because it contains two nega-

tives. The first one is that you have bad luck and, even worse, it contains the idea that luck is the major determiner. YOU are the major determiner of what happens in your life! Luck has little or nothing to do with it. So, if you want to talk about luck at all, we'd rather have you say things like, "With my luck, if I wash my car, it won't rain for a week."

- I hate....(fill in the blank again.) Hating anything or anyone just takes energy. Concentrate on what you love, or at least on what you like.

OK, you get the idea. And remember, as we discussed in Chapter 2, if those negative ideas do slip into your head or even out of your mouth, just tack on the phrase, "but it doesn't matter." One final thought to help you get the hang of positive self-talk. You might try telling a few people about your efforts to use only positive phrases and ask them to remind you if you slip. This will help you and, incidentally, it will help them too, since they will become more sensitive to their own self-talk as they try to help you. By the way, if you want to read more about using self-talk, look at the book by Shad Helmstetter that we included in the reading list at the back of the book.

 Physical Preparation

Week 6 Training
Day 1: 4 miles
Day 2: 5 miles
Day 3: 4 miles
Day 4: 11 miles
Total for Week: 24 miles

This week you increase your weekly mileage by three miles. You add one mile to the two shortest days, making them 4 miles each and one mile to the long day, making it 11 miles. To this date you have already run 4, 5, 6, 7, 8, and 10 miles, so the two 4-mile days will be a piece of cake. You won't even notice the increase.

The long day is increased to 11 miles. Can you believe it? You have only been on this program for six weeks and you're almost halfway to a marathon. Just a reminder regarding the day before and after the long day. Because the mileage is getting long enough to cause significant energy depletion, it is important that you eat well throughout the week and that you conserve your energy the day before the long run. The day after the long run should be a rest day so that you can begin the recovery process. The 11-mile run will cause trauma to the muscular and skeletal systems and they need to begin the repair process as soon as possible. If you have been having any nagging aches and pains, it may be useful to take 400-600 mg of ibuprofen after the long run as a preventive measure to reduce discomfort the rest of the day.

Nutritional Principles

Nutrition has received a lot of press in the past several decades in this country, primarily related to its potential impact on health. Proper nutrition is one of the most important factors for obtaining and maintaining good health. Likewise, when training for a marathon, nutrition has a very important role. Good nutrition ranks right up there with fluid replacement and the actual training. In fact, without at least adequate nutrition, the training could not be done.

What role does nutrition play in performing exercise? A little fundamental exercise science is in order to be able to understand how important nutrition is. It all starts with the basic function of skeletal muscle, which is to develop force or to "contract." It is the repetitive contraction of muscles pulling on the skeletal system that propels you in running as well as any type of movement. We could not move our bodies or body parts without the contraction of muscle. In order for the muscle to contract, there has to be a relatively constant supply of chemical energy available to the muscle. Specifically, this chemical energy is adenosine triphosphate or ATP. ATP is to the muscle what gasoline is to your car's engine. The chemical energy in the form of ATP fuels the mechanical machinery in the muscle that produces the contraction.

In each muscle there is only a small quantity of ATP available for the muscle to use. This "stored" ATP will last for just a few seconds and more ATP must be continuously manufactured if muscular contraction is to continue for longer than a couple of seconds. When you go out on a 3-mile run, your muscles are continuously making ATP throughout the run. As quickly as it is made, it is used to fuel contraction and then more has to be made.

The process by which ATP is made in the muscle is referred to as being either anaerobic or aerobic. The distinction between these two processes is whether oxygen is used in the process to make ATP. Anaerobic means "without oxygen," and in using this process, ATP is produced in the body without having to use oxygen. Aerobic means "with oxygen" and this process requires the use of oxygen to make ATP. The role of aerobic and anaerobic processes for making ATP will be discussed later in this section. For now, the important point is that regardless of whether we are using aerobic or anaerobic processes, the goal of both is to make ATP.

To make ATP, the muscle uses carbohydrates, fats, or protein. Because they are used to make ATP, these three nutrients are referred to as the energy nutrients. Although all three energy nutrients can be used to make ATP, most ATP is made from carbohydrates and fats. As long as we are eating enough carbohydrates and fats, protein is not used to make significant amounts of ATP. We are getting a little ahead of ourselves though. In order to understand the importance of good nutrition, a brief introduction to nutrition is necessary.

There are six nutrients that the body needs in order to function normally. They are carbohydrates, fats, protein, vitamins, minerals, and water. Carbohydrates, fats, and protein are energy or caloric nutrients because they provide a source of energy that can eventually be transformed into ATP. Vitamins, minerals, and water do not directly provide any energy to the body but they are essential for all the chemical reactions that do produce energy. Without adequate amounts of vitamins, minerals, and water, all the carbohydrates, fats and proteins would be almost useless.

The runner's nutritional concern should be focused on both short-term energy provision and on long-term health and optimal functioning of the body. In the short term, the primary concern is with the nutrients that provide energy for muscular contraction. For example, there would not be any serious impact of eating foods that provide adequate energy but poor vitamin and minerals for a few days. But if inadequate vitamins and minerals were consumed on a regular basis over weeks and months, then health and performance would start to be compromised. So, looking at the big picture, a runner should attempt to ensure that adequate amounts of calories, vitamins, and minerals are consumed on a daily basis. The topic of water was discussed in detail in Chapter 5 but as a reminder, adequate fluid consumption is critical each day.

Carbohydrates, fats and proteins can all be used as a source of chemical energy that can eventually be converted into ATP. The amount of energy contained in each of these energy nutrients is dependent on which nutrient you are talking about. Each gram of carbohydrate and protein contains four kilocalories of energy and each gram of fat contains nine kilocalories of energy.

Carbohydrates. The most important energy nutrient for the marathon runner is carbohydrate. Carbohydrates become the predominant food source from which ATP is made when you exercise at moderate to high intensities. Compared to fat, when carbohydrates are used to make ATP, it takes less time to make ATP and more ATP can be made over any given time period. The faster you run, the more ATP you need compared to running at a slower pace. Therefore, the faster your running pace, the greater the need to have carbohydrates available to the muscle.

Another reason carbohydrates become the preferred fuel by the body when exercising at higher intensities is that carbohydrates can be used to make ATP both anaerobically, when the oxygen supply is not completely adequate, and aerobically. Since both aerobic and anaerobic breakdown of carbohydrates occurs, greater amounts of ATP can be made in less time using carbohydrates compared to fats.

Unfortunately, all carbohydrates are not created and used equally by the body. The two things all carbohydrates have in common is that each gram contains 4 kilocalories and by the time they are completely digested and made available to the muscle, they are all converted to glucose. Glucose is the common starting point for carbohydrate metabolism. If you eat a baked potato, it winds up as glucose. If you eat a bagel, it winds up as glucose. If you eat table sugar, it winds up as glucose. All carbohydrates wind up as glucose and glucose is primarily what active muscles use to make ATP. Glucose is called a "simple sugar" meaning that it isn't broken down into anything simpler before the body can use it. A potato is a starch or more correctly a "complex carbohydrate or sugar" meaning that before it can be used by the muscles it has to be broken down into a more simple chemical form. That more simple chemical form is glucose.

If all carbohydrates wind up as glucose, then why aren't all carbohydrates considered to be nutritionally equal? The two things that differ about carbohydrates are that they are digested at different rates and therefore glucose becomes available to the body at different rates, and they contain varying amounts of other nutrients, in particular vitamins and minerals. Simple sugars are digested more quickly and are made available to the muscles rapidly compared to most complex carbohydrates. In general, complex carbohydrates are digested less rapidly so that their energy availability is spread out over a longer period of time. In most individuals, this rate of appearance of carbohydrate as glucose doesn't have a large impact unless you are eating the carbohydrate in order to supply energy quickly, as during a long training run or the marathon. In this case, the quick appearance of glucose can be a definite advantage. This is why fluid replacement drinks contain simple sugars like glucose and fructose.

The biggest potential difference between simple and complex carbohydrates as mainstays of your diet is that complex carbohydrates usually provide a much higher level of vitamins and minerals than do simple carbohydrates. Think about where you get most of your simple sugars in your diet. They come predominantly from "sweet" things like candy, pop, ice cream, pastries, etc. These types of foods generally have little additional nutrition in the form of vitamins and minerals. On the other hand, most complex carbohydrates come from vegetables, cereal, and grain products and these foods generally have high quantities of vitamins and minerals.

From an energy provision standpoint, it doesn't make much difference whether you consume complex or simple carbohydrates. However, from a total nutrition standpoint, it does make a difference. In the long run, total nutrition is important for both performance and for health. Therefore, you should try to get most of your carbohydrates from complex sources. The exception to this is fruit. Most fruits contain fructose which is a simple sugar but they also contain good amounts of vitamins and minerals. So fruits, even though predominantly a simple-sugar source, can be treated as though they are complex carbohydrates.

What is the optimal amount of carbohydrates to eat? The answer to this question is best expressed relative to the total number of calories you eat. Carbohydrates should make up a certain percentage of your total daily calories. Most experts recommend that carbohydrates should make up 50-70% of your total calories consumed. For example, if you need 2000 kilocalories per day to maintain your body weight, you should eat 1000-1400 kilocalories of carbohydrates per day. Since each gram of carbohydrate contains 4 kilocalories, 250-350 grams of carbohydrates should be consumed each day.

Table 6.1 indicates the good and not-so-good sources of carbohydrates and Table 6.2 lists some of the best carbohydrate sources and the number of calories in a common serving. Begin to be more selective in your choice of carbohydrates. Reduce the amount of simple sugars you consume and increase the amount of complex carbohydrates. Your running and your health will benefit.

Glycogen. Glycogen is the way your body stores carbohydrates for future use. Chemically, glycogen is just individual glucose molecules that are chemically linked together in chains so they can be more efficiently stored. The two primary places in the body that glycogen is stored are in the liver and the skeletal muscles. When you eat a meal containing carbohydrates and the carbohydrates are digested and converted into glucose, the glucose is predominantly taken up by the liver and skeletal muscle and most is converted into glycogen and stored. If you happened to be exercising at this point in time, some of the glucose entering the muscle could immediately be used to make ATP but this would tend to be an exception rather than the rule. The likelihood is that, following a meal, there would not be a high demand for producing ATP in the

Table 6.1 Sources of Carbohydrates

Good Sources of Carbohydrates	Poor Sources of Carbohydrates
spaghetti, noodles, macaroni with tomato sauce, rice, potato, yams, stuffing without butter or gravy, lentils, chili beans, split peas, bread, muffins, bagels, French toast, pancakes, cereal, jam, jelly, honey, syrup, bananas, pineapples, raisins, figs, apple crisp, date squares, fig newtons, fruit juices, sherbet, ice milk, frozen yogurt	pizza, lasagna with lots of meat and cheese, french fries, fried rice, buttery potato, casseroles with rich sauces and gravies, donuts, croissants, danish pastry, eggs and breakfast meats, butter, margarine, cream cheese, cookies, cakes, pastries made with lots of butter, alcohol, milk shakes, frappes, ice cream

Table 6.2 Foods High in Carbohydrates and Low in Fats			
Selected High-Carbohydrate Foods	Energy (kcal)	Carbohydrates (g)	Fat (g)
Apple, medium	81	21	0
Grapes, 1 cup	58	16	0
Strawberry Yogurt, 1 cup	257	43	3.5
Peas, cooked, 1 cup	110	19	0
Applesauce, 1/2 cup	97	26	0
Banana, medium	105	27	0
Corn, cooked, 1/2 cup	88	21	0
Baked Potato, large	139	32	0
Raisins, 2/3 cup	300	79	0
Whole Wheat Bread, 1 slice	61	11	1
White Bread, 1 slice	64	12	1
Whole Wheat Bagel, 3" diameter	165	28	2
Corn Bread, 1 piece	198	29	7
Noodles, egg, 1 cup	178	33	2
Rice, Long Grain, 1 cup cooked	225	50	0
Corn Tortilla, 6" diameter	67	13	1
Spaghetti with Tomato sauce, 1 cup	179	34	1.5

muscle and most of the glucose would be stored as glycogen. Later, when you do exercise, the glycogen in the muscle is converted back to glucose and used to make ATP.

The glycogen in the liver has a different primary purpose than the glycogen in the muscle. The liver glycogen is used to maintain normal levels of glucose in the blood. This is extremely important because glucose in the blood (commonly called blood sugar) is the nutrient that the brain and nervous system require for normal function. Think about how you feel when you go too long without eating. You may become tired, irritable, light-headed or have any number of other symptoms indicating low blood sugar. Low blood sugar occurs when the liver runs out of glycogen due to not eating carbohydrates. Low blood sugar also affects exercise because the nervous system controls the muscular system. When the nervous system isn't functioning normally, the muscular system doesn't function normally. Therefore, it is important for the runner to maintain adequate amounts of liver glycogen.

One of the major problems with carbohydrates is that the body cannot store huge amounts. Compared to the ability to store fat, the body has a very limited ability to store carbohydrates. If all the carbohydrate depots in the body were maximally filled with glycogen, you would have about 1500-2000 kilocalories available. But in actuality, probably 25-50% of this total is not available to runners to provide ATP for running because it is located in muscles not used in running. Remember, once glucose enters a muscle cell, it is trapped inside that muscle cell and no other muscle cell, let alone a different muscle, can use it. The quadriceps cannot use the glycogen stored in the triceps and vice versa. Therefore, the glycogen stored in muscles not used in running does not benefit the runner.

So, how far could you run on, say, 1500 kilocalories from carbohydrate that would be available in your body? If carbohydrate were the only fuel being used, which it is not, then 1500 kilocalories would allow an average-size male to cover about 12-15 miles (each mile requires 100-125 kilocalories). Obviously, you could not cover 26.2 miles using just the stored carbohydrates you have. In the real world, both carbohydrates and fats are used when you run but this scenario does illustrate the importance of eating carbohydrates on a regular basis. You have to restock your carbohydrate stores quite frequently because you cannot store very much.

As mentioned, carbohydrates and fats share the major burden of supplying chemical energy to make ATP. As you may have already guessed, you have a much greater capacity to store fats than carbohydrates so that the quantity of fat available is never an issue. The average 150-pound male runner who may be 12-15% body fat would have 13-18 pounds of fat available for energy which translates into approximately 53,000-73,000 kilocalories, enough to cover 530-730 miles of running. A typical female runner weighing 120 pounds with 20-25% body fat would have 10-16 pounds of accessible fat accounting for 41,000-65,000 kilocalories, or enough to cover 546-866 miles of running. As you can readily see, most of us have more than enough fat to supply energy, sometimes more than what is consistent with good health.

Fats. Fats are important to the body because they are used in many structural and chemical processes. Everyone needs to consume some fat. Unfortunately, we sometimes consume far more fat than we need and this causes a potential health problem.

Fats are the other primary food we can use to make ATP. Unlike carbohydrates, fats can only be used to make ATP aerobically and because of this limitation, fat cannot be used to make as much ATP over a given time period as carbohydrates can. When you have plenty of oxygen available to the muscle, the body preferentially makes more ATP from fat than from carbohydrates because you have a lot more energy stored as fat than as carbohydrate. The body conserves its supply of glycogen whenever it can and using fat to supply part of the energy for muscular contraction is one way it does so.

Because of the way we generally eat, most of us get plenty of fat in our diets. The average American consumes 35-50% of total calories as fat. This is why we usually have plenty of storage fat. In order for a runner to get adequate amounts of carbohydrates and protein, normally the fat has to be reduced. Reducing fat consumption will be beneficial from both a performance and a health perspective. Optimally, fats should account for 30% or less of your daily caloric intake.

Not only do we often eat too many fats, but we also tend to eat the wrong kinds of fat. The unhealthy kind of fat is saturated fat, which is found in animal products (meat and dairy products). Unsaturated fat, found mostly in vegetable and grain products, is the more desirable type of fat to consume. It doesn't matter which you eat from the point of view of energy production, but unsaturated fats are much more healthy for you. So when you have a choice between animal fat and vegetable fat, vegetable fat is the healthier choice. There is one exception to this general rule. The tropical oils (palm and coconut oil) are highly saturated even though they are not animal fat. So it is best to stay away from these tropical oils as well as animal fat.

Protein. As previously mentioned, protein is not ordinarily used as a fuel to make ATP for muscular contraction. The primary purpose of protein is to build, maintain, and repair tissue. Because running is a traumatic activity and there is significant tissue damage that results from running, protein is essential in the diet of the runner. Protein helps your muscles and bones recover from all those miles of pounding.

The type of protein that is most necessary is called complete protein. Complete protein is protein that contains all the essential amino acids that the body requires for normal function. These amino acids are the end products of protein digestion and are the building blocks for many things in the body. The essential amino acids are the ones the body can't make from any other source. Complete protein comes predominantly from animal sources like meats, dairy products, and eggs. Vegetable sources of protein generally lack one or more of the essential amino acids.

The typical runner training for a marathon needs about 0.5-0.7 grams of protein for each pound of body weight per day. So a 120-pound female would need 60-84 grams of protein each day while a 150-pound male would need 75-105 grams per day. The majority of the protein should be from complete protein or if animal products are not consumed, careful planning should go into making sure all the essential amino acids are consumed by eating the appropriate combination of vegetable sources of protein.

Table 6.3 lists common sources of protein and gives a rating of how complete they are. Unfortunately, many of the good sources of protein are also high sources of saturated fat. If animal products comprise a large portion of your protein, be selective in choosing the lower fat sources. Poultry and fish usually have less

Table 6.3 Common Sources of Protein			
Food	Amino Acids	Average Serving	
		Grams of Protein	Serving Size
Milk Exchange			
Milk, skim	complete	9	8 oz.
Cheese, cheddar	complete	7	1 oz.
Yogurt	complete	8	1 cup
Meat Exchange			
Beef, cooked, lean	complete	24	3 oz.
Chicken, cooked, white	complete	24	3 oz.
Fish, cooked, white	complete	21	3 oz.
Eggs	complete	6	1
Vegetable Exchange			
Beans, medium	incomplete	1	1/2 cup
Carrot, medium	incomplete	1	1
Peas, green	incomplete	4	1/2 cup
Potato, baked, medium	incomplete	3	1
Fruit Exchange			
Banana, medium	incomplete	1	1
Orange, medium	incomplete	1	1
Apple, medium	incomplete	1	1
Starch/Bread Exchange			
Bread, wheat	incomplete	3	1 slice
Bread, white	incomplete	2	1 slice
Macaroni, cooked	incomplete	3	1/2 cup
Navy Beans, cooked	incomplete	7	1/2 cup
Peas, split, cooked	incomplete	9	1/2 cup
Spaghetti, cooked	incomplete	3	1/2 cup

fat than red meat, but by being selective in your choice of red meat, you can get good protein with minimal fat. Choose the leaner cuts of red meat like round steak instead of T-bone. Eat low-fat luncheon meats and drink skim milk. These kinds of dietary changes will help ensure your protein intake is adequate while your fat intake is minimized.

Mixing and Matching. As a percentage of total calories consumed, protein should comprise 15-20%, fats should comprise less than 30%, and carbohydrates should be the remainder. If you stick with these minimal guidelines, carbohydrates will be 50-55% of your total calories. Ideally, you should decrease fats even more and increase carbohydrates even higher. Your protein is the constant in this relationship and the carbohydrates and fats are inversely related. As fat consumption as a percentage of total calories goes down, carbohydrate consumption should go up.

It was mentioned before that both carbohydrates and fats are used to make ATP. Under what conditions is each used and how does this relationship change? Several factors determine how much carbohydrate and fat are used to make ATP. The factors are the intensity of the exercise, the duration of the exercise, the type of diet you are eating, and your level of conditioning. A brief explanation of each follows.

Energy and Intensity. At rest, the typical individual on a typical mixed diet will use about 70% fat and 30% carbohydrate for making ATP. As the intensity of the exercise increases, the proportion of fat decreases and carbohydrate increases. When you are working at about 50% of your capacity, a level that most people would consider a fairly easy effort, you are using about 50% carbohydrates and 50% fat. As you continue to increase your intensity, you increase the proportion of carbohydrates and decrease the proportion of fats. At the level that elite marathoners run (like a 2:10-2:20 marathon), they are burning about 70% carbohydrates and 30% fat during the first half of the marathon before their carbohydrates start to deplete. An activity like running 1/4 to 1/2 mile as fast as you could would use 95% carbohydrates and only 5% fats. So the basic rule is the higher the intensity, the more carbohydrates you use.

Energy and Duration. The longer the duration of the exercise at any intensity, the proportion of fat use goes up. This happens because as carbohydrates begin to deplete, fat has to be used more. Ideally, marathoners hope that they don't run out of carbohydrates until the end of the race. However, they often run out before that and, as a consequence, they experience a phenomenon often called "hitting the wall." When you hit the wall, you have to slow your pace and the work becomes much more difficult. When fats are the major source from which to make ATP, you just can't run as fast. You can continue running, just at a reduced speed.

Energy and Training. The more trained or fit you are, the more fats you use at any level of effort. Training increases your ability to use fats at higher intensities. This is a very advantageous adaptation for marathoners because it allows you to conserve your carbohydrates for later in the run and you are not as likely to run out of carbohydrates.

Energy and Diet. Eating a high-carbohydrate diet increases the proportion of carbohydrates you use. Eating a high-fat diet increases the proportion of fats you use. This type of change occurs fairly rapidly and it actually begins to occur right after a single meal. If your diet consists of a high proportion of carbohydrates on a regular basis, then you will burn more carbohydrates for energy all the time, at rest and during exercise and the same is true for fats. There have been several recent reports in the sceintific literature that have concluded that more aerobic work can be done if a diet higher in fat (45-50% fat) than is typically recommended is consumed. These reports contradict decades of traditional nutritional knowledge about the benefits of consuming a high-carbohydrate diet for long duration activities like running a marathon. This new information has not yet been subjected to rigorous replication by other scientists and the consensus among many nutritional experts is that a high-carbohydrate intake is still the appropriate path to follow. Certainly, from an overall health perspective, a high-fat diet is not recommended.

Diet and Weight. In addition to eating adequate amounts of protein and carbohydrates, another key to optimal nutrition is eating the proper number of total calories. Many people who begin exercising or who have thoughts of running a marathon may have grandiose ideas of losing large amounts of weight. Such expectations sometimes far exceed reason and the limitations imposed by physiology. The key to weight loss is a combination of caloric reduction and an increase in caloric expenditure. Either by itself makes success far less likely. In training for the marathon, you will be automatically increasing your caloric expenditure. Combining this with a modest reduction in caloric intake would produce even larger weight loss.

Consider that the total energy expended during the entire marathon training program is approximately 41,800 kilocalories or the equivalent of 12 pounds of fat. So if you didn't increase your caloric intake above that which maintained your weight before your started training for the marathon, and went through the entire training program, you could reasonably expect to lose about 10-12 pounds. If however, you decreased the number of calories necessary to maintain your weight before training by 500 kilocalories per day, you could lose and additional 16 pounds. Sounds easy, right?

The potential problem with this approach is that it becomes easy to increase your caloric consumption rather than decrease it because the amount of exercise you will be doing tends to stimulate the appetite. This is another reason it is important to decrease your consumption of fats and increase your consumption of carbohydrates. You can eat much more bulk with carbohydrates than with fats and the bulk tends to suppress the appetite. You can actually eat more and get fewer calories. As long as you keep your carbohydrates at an adequate level, your caloric deficit will use some to the stored fat you have and thereby reduce your total fatness.

Vitamins and Minerals

Vitamins and minerals complete the nutrition picture for optimal functioning of the body. Most of you are going to be interested in your overall health in addition to running a marathon. In fact, as you begin to see and feel the changes in your body resulting from the running, you will be that much more motivated to do everything you can to promote good health and well-being for the long haul. If you have not been a regular exerciser before, this program can be the start of a lifestyle in which you are committed to attaining and maintaining optimal health. Good overall nutrition is a major part of this effort.

Vitamins are complex organic compounds that are involved in almost every metabolic process in the human body. Minerals are inorganic elements found in nature that are essential to life. Vitamins and minerals are intimately involved in structural and chemical functions of the body. Adequate vitamin and mineral intake comes from eating a wide variety of foods from all the food groups. As mentioned earlier relative to carbohydrates, good sources of vitamins and minerals generally are found in complex carbohydrate sources as opposed to simple carbohydrates (remember the exception is fruit) and in animal products. The more processed a food is, the less will be the vitamin and mineral content unless the processed food is fortified with vitamins and minerals, as in many breakfast cereals. Everything else being equal, raw and unprocessed foods will give you more vitamins and minerals.

Research has consistently supported the concept that if people get adequate vitamins and minerals from their foods, there is no need to take vitamin and mineral supplements. But this is a mighty big if! The problem is that studies evaluating the nutritional intake of the average individual have found that most of us do not get adequate vitamins and minerals in our diets. Studies on athletes have come to the same conclusion. Many, if not most of us, do not eat nutritionally adequate diets. Also, there is relatively recent information that strongly suggests that the recommended daily amount (RDA) for some of the vitamins and minerals is actually too low, a fact which only compounds the potential problem of inadequate vitamin and mineral intake.

So what is the solution to this dilemma? Our recommendation is that, unless you are very confident that you are consuming a nutritionally adequate diet, you should take a one-a-day type vitamin and mineral supplement which usually provides no more than 100% of the RDA for the vitamins and minerals.

These are inexpensive and the amount of vitamins and minerals is not enough to cause potential problems with taking too much. They are like a nutritional insurance policy. They are there if you need them.

There are several specific vitamins and minerals which deserve special consideration. Recent nutrition research has provided a basis for reassessing traditional thought concerning the RDA for certain vitamins and minerals. Although the evidence is not absolutely conclusive at this point in time, it is sufficient for you to give some extra consideration to these issues.

Antioxidants. During the normal chemical processes that produce ATP in the cells, potentially damaging substances called free radicals are produced. These free radicals can damage different parts of the cell including the cell membrane. We normally have body defenses which can adequately handle free radicals. However, when a person exercises a lot, free radical production is increased. The current controversy is whether this increase in free radical production increases the risk of cell damage.

Nutritional antioxidants comprise a broad range of essential and nonessential nutrients that can aid in the detoxification of potentially damaging free radicals. The best known of these antioxidants are some of the vitamins and minerals that we should be consuming on a regular basis. The most well researched antioxidants are vitamin E, C, and beta-carotene (a vitamin A precursor). One of the concerns that has been raised by some is whether individuals who exercise on a regular basis need more of these antioxidants than normal. If there is also a likelihood that you may not be getting even "normal amounts" of these vitamins in your diet, then there could certainly be some benefit to supplementing your intake of antioxidants.

Calcium. Calcium is the most abundant mineral in the body, accounting for about 2% of the body weight. As you are probably well aware, calcium plays a critical role in bone formation and bone strength. Running is an activity that has the potential to increase your bone strength but only if your calcium intake is adequate. However, if your bone strength is low when you begin running, the trauma of running can increase the likelihood of injuries involving bone, like stress fractures. Unfortunately, runners tend to be at higher risk for inadequate calcium intake, especially female runners. The long-term unfortunate outcome for many that do not consume adequate calcium is osteoporosis later in life.

Make sure your consumption of calcium is adequate. The current RDA for adults younger than 25 years is 1200 mg per day. For adults 25 years and older, the RDA is 800 mg. There are many experts who think these RDAs are too low and that adults need between 1200-1500 mg of calcium daily.

If you do not eat or drink dairy products it is unlikely that you are consuming adequate calcium without supplementing. Table 6.4 lists the calcium content of some common foods and it is pretty clear that if you do not eat or drink milk, yogurt or cheese, it is going to be difficult to get enough calcium. Evaluate your diet and identify the primary sources of calcium. If you are not getting enough, either make an effort to eat more of the right kinds of food or supplement with calcium.

Table 6.4 Calcium in Selected Foods		
Food	Approximate Measure	Calcium (mg)
Milk, skim	8 oz.	300
Milk, whole	8 oz.	290
Cheese, cheddar	1 oz.	213
Yogurt, lowfat	4 oz.	225
Ice Cream	1 cup	176
Chicken	3 oz.	11
Beef	3 oz.	10
Egg, large	1	51
Peas, cooked	2/3 cups	25
Spinach, cooked	1/2 cup packed	89
Broccoli, cooked	1 cup	136
Apple, medium	1	10
Orange, medium	1	54
Bread, white enriched	1 slice	21

Iron. Iron is a trace mineral that is involved in oxygen transport and aerobic metabolism. Iron is one of the components of hemoglobin, the compound that attaches to oxygen and carries oxygen around in the blood. Without hemoglobin to transport oxygen, we could not survive. Because the optimal transport of oxygen is so important to the runner, iron becomes one of the key nutrients that runners should make sure they are getting in their diets. Various research studies have found that as many as 50-80% of female athletes, particularly endurance runners, are at risk of iron deficiency. The reason this may be so high in runners is that endurance athletes, especially females, tend to reduce their caloric consumption in order to maintain a lower body weight. In so doing, they do not eat enough meat and most of us get most of our iron from meat. At the same time, the trauma associated with running probably increases iron loss.

Dietary iron comes in two forms, heme iron found in animal products like meat and nonheme iron found in plants. Heme iron is absorbed more easily by the body compared to nonheme iron and is the preferred iron source. Table 6.5 lists the iron content of selected foods. The current RDA is 10 mg for teenagers and adult males and 15 mg for menstruating teenagers and adult females. Take a look at your diet and get a feeling for the amount of iron you are consuming. If you do not eat much meat, your iron intake is likely to be low. Bread, cereal and other wholesome carbohydrates are good sources of iron if the words "enriched" or "fortified" are on the food label. In general, grain products offer very little iron, and because the iron is nonheme iron, it is poorly absorbed. Consuming animal protein along with nonheme iron sources enhances the absorption of the nonheme iron. Vitamin C also enhances the absorption of iron.

Table 6.5 Iron in Selected Foods		
Food	Quantity	Iron (mg)
Liver, cooked	4 oz.	10
Beef, roasted	4 oz.	6
Pork, roasted	4 oz.	5
Turkey, roasted dark meat	4 oz.	3
Tuna, canned, light	6.5 oz.	2
Chicken Breast, roasted	4 oz.	1
Haddock, broiled	4 oz.	1
Egg, large	1	1
Prune Juice	8 oz	3
Apricots, dried	12 halves	2
Dates, dried	10	1
Raisins	1/3 cup	1
Spinach, cooked	1/2 cup	2
Green Peas, cooked	1/2 cup	1
Broccoli, raw	1/2 cup	1
Baked Beans	1/2 cup	2
Kidney Beans	1/2 cup	2
Dry Cereal, fortified	3/4 cup	18
Spaghetti, cooked, enriched	1 cup	2
Bread, enriched	1 slice	1

PART 3   And Monkey Hear, Too

We humans are marvelous creations. Not only do we have mental monitors the likes of which technology will never duplicate, but we come with the most sophisticated sound boards imaginable. What visualizations are to the monitor, self-talk is to the sound board. While each of these cognitive components is extremely powerful on its own, when combined they constitute the programming language of the brain and are strong enough to control the entire system...that would be you.

As was explained earlier in the chapter and the following examples will show, the brain believes what it is told and alters behavior to match so that the system is not in a state of dissonance. It is a report-response feedback loop that is automatic and continuous. So as long as you are constantly talking to yourself anyway, why not be telling yourself something that will be self-promoting rather than self-destructive. All this takes is a heightened awareness of your self-talk content and a little practice to replace the negative self-talk with positive.

The following analysis of my self-talk over the course of the training program reveals some interesting changes in content, the position of the "voice," and the perceived location of control. As you read, keep in mind what was said earlier about self-talk essentially being the equivalent of self-programming. What kind of reality was I creating for myself as a result? An even better exercise would be to ask yourself that same question about your own self-talk.

When I was out walking in the pretraining stage prior to the start of the running schedule, I would say to myself, "You can do this, you can do this," in a commanding, berating voice which almost seemed to be outside of myself. The voice I was hearing was distant, uninvested, and impersonal. With every step the voice grew more stern and loud until I would mentally collapse under its assault. Then I would think, "You're dreaming. You'll never be able to do this. This is hopeless."

Buying the training shoes was the first turning point (of many) in my self-talk. Once I started walking in the best fitting, feeling, and most expensive pair of shoes I'd ever owned, I started thinking, "You are worth it." It became a chant in time with my steps, and initially the "voice" saying it seemed to be outside of myself, but was warmer and more supportive.

During the first two weeks of the training schedule, the position of the voice changed from detached and critical to more like that of a coach, cheerleader, or ally. While it remained outside of the personal "I," it did not seem as distant and critical as before. "Pull through...keep going...you're all right...push out...keep going...you can do this...looking good..." comprised my chants which would vary in intensity and duration with my activity level and how I felt.

In the third week of training, the first person "I" emerged and was intermittent with the "You" of the second person. I found myself saying things like, "It's OK...Looking good...I can do this...You're all right...Just keep going...I'm running!" When spoken in the first-person, the chants were primarily in response to the running situation of the moment; while it sounded like the location of control was internal, the power of the moment continued to lie outside of myself. I was still giving away control to the external situation.

A real breakthrough happened in week four when I consciously assumed control of my self-talk. As "I" permanently replaced "You," the self-talk changed from outside-centered, hypnotic mantras to more of a self-dialogue about the running. I became my own coach, best friend, and greatest ally as I assumed an internal locus of control. Through friendly self-affirmations such as, "I am running. I can do this. Good. I want to run. I'm glad I am doing this. This feels good. I like running," I took back the power that I had previously been giving away. By consciously determining the words I was controlling the situation, whereas before it had controlled me.

Despite this discovery, there were times when I regressed to situation-based, negative self-talk spoken in the second-person "you." It seemed worse when I was under a lot of deadline pressures and had other things I felt I should have been doing instead of running. As long as I mentally carried the weight of those "shoulds" with me, running was an effort-laden ordeal. As soon as I mentally "shelved" everything else and focused just on the running, things went much better. As an example, I clearly remember the first 14-mile run. I had had a lousy week. It was mid-term, assignments were due in every class, my kids were acting out, I was struggling just to keep my head above water, and we had to do this 14-miler. I remember thinking, "That's over half a marathon!" The following entry from my journal summarized what happened:

> *What a lousy run! It was my worst yet. I walked more times today than I have all the other times combined. I just could not keep myself going. Physically I was OK, but I kept hearing a voice saying, "This is stupid! This is totally stupid. Why would anyone want to run 14 miles?" And when my conscious mind couldn't come up with an answer, I would stop running and walk. I walked a lot. I couldn't seem to come up with a positive answer to counter and squelch the negative self-talk.*

It was the worst run of the entire training schedule.

A week later I had the best run of the entire training schedule — and it was another 14 miler! One of the things that contributed to the dramatic change was the self-talk I had started using earlier that week. I adopted a modified version of a personal paragraph that Dave had shared in class that week. Mine went: "I am a marathoner. Thirty miles a week. I love to run. I'm mind-body strong. Get stronger every day. I will not stop." This was said (often out loud) in synch with my steps, and quickly replaced all other self-talk. Never after did my running seems as effortful as it had only the week before.

I continued to refine the last line of my paragraph over the remaining weeks. Changing the negative-based "I will not stop" to the positive-based "I can do this" helped to substantially decrease the number of times I walked.

Use of the paragraph progressed to the point of being automatic. Sometimes I found that I had gone on to thinking about something else, but could still hear it being repeated in my mind on its own - almost like listening to a song while thinking about something else.

By marathon day my paragraph was: "I am a marathoner. 30 miles a week. I love to run. I'm mind-body strong. Get stronger every step. I am doing this because..." and it would repeat itself. I said this for 20 miles until I hit "The Wall." After that my self-talk changed, and you'll read about that in a later chapter.

This analysis suggests that self-talk is a barometer of one's locus of control. Where the locus of control lies, so too lies the power over one's cognitions and ensuing self-concept. When I look back at how my self-talk changed over the course of training, I can see that in terms of self-concept I went a lot further than 26.2 miles!

Jennifer Haglund, who was a miler and two-miler in high school, had this to say about self-talk:

Positive self-talk was the most helpful strategy for me. "I am a marathoner" made me really believe it was going to happen. I made signs and hung them on my walls; I even took them with me when I went home for the weekends. It was great.

Julie Stone remembers:

I found that saying over and over in my mind a word pattern in an order really helped. " I can, I can, I can....she can...we can... you can." Saying this really helped to focus and stay in sync.

Heidi Brandt used a different kind of self-talk which for her proved to be just as effective:

I sang to myself all the time. Queen's "We are the Champions," and Green Day's "When I Come Around." Sometimes I'd sing the cheer, "We got spirit!"

Jane Mortenson, who as we described earlier was battling cancer, offers this:

When I felt the running was really hard I used several mantras: "I am a marathoner; I can do this; I'm so glad I'm not hooked up to a respirator." That had a way of quickly putting everything in perspective and reframing the activity as fun and a gift to be able to be in a marathon.

Sometimes I would use a mantra, but change the noun at every mile like, "My heart is getting stronger," "My lungs are getting stronger," "My legs are getting stronger." I really felt that by telling myself I was getting stronger, I was.

I also would go through the alphabet and think of things I was grateful for. A was for Active, B was for Bold, C for Courage.... I could get through several miles with this little game.

Patti Hasty Rust reflects:

Positive self-talk can really help you with all areas of your life. It helps you to just have a better outlook on life in general; not just to get you through a marathon, but the day-to-day things you deal with.
Also, it is important to feed off the positive support and encouragement of others. Remember the things they say and incorporate them into your self-talk.

If you haven't already written out your paragraphs and posted them in conspicuous places, do that now. Visualization and self-talk are two of the most powerful mental techniques you can use. And you will need to use them.

General Tips From the Marathoners — Week Six:
- In the beginning my body fat was too low. I didn't eat enough. Dr. Dolgener had me eat Dairy Queen and french fries. Eventually it got to be a routine for Friday night. I started to feel the difference later on in the training.
- After I'd been running for awhile, I got my cholesterol checked, and the results were really good. They asked me if I exercised a lot. I thought, "Wow, it really does help!"

	Scheduled Distance	Actual Distance	RPE
Day 1	4		
Comments:			
Day 2	5		
Comments:			
Day 3	4		
Comments:			
Day 4	11		
Comments:			

Total Miles This Week_____Cumulative Total_____

Chapter 7:

W e e k   S e v e n
Closing in on Half-Way There

You have done enough running now to know that there are times during your runs when you are focused and concentrating on what you are doing and there are other times when you are "spacing off." You may like the times when you are spaced off because the time seems to go quickly and, sometimes, before you know it, you are finished with your run. In Chapter 11 we will discuss what are called associative and dissociative mental techniques that you can use, but for now we want you to learn to concentrate when you need to do so (and you WILL need to do so in the marathon).

You may have had the following experience late in some of your long runs. Let's say it was one of the last few weekends, maybe last weekend during that 11-mile run, when you had completed about 9 miles of it. You were running alone and you were getting really tired. You started slowing down. Maybe you even started shuffling along, hardly running at all. You were still moving, not wanting to walk, but you were losing your running form and feeling like you could barely move. Then, suddenly, you saw someone you knew coming the other way. From somewhere deep inside you found some energy, you lifted your head, your knees came up a little bit, you increased your speed, smiled and waved to your friend. And, just for a minute or so, you felt pretty good again. What was going on there?

The answer is that before you saw your friend, you were losing your focus or your concentration. Fatigue can do that to us. But when you saw your friend, you found new energy, concentrated on your running form and were able to resume it pretty well. That should tell you that the fatigue you were feeling was only partly physical. It was also partly mental. The physical part of it, even if we take care of hydration and eating right and all the other aspects of it, is still inevitable as we keep increasing the length of our runs. You are going to get tired. That's just part of getting stronger. We have to push ourselves to reach the goal. But the mental part of it is, in large part, avoidable. We can learn to be better at maintaining our concentration and that will help us maintain our running form and thus our speed. It will also, because behavior change leads to attitude change, make us feel stronger psychologically. When we are running with better form it makes us feel more confident.

What happens when you lose your concentration is that you are using only a portion of your physical capability. Think of it this way. If you have 50 units of talent or ability and you are not using 25 units of it, it is as if you had only 25 units of ability. The difference between athletes who perform well consistently and those who perform well on only a few occasions is often not the amount of raw ability they have but the ability to concentrate on the task at hand in order to use all of the ability they possess. In some sports, consistency is less important than in others, but in your sport, endurance running, consistency (and therefore the ability to focus and concentrate) is extremely important.

The ability to focus on just one thing for an extended period of time is a problem for many people, perhaps in part because the lifestyle that has become predominant in America is one which involves a fairly rapid pace and, often, doing more than one thing at a time. If your life is like that, you may need to work on your focus and concentration abilties in order to be able to make the best use of all of your training on marathon day. This will be especially important during those last 6 or 8 miles of the marathon, when fatigue will make it even more difficult to maintain your pace.

So, how can you become better at maintaining your concentration? As with everything else we are doing, it will take some practice, but you will see some improvement rather quickly by doing the following exercises. We recommend that you do Exercise #1 (The Number Concentration Table on the next page) several times every other day for the next few weeks. All you do is cross out the numbers in order, beginning with 00 and continuing up to 99. Obviously, you will need to make some copies of it before you mark on it. It seems to work best if you time yourself and keep track of how long it takes you to do it each time. This will help you track your progress and, when you get to the point at which you can do it very rapidly, you should make up a new table with the numbers in a different pattern so that it remains a concentration exercise, instead of a memorization exercise.

Another easy and convenient way to improve your concentration skills is to take a newspaper and give yourself the task of crossing out all of a certain

06	50	13	84	57	33	90	46	68	18
38	72	19	67	04	44	01	60	87	29
61	10	58	92	27	75	35	95	22	83
26	31	64	48	08	55	98	40	78	71
54	00	41	97	14	51	81	12	03	36
15	66	86	70	20	79	93	32	53	62
76	23	94	17	37	85	39	88	07	25
47	82	63	02	73	09	65	99	42	59
05	34	11	56	89	24	96	16	91	45
21	74	52	43	28	77	49	69	80	30

Exercise 1

letter in the text of one or several articles. First try, for example, crossing out all the u's you can find. Then try to cross out all the t's. And then, when you get better, try crossing out all the f's. The f's will be more difficult because they are sometimes pronounced as v's and this will make them more of a challenge.

Another way to get better at focusing is to play the old game of concentration with an ordinary deck of playing cards. Just spread them out face down on the floor or on a table. Then turn one over, look at it, turn it back over (try to remember what and where it is), then turn over another one, and another...looking for matches. If you can get somebody else to play this game with you, it can be competitive and fun and good focus practice at the same time.

There are also some ways you can improve your concentration and focus skills by using ordinary objects around you. Try this. Go and get your running shoes. Now take one of them in your hands and study it carefully. Examine it in great detail. Look for marks on the sides and the uppers. Turn it over and look carefully at the bottom. Study how it is worn differently in different parts of the sole. Memorize the tread pattern and try to visualize it in your mind. When you have studied it completely, put it down and pick up its mate. Look for differences between the two such as different marks and different tread wear patterns. You can do this exercise with any ordinary objects that you see every day but do not usually attend to. Or, if sounds interest you, you may want to sit quietly (either indoors or out) and concentrate on what you hear. Try to do this for several minutes. Work hard at not letting anything else (such as other thoughts) interfere with your listening. Some people enjoy using their sense of touch to develop their ability to concentrate. Try walking around your house touching things slowly and feeling for textures or perhaps you might try smelling things. The point of all this is to train yourself to focus and to resist distraction.

One more idea is to use your own body to learn to concentrate. Try this. Try to tighten the muscles in your big toe without tightening the muscles in your calf. Go ahead and try it right now. It's not easy, is it? A good way to improve your ability to concentrate is to work on doing that until you can do it easily. If you succeed, then try tightening the muscles in arch of your foot without tightening your calf muscles, etc. You can work on doing it with your hands and arms too. We'll discuss this technique more in Chapter 10.

We are trying to give you lots of different ways to do this because we have found that most people think some of these things are silly and find others interesting and useful. Perhaps you will make up your own ways to get better at concentrating. Whatever works for you is what you should use, but use something, because, believe us, you are going to need to be good at focusing on the task at hand on marathon day.

 Physical Preparation

> ### Week 7 Training
> Day 1: 4 miles
> Day 2: 6 miles
> Day 3: 4 miles
> Day 4: 12 miles
> ### Total for Week: 26 miles

Your total distance for the week will be just 2 tenths of a mile short of a marathon. In effect, you will run a marathon this week, just not all at one time. The mileage on the moderate day is increased by one mile to 6 miles and the long day is increased by one mile to 12 miles. Not counting the last two weeks of training which are taper weeks, you will be half through your training when you finish your 12-mile run this week. Progress has been consistent and if you maintain the training schedule, you will be ready for the marathon in nine weeks.

In the previous six chapters, we have discussed the physiological impact of your diet and fluid intake. As you enter the last half of the training program and the mileage becomes longer and longer, nutrition and fluid intake become even more important. Now is the time to make a concerted effort to maximize your chances for success by eating and drinking appropriately.

Rest and Recovery

Throughout the first six weeks of training, your body has been adjusting and adapting to the running. It may be that by now, many of the early aches and pains have gone away and you feel pretty good. There may still be some stiffness and soreness following the long run, but for the most part your training has progressed to the point that it may be pretty much pain-free. On the other hand, you may still be adapting and because each week brings on additional stress, each week brings on additional aches and pains. No two people will adapt in exactly the same way. There are many factors which dictate exactly how you will adapt, and just because you have a few more aches and pains than someone else does not mean something is wrong with you.

This process of adapting to the increased running is referred to as a chronic training response. The human body is a marvelous piece of machinery. It is very pliable and adaptable. In common exercise jargon, you are going through a program of progressive overload. This simply means that, on a weekly basis, you are gradually asking your body to do more and more work. The three physiological systems that are primarily being overloaded are the muscular system, the skeletal system, and the cardiorespiratory system. Week by week, as you increase your mileage, these systems are adapting and getting better at doing what they are supposed to do. They are becoming more efficient at what they do as well as increasing their total capacity for performing their specific functions.

In training programs, we often focus on the act of the training itself, like the running you are doing. We sometimes do not consider the other half of the program that is just as critical as the actual training. The other half is the recovery period. A training program is really a cycle of imposed stress followed by recovery from the stress. The cycle is then repeated, sometimes every day, sometimes every other day. It is the combination of the imposed stress and the recovery period that actually produces the adaptations that occur in the body.

The two keys to optimal training are to impose the right amount of stress (mileage in your case) and to allow adequate recovery from the stress. Our experience has shown us that if you stick to our training schedule, you will be getting the right amount of stress. The proper amount of recovery is more under your control. Recovery includes three areas, energy recovery, fluid recovery, and general cellular recovery which comes with adequate sleep.

In previous chapters, the topics of nutrition and fluids have been discussed in detail. Without adequate caloric and fluid consumption, you will not recover day to day. You may have noticed already that by the end of the week of training you may feel more fatigued than you did at the beginning of the week. If this is occurring on a regular basis, it may be due to inadequate carbohydrate consumption throughout the week. The scenario may be that following the long run of the week you have a day of recovery on the weekend during which you eat and rest more than you do during the week. This will promote greater glycogen storage so that you begin the week fairly stocked with glycogen. To fully restore glycogen after a depleting run takes about 24 hours assuming your carbohydrate intake is adequate. However, if you do not continue to eat adequate amounts of carbohydrates during the week, your glycogen stores will decrease throughout the week and by the end of the week you will be more fatigued than you were at the beginning of the week. The way to prevent this scenario is to consume adequate carbohydrates each day throughout the week.

The scenario regarding hydration parallels the above pattern with carbohydrates. If you do not drink adequate fluids every day throughout the week, you may gradually dehydrate by the end of the week. Dehydration reduces your ability to adapt to training and decreases your desire to train. Also, depletion of glycogen combined with dehydration can cause double trouble.

Adequate sleep plays a central role in the body's overall ability to recover from the previous 15-18 hours you have been awake. Even if you were not training, adequate sleep would be important to normal body function. The additional stress imposed on the body by training for a marathon makes adequate sleep even more important. The major question is how much sleep is enough? There is no simple answer to this question. Different people require different amounts of sleep. Most require 6-9 hours each night. The important thing is that you combine adequate sleep on a regular basis with the nutritional and fluid requirements. A lack of any of these three can cause problems and the problems can be compounded by coexistence of two or more.

Missing a few hours of sleep here and there during the training program will not have a significant impact. But, not getting sufficient sleep on a regular basis can lead to more ominous consequences. Training adaptations will be diminished and even reversed. So pay attention to your sleep, just like you pay attention to your eating and drinking. You need to make adequate sleep a priority, not a luxury.

Overtraining. Some athletes reach a physiological and mental state referred to as overtraining. Normally, overtraining is due to doing more training than the body can recover from. The general philosophy of these athletes is that if a certain amount of training is good, then more must be even better. So instead of running 30 miles a week, they start running 50 miles a week, then 80 or even 100 miles a week. But the body has a limit to what it can tolerate and too much stress causes a response opposite to the one you are hoping for. Overtraining can also result from not enough recovery. The training is not absolutely too much, but it is too much relative to the amount of recovery. An athlete could become overtrained by not getting adequate recovery as well as by doing too much training.

Experience has shown us that the amount of training you are doing in this program is just enough for you to be successful in completing a marathon. So, in order not to become overtrained, you need to provide sufficient rest and recovery for the amount of training you are doing. Table 7.1 list some of the symptoms of overtraining or incomplete recovery. One of the most objective and consistent symptoms is an increase in resting heart rate. This is a good way to objectively track your recovery. What should happen over the course of the training is that the resting heart rate should go down. If the resting heart rate goes up, overtraining or insufficient recovery is a likely cause. You need to be careful to measure your resting heart rate under the same conditions each day. The best time to do it is in the morning after you wake up but before you get out of bed.

The other more subjective symptoms listed can be important indicators of overtraining as well but many of these symptoms occur periodically even when you are not overtraining. For example, it is very common to feel more tired on some days than on others. Periodic feelings of tiredness are not necessarily due to overtaining or inadequate recovery. However, if the listed symptoms are prolonged, then overtraining or inadequate recovery is certainly a possibilty. If you follow our program, you are not likely to become overtrained. Please don't think

Table 7.1 Symptoms of Overtraining
Increase in resting heart rate
Retarded recovery of heart rate after exercise
Decreased performance
Amenorrhea
Weight loss
Increased incidence of infections
Increased perception of effort for a fixed amount of exercise
Persistent muscle soreness
Disturbance of normal sleep patterns
Increased anxiety and depression
Decreased sex drive

that if our program is sufficient for you to complete the marathon then more training will be even better. Just trust our experience with hundreds of runners and stick to our program.

PART 2 Turning Points

I distinctly remember the class lectures pertaining to the issues discussed in this chapter. It seemed ironic and slightly sadistic that we would be hearing about the importance of sleep and not overtraining right at mid-semester when most of us were probably putting in long nights studying for mid-term exams or finishing papers. I remember how we rather sheepishly took off our shoes and at the instructor's prodding studied the fine nuances of each in spite of the apparent silliness of doing so. I recall thinking that now that we were pretty well into the training program, the instructors must be having to come up with filler material so that they have something to talk about until we got closer to the actual marathon. I was wrong.

What I didn't appreciate at the time, but do now, is that this material sets the foundation for the next four weeks of training. This is not silly, filler material. It is critical that you take it seriously because subsequent instructions and techniques build upon it. It is at this point in the training that things can start to happen: aches and pains that weren't there before, bouts of bronchitis or sinus infections, blisters or chafing problems due to the increased mileage.

At a point in the training where you might begin to feel fairly comfortable with the training routine and think you can start to relax and focus on other things, is just the time when you don't want to do that. It is important that you maintain your focus and work at increasing it by doing the exercises suggested in order to stay injury-free, and be ready to make the most of the mental conditioning techniques to come.

There is no doubt that training for a marathon involves time - something which most of us already feel we don't have enough of. The next six weeks comprise the most time-consuming section of the program. It is during this time that many participants experience turning points in their training...an existential rededication of sorts. With that in mind, now would be a good time to remind yourself just why you decided to do this program.

If you're having trouble remembering, maybe this will help:

Training for and running a marathon is not a single event; rather, it is an experience. It is a discovery of self that will forever change your perceptions, perspectives, priorities, and possibilities. You will meet yourself at what you thought were the boundaries of your potential and endurance and watch in awe as they evaporate to reveal only open expanse. To know that the only boundaries in life are those which we create ourselves is a discovery which can not be taught — it must be experienced. For once you have seen the view from the mountain top, living a life of voluntary blindness is no longer an option.

Focusing is always harder when you have lots going on in your life, so we thought you might like to hear some thoughts from past participants on the issue of time and how they managed to incorporate the training into their schedules.

As the managing editor of news operations and chief anchor person for a local television channel, working within a tight schedule was nothing new to Ron Steele:

> *The hardest part of this training program is making the time to do it. It's not the running itself...it's finding the time. We are all so busy. I work second shift. My three children were in school during the day and my wife went to work early, so I did all my running in the morning or at noon and then I went to work. There were certain days when I had some work which involved traveling and that made it more difficult, but I always made it up. I never missed a day of training. It comes down to just making the time. There is always time enough for what is important.*

> *A lot of people sit back and say, "Why do you waste your time doing that? Why would you want to do that anyway?" To me, this type of activity reveals a basic side of a person. You're out there pitting yourself against nature. It's just you and the pavement. You are surrounded by other people, but they really don't matter because you're not racing against them. You're not racing against the clock. It's just you throughout and you run until you're done.*

Eric Johnson reported:

> *My time management was great during marathon training. I want that semester back! I didn't waste my time playing video games or anything. I was taking 19 credit hours, I was a Resident Assistant in the dorm, and I had a job. I could do it all!*

As a nontraditional student, Patti Hasty Rust was even busier than most of her classmates as the following account suggests:

> *It's amazing to me when I look back at all the things I had going on while I was training for the marathon. Not only was I working, but I*

had a lot of additional responsibilities given to me at work on a temporary basis because my supervisor was working on a special project. So I ended up supervising several people and was working on a major project myself. I was also on some committees at church that took a lot of time. Plus I had my responsibilities at home to my husband and my one-year-old son, and was attending graduate classes toward my MBA at that same time.

I probably had more demands on my time than at any other time in my life, but when I look back on it, it seems to me that training for the marathon actually helped me get through it. I don't know how to explain that exactly, but I really think it gave me a better mindset toward everything I was doing at the time, and helped me manage it and deal with the stress better than I would have if I hadn't been involved in the marathon class.

Although throughout most of the class I felt pretty confident that I would be able to complete the training and run the marathon, there were a couple of times when I had second thoughts and even considered dropping out. I had to miss one of the longer Saturday runs because my young son was in the hospital with a respiratory virus and both my husband and I ended up with the flu. My son had been sick quite a bit that winter and at that point I remember thinking, "What am I doing in this class when I have my son to take care of? Shouldn't I be there for him instead of out running?" When I called Forrest and left a message that I wasn't going to be able to make the run, I guess I was really considering dropping out.

We got past the weekend and got our son back home. By the time I had a chance to talk to Forrest I was feeling a little better. I reminded myself that by running, I was giving my son a healthier and happier mom. Even though he was too young to realize it then, I hoped that possibly I might be setting an example which would be helpful to him later in his life should there come a time when he faced what seemed to be an unreachable goal. Still, I had real concerns about how having missed that long run would hurt my chances of finishing the marathon and whether or not I should even continue. He was great. He listened to my concerns and assured me that in the whole scheme of things missing one or two runs (even long runs) was not enough to undo all the rest of the training. He suggested I just try to run a little bit extra that week to make up for it and not worry about it. I did that and felt I was able to get right back into it and having missed that long run didn't seem to affect me at *all. That Saturday I did the long run just like nothing had happened. In a way, I guess that was kind of a turning point for me. I mentally rededicated myself to doing this and never looked back.*

Ron Steele's turning point happened on one very cold winter day:

I remember having to do one of the long runs on a day when there was a bitterly cold headwind blowing out of the west. It was a terrible day to have to be running. It was in the middle of February, and they were absolutely the worst conditions I've ever run in. I remember thinking that if I could make it through that run, the marathon would be a snap. Every step was sheer misery; I really had to use all the mental techniques I knew at the time to get through that run. It was so tough. But I did it...we all did it. I think that was kind of a turning point for a lot of people in that class.

Kathy Schneider remembers:

On the long run in week eight I thought my total time was really slow because I had a bad running day, but I checked my seven-mile run from near the beginning of the semester and realized I had quickened my pace! After that I was psyched!

As has been mentioned several times, this program is designed to give the basic non-runner just what is needed to successfully complete a marathon. I call this the "Goldilocks" principle — not too much, not too little...just right. If you are practicing both the physical and mental components as described in the program there is a very good chance that you are feeling better than you ever have in your entire life. Your energy level is up, you are enjoying better and more restful sleep, you're hungry for the "right" things for once and drinking more water. Your clothes are fitting better and perhaps you have even lost a little weight. You are feeling better about yourself than you have in a long time, more relaxed, more confident. Maybe you have even noticed that you don't seem to be as anxious or depressed as you used to be. Even though you have all the same demands being made of you, in general you seem to be handling things better. Congratulations! You're in the "Goldilocks Zone" where you're not under- or over-training, but are training just right.

That's what Kathy Schneider was talking about when she shared the following:

I've always been an energetic person, but sometimes I get sick and run down. Throughout training, though, I went out with friends just about every Friday, then I came home to clean the dorm (I was the weekend custodian and liked to do the cleaning while everyone else was sleeping), and then go with the class for the long run of the week on Saturday morning at 8:00 am. After the run, I usually got some sleep. Never in my life have I had that much physical energy!

Patti Hasty Rust shared the following observation regarding the connection between sleep and diet:

After the Saturday long runs I would go home and sleep for several hours. I just felt really out of it. This continued until I started eating the right things, especially carbos, and drinking enough. Then the runs didn't seem to take so much out of me and I could recover more quickly.

Ron Steele had this insight to share on the subject of overtraining:

I knew that when I got sick I was overdoing it in the course. It's one of my barometers for the stress of overtraining.

You are headed into an exciting time of the training. Take care of yourself so you can enjoy it.

General Tips from the Marathoners — Week Seven:

- A lot of people report that the first one to three miles are the hardest of any run. It seems like it takes a while to get warmed up and get going. If you are having this same experience, it's normal. Try using the mental techniques, such as positive self-talk and visualization, right from the beginning and that should help you get into the groove more quickly.
- I make it a point not to look up at hills. I look down at my feet so that I can't see the rise. It really helps.
- I, too, discovered that when it came to running up a hill I did better if I focused only on my feet. If you think about it, slope is relative to the big picture. If you can't see the big picture, your mind doesn't know you are going up a hill. By focusing on your feet and doing lots of positive self-talk about how strong you are, you keep yourself from being intimidated by the hill.
- Taking ibuprofen before and after the long runs really helps. It can keep the swelling down in your knee and hip joints.
- It's absolutely critical that you stay sufficiently hydrated during the long runs. An alternative to carrying water or sports drink is to run a route that passes the same point (like your house, for instance) several

times so that you can set out bottles of fluid ahead of time and just grab one as you run by. For those participants who have children, a great way to get your children involved in your training is to give each a turn at accompanying you on a bicycle in order to carry your water or have them take turns manning water stops set up along your route.

- A great way to improve your concentration is to play the children's game "Memory." The concept is the same as Concentration with a deck of playing cards, but the pictures are more fun. Plus, if you have children play it with them...they don't need to know you're doing it as a part of your marathon training!
- As a class we really did take our resting heart rate first thing each morning, and it really did go down. Start doing this. It is a great first reminder each day that you are a marathoner. It helps you get out of bed with a positive attitude.

	Scheduled Distance	Actual Distance	RPE
Day 1	4		

Comments:

Day 2	6		

Comments:

Day 3	4		

Comments:

Day 4	12		

Comments:

Total Miles This Week_____Cumulative Total_____

Chapter 8:

Week Eight

Going Over 150 Miles of Training

 PART 1 **Achieving "Flow"**

Sometimes athletes describe an experience they have had while participating in their sport that seemed to them almost like being in some sort of dream state. Everything seemed exceptionally easy to do. Everything they tried seemed to work well. Basketball players who have had the experience say everything they shot went in the basket effortlessly. Golfers say all their shots seemed perfect. Football players say they felt as though they could see the whole field clearly and their bodies just seemed to know what to do automatically. And distance runners who have felt this way say it seemed to them as if they could have run forever without ever getting tired. "It just felt like I was floating," one of the people in our class said when she achieved "flow."

What IS this experience? How can we explain it? And, most importantly, how can we create it at will? The experience of "flow" was first described using that term by a psychologist named Mihaly Csikszentmihalyi. In his 1990 book, *Flow: The Psychology of Optimal Experience*, he defined it as, "being so involved in an activity that nothing else seems to matter." (p. 4) A couple of pages later, he also described it as "the way people describe their state of mind when consciousness is harmoniously ordered, and they want to pursue whatever they are doing for its own sake."(p. 6)

Csikszentmihalyi and others have studied the flow phenomenon for years and they are convinced that "moments like these ..are not the passive, receptive relaxing times..[they] occur when a person's body or mind is stretched to its limits in a voluntary effort to accomplish something difficult and worthwhile.

Optimal experience is thus something that we make happen." (p. 3)

The immediate value of such experiences for us as we train for and run the marathon is that people tend to perform whatever activity they are involved in REALLY well when they are in the flow condition. So, if you can achieve it, you will run at your very best! The reason people perform well in this condition is that flow requires complete involvement in the activity at hand. So all of their resources are focused on the task they are performing; all of their energy, all of their ability, all of their motivation. This provides us with a very important clue as to how to achieve this state and it relates to what we discussed in Chapter 7, that is learning to focus and concentrate. But let's be even more specific here. The whole training program you are following has been designed with creating conditions for you under which the flow experience is likely to be attained.

Csikszentmihalyi suggests that even very simple physical acts (such as running) can be approached according to a series of steps that will likely produce the flow experience. He identifies those steps as follows: (a) Set an overall goal and a number of subgoals, (b) have ways of measuring progress in terms of those goals, (c) learn to concentrate on what one is doing and to make finer and finer distinctions in the challenges involved, (d) work on continuing to develop, and (e) keep increasing the challenge to avoid boredom. Does that sound like your training program? The major responsibility you have, in addition to following the program, is to work on item (c), that is to learn to focus on running while you are doing it! You may find this easiest to do when running alone. Try to think about your form, your rhythm, your breathing, your pace, your foot plant. Work on those mental tapes you have constructed. If you are running with someone else, and you want to talk, try to talk as much as possible about running, (remember....focus on the positive). Try running with someone else and NOT talking, but rather focus on matching stride and pace, or on taking turns leading the way up hills. One of your authors experienced some of his best flow experiences while marathon training with three other runners along country roads in single file. Each mile, the leader would rotate to the back and the next person would lead for one mile, just as bike racers do. Each of us worked on matching the others in rhythm and stride length. We were like one well-oiled, smooth-running machine!

Flow and Fun

One of the most exciting aspects of achieving flow is that it is often truly FUN! Have you ever thought about what makes something really fun? Think of the last time you had fun. Where were you? What were you doing? If you are like most people, you were so involved in whatever you were doing that you were unaware of time passage, unaware of whether you had anything else to do, unaware of anything other than what you were doing at the time. When we are not focused completely on the moment, it is not possible to have fun because we are so distracted that we cannot fully experience things. Some people are like that...never entirely present ANYWHERE...because they are always thinking of where they need to be next or what they need to be doing. And, as a consequence, they don't have much fun. We tend to have the most fun under exactly the same conditions as those under which flow occurs...total focus on the activity in which we are engaged. So, you will do your best running AND have the most fun running when you are in flow! Doing things well IS fun, isn't it? So, we hope you are having fun getting ready for this marathon. If you are having less fun doing this than you would like to have, or less fun in life in general than you would like to have, you might want to pick up Csikszentmihalyi's 1997 book called *Finding Flow* and read it. The complete reference is included in our reference list at the back of this book.

 Physical Preparation

> ### Week 8 Training
> Day 1: 4 miles
> Day 2: 6 miles
> Day 3: 4 miles
> Day 4: 14 miles
> **Total for Week: 28 miles**

The three shorter runs this week are the same as last week. By now the four- and six-mile runs probably seem rather easy, and they should. This week is the half-way point of the training program and at the end of this week you will have run farther than a half-marathon in a single run. Think of how you felt in the first week of training when you ran your first five-miler. At the completion of that five-miler, if you would have asked yourself the question "Will I really be able to run three times this distance in just seven more weeks?" Well, you will. After completing the 14-mile run at the end of this week, you can really visualize yourself successfully completing the marathon in just eight more weeks. After all, you are going to have to run only twice as far, rather than three times as far. You will be able to do it.

If you haven't already done so, you need to start practicing drinking every 15-20 minutes and determining what kind of fluid you tolerate. If you haven't tried something like Gatorade yet, try it. It will probably help you as the distance continues to get longer. The more you practice the habit, the better you will get at it. Drink 6-8 ounces each water stop to get used to having some fluid in your stomach while running.

Cross-Training and Other Training Methods

Cross-Training. Cross-training was briefly discussed in Chapter 3 in the context of injuries. Recall that cross-training is using other methods of training to accomplish the same general outcome. For example, there are many different types of exercise you could do to train the cardiorespiratory system, like bicycling, swimming, cross-country skiing, etc. Like running, all these activities train the heart to be a better pump. Your heart gets stronger and capable of pumping more blood per minute. So, if your objective were to improve cardiorespiratory function, any of these methods could be used. However, these activities would not have the same capacity to improve your running because they all use different muscle groups and training the specific muscle groups is important to performance success. To achieve optimal improvement in a specific activity, the best thing to do is that activity itself. Runners should run, bicyclists should bike, swimmers should swim, etc. This is referred to as the principle of specificity.

Of what value is cross-training? First, cross-training can provide a valuable means of continuing to train the systems of interest if you become temporarily incapable of doing the specific type of activity you are training for. The most obvious example would be in the case of an injury. If you hurt your foot and could not run, swimming or bicycling might be something you could do. At least you could maintain the cardiorespiratory system. The specific muscles used in running would not receive as much benefit, but given the circumstances, these other activities are quite effective.

The second way in which cross-training could be useful is in situations where you might want to do more total work than you are capable of in the specific activity you are training for. For example, running is a very traumatic activity and some people just may not be able to do all the mileage necessary to complete a marathon, or whatever the distance of interest is. There may be some orthopedic limitations or other conditions that will just not allow you to do the necessary mileage. But, you may be able to run half or three-fourths of the mileage and then do some other, less traumatic type of exercise along with the running. In other words, you do the same total amount of work but you are splitting it up between running and a second activity. This is a smart approach if you know that you have injury problems after you get up to a certain mileage. Again, you will not have all the specific training effects that just running will give you, but it will be more beneficial than just reducing your mileage.

A third way cross-training may be beneficial to the runner is in situations of overtraining. Of course, if you are following our program carefully, overtraining should not occur, but if it does, you can sometimes switch to a different form of training for a while rather than just stop training altogether. By performing a different activity, you reduce the specific stress on muscles while still benefiting from the new activity. A runner might switch to swimming or bicycling, both of which would maintain the cardiorespiratory system but which also significantly reduce the trauma to the body in general.

Resistance Training. There has always been a certain amount of controversy surrounding the relationship of resistance training to running. Should distance runners also do resistance training? Will resistance training benefit the runner? The answer is not so straightforward and simple as we would like it to be.

Endurance running is not an activity that requires high levels of strength. Although a certain amount of strength is necessary, a large strength capacity is not necessary or even desirable. The role that muscular strength plays in endurance running capacity can be easily seen by looking at elite distance runners. Elite distance runners are thin and, if anything, under-muscled, not over-muscled. In particular, the upper body of elite distance runners often appears almost emaciated. Why is this the case?

Excess body weight that does not contribute directly to an increased running ability is a detriment to distance runners. It doesn't matter whether this excess weight is in the form of fat or muscle. The reason is that just to carry more weight in any form requires more ATP, ATP that could be used to increase the speed of running if there were not excess weight. Imagine yourself strapping on a 20-pound backpack and going out for your normal training run. Do you think it would be harder to run at your normal pace with the extra 20 pounds? Of course it would. In fact, you could not run at the same pace with the extra 20 pounds.

Elite runners do not want to "bulk up" with unnecessary muscle mass. They need a certain amount of muscle mass, particularly in the legs, but heavily muscled legs and upper body, if anything, will be a disadvantage. Many elite distance runners will do some resistance training which is classified as muscular endurance training as opposed to strength training. The object is primarily to increase the endurance of the muscles, not the muscle size and weight. Muscular endurance training differs from strength training primarily with respect to the amount of resistance used and the number of repetitions performed. This will be discussed in more detail in a later section.

Obviously, there are many major differences between elite endurance runners and most of you who just want to complete a marathon and maintain good overall fitness. In order to attain and maintain overall fitness, you should do some resistance training as part of a complete training program. In the big picture, muscular strength is a fitness component that will improve your life in many ways. Also, for the novice runner trying to run a first marathon, doing some resistance training can decrease the likelihood of injury. Everything else being equal, the stronger a muscle is the less the stress any activity will impose on that muscle. The lower the amount of stress, the less the likelihood of injury.

For the novice marathoner, the questions really is "How much time can I afford to spend on resistance training relative to its contribution to my running performance?" Adhering to the running schedule takes a committed effort and considerable time. How much additional time can or should you spend doing resistance training? There is no question that you should not take away from your run training time in order to do resistance training. Resistance training, when performed, should be in addition to the required run training time. Relative to the goal of finishing the marathon, running training is far more important than resistance training.

A Runner's Resistance Program. Because of the time commitment in doing the run training program, most of you are not going to want to or be able to spend a lot of time doing resistance training. However, there are some helpful exercises that would probably benefit the novice marathoner specifically, and runners in general. The major objective of a runner's resistance program is to increase muscular endurance and strength of the muscles that will be of greatest benefit to a runner. You are not trying to develop large, bulky muscles. The type of training recommended will develop adequate muscular strength and endurance in the muscles beneficial to running.

The exercises discussed below are exercises that can be done using just the body weight or hand-held dumbbells. The idea is to make them as simple and accessible as possible so that you will be more likely to do them. More extensive weight training equipment could be used, for instance barbells and weight machines, but they are not necessary.

The muscle groups that are most important to the runner are the calf (gastrocnemius and soleus), the hips (gluteus maximus), the thigh (quadriceps and hamstrings), the abdominal, the lower back, the shoulders (pectoralis major, deltoids, latissimus dorsi), and the arms (biceps and triceps). Figures 8.1 through 8.9 show the recommended exercises for each area.

Special mention should be made regarding the abdomen and the low back. Many runners suffer from some type of low back problem that might have developed from running or even existed prior to starting to run. Running is hard on the back, particularly if the supporting structures are not well developed. The muscles of the abdomen and the low back are critical to maintaining proper structural alignment in the back so that back problems are less likely to occur. Maintaining good muscular strength, endurance, and flexibility (see flexibility discussion in Chapter 4) in these muscles is a must for the runner wanting to avoid back problems.

For the exercises described in figures 8.1 through 8.9 in which a dumbbell is used, 15-25 RM should be performed. (An RM is a repetition maximum or the greatest amount of weight that you can perform the indicated repetitions with.) The only way to determine how much weight you can use to perform a certain number of repetitions with is through trial and error. Pick a weight that seems reasonable and see how many repetitions you can do. If you can't do the desired number, decrease the weight and try again. If you can do more repetitions than the desired number, increase the weight and try again. Depending on your time availability, at least 1 set (a set is performing the designated number of repetitions without resting) should be done, and as many as 3 sets could be done for optimal results. You should rest about 2-3 minutes between sets of the same exercise. As you are able to do more than 25 repetitions with the designated resistance, increase the resistance to bring the repetitions back down to 15 and work your way back up to 25. For the exercises using your body weight, start with the easiest position until you can do 25 repetitions. When you can do 25 repetitions of the exercise, advance to the next harder position until you can do 25 repetitions in the harder position. When you can do 25 repetitions in the most difficult position, then you will have to use external weights to continue to improve.

Special Considerations for Low Back Problems. As mentioned above, running is a traumatic activity that can really put a lot of stress on the back. In addition to muscular strength, muscular endurance, and flexibility, there are two additional activities that can be useful in preventing and treating low back problems.

Running exerts tremendous compressive forces on the vertebrae and the vertebral disks that separate the vertebrae. This type of repeated compressive loading of the spine can be a cause of low back problems if there is malalignment of the spine or if the supporting structures are weak. Therefore, periodic unloading of the spine can be helpful in reducing the compressive forces on the spine. Unloading the spine can be accomplished by hanging by the hands or legs from a bar and letting the body weight unload the spine. In both these hanging maneuvers, the weight of the body tugs on the spine in the opposite direction compared to when you are running, and the result is that the spine is unloaded.

If possible, hanging should be done after each run, just like stretching. Hang for a cumulative time of 3-5 minutes even if you have to hang for multiple shorter periods. If you are not able to hang from your hands or your legs, getting on an abdominal slantboard and just lying in the upside-down position would be effective.

PART 3 | Getting In the Flow

If it is possible for a person to be in love with a state of being, I am in love with flow. It is a condition that feels like a perfectly stressless place: a place where time stops and only the moment exists: a place comprised of moments full of purpose without pressure, where output effortlessly matches input. It is a place that is mysteriously cool and warm, exciting and relaxing all at the same time,

Figure 8.1 Abdominal muscles (rectus abdominis)

a) Lie supine with the knees bent so feet are flat on the floor.

b) Cross the arms across the chest and raise your shoulders completely off the floor.

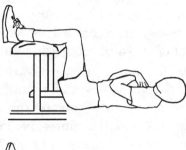

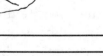

c) and d) To increase resistance and make the exercise more difficult, place the feet on a bench or chair. To add additional resistance, place the hands on the side of the head with the elbows pointing outward. For even greater resistance, place the arms outstretched about the head. To continue adding resistance, hold a dumbbell or other weight high on the chest.

Figure 8.3 Biceps

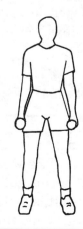

a) Holding a dumbbell or other weight in both arms.

b) Bring the one hand to shoulder level by flexing at the elbow and, while returning this hand, flex the other forearm in a similar fashion. Repeat in an alternate fashion.

Figure 8.2 Arm and shoulder muscles (triceps, deltoid, pectoralis major)

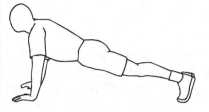

a) Perform typical push-ups.

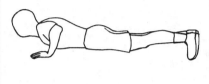

b) Try to keep the body straight as it is lowered down and then pushed up. Repeat.

c) To make the exercise easier, use the knees as pivot points instead of the feet.

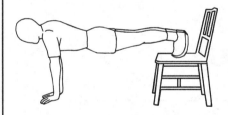

d) To increase the difficulty, place the feet on a chair, bench or step. The higher the chair, bench or step, the more difficult the push-up.

Figure 8.4 Triceps

a) Sit on a bench or chair and hold a dumbbell or weight directly overhead with both hands.

b) Slowly lower the weight behind the neck and return over the head. Repeat.

Figure 8.5 Upper back and biceps

a) Place your left knee and left hand on a bench or chair while keeping your right knee slightly bent and right foot on the floor. Hold a dumbbell with the right hand.

b) Keeping the back level, pull the dumbbell straight up to the shoulder. Return and repeat.

Figure 8.6 Top of shoulders (deltoids)

a) Stand erect while holding a dumbbell or weight in each hand.

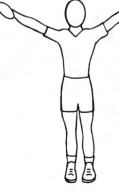

b) Raise both arms out to the side to slightly above horizontal. Repeat.

Figure 8.7 Thigh (quadriceps)

a) Stand erect with dumbbells held in both hands.

b) Take a giant step forward with right leg and lower your body until the right thigh is parallel with the floor. Stand back erect and repeat with the left leg.

Figure 8.8 Thigh (quadriceps) and buttocks (gluteals)

a) Stand erect with dumbbell held in each hand. Place the left foot on a bench or step.

b) Step up and then step back down with the right foot. Repeat with the opposite leg. The higher the step, the more difficult the exercise.

Figure 8.9 Calf (gastrocnemius and soleus)

a) Stand erect while holding a dumbbell in the left hand with the left toe on a stable piece of lumber or on a step. Use the right hand for balance. Keep the right foot raised.

b) Raise up on your toes and then lower the foot back down.

where anything and everything is possible. There are no boundaries or limits.

Most of us have experienced flow without knowing it. Think of the activities you would rather do above any others; those things you enjoy doing just for the sake of doing them. These are the activities that fill rather than drain, where there is a sense of peace and quiet inner joy. Although you may be working hard, it doesn't feel like hard work, it feels like play. That's flow.

When we are in flow, everything else melts away and time passes unnoticed. We are so in synch with what we are doing that it's almost as if we merge with the activity and it feels so good we don't want to stop. That's why flow is fun, highly addictive and easy to love. In a lot of ways, flow is like being in love; pleasantly all-encompassing, energizing, joyful. Things look and feel different, life is good and you wish it would last forever.

The best news is that flow is a state you can create at will. You create it out of your mind through the concentrated use of positive self-talk and visualizations under a state of low arousal. When practiced within a body physically able to enact the "as if" self-programming, flow is the result.

Are you starting to get the sense of how everything you've been told so far is beginning to come together at this point? Think of the mental and physical training pieces you've been given. Mentally: locus of control; focusing on the positive; importance of low arousal; acting "as if;" the use of visualizations and self-talk; and the importance of focus and concentration. Physically: pace; shoes and clothing; correct running form; how to breath properly; avoiding running injuries; overtraining and cross-training; stretching; proper nutrition, hydration and rest. It's like you've been working on both sides of a puzzle at once and now have the connecting pieces that will join the two sides together so that you can start to appreciate the big picture. That metaphor is a good description of what happens during flow. Flow is produced when the mind and body are perfectly synchronized and as a result you are elevated to a higher state of being.

For me, flow was most easily created when I ran alone, which was never a problem since everyone else ran at a faster pace than me and I was, therefore, always alone at the end of the pack. Maybe that's part of the reason I became so good at achieving it. Once I got by those first (awful) miles and felt like I was physically and mentally warmed up, it didn't take too much longer before I was in flow.

I would clear my mind of everything but the moment at hand. I narrowed my focus by looking at my feet or at the ground ten feet ahead of me. I blocked out everything external and went inside myself. I felt my feet hit the pavement, my knees lifting my legs at the hip, my arms loosely mirroring the angle of my legs. I matched my breathing to my steps. Once I knew that I was physically in the groove of my pace, I shut my head off except for the positive chants that became the background music to the visualizations. I watched the ground, but what I was really experiencing were the sights and sounds playing on my internal screen. Sometimes I would run for several minutes before realizing that I had been so inside myself that I had passed whole sections of the course without really seeing them. It was as if I were on automatic pilot.

I got so good at achieving flow that I started experimenting to see how far into it I could get. I discovered that the more I restricted external distractions, the richer the experience became. I tried to narrow the environmental stimuli by first squinting, then taking turns closing one eye and then the other. By the time we got into the longer Saturday runs, I was running with both eyes practically shut, except for one sliver I kept open so I could guide myself by way of the edge of the sidewalk. The flow was awesome!

The fall wasn't. I tripped over a raised section of sidewalk and went down hard. I'm sure to passing motorists it looked quite comical, but I wasn't laughing when I realized I had twisted my back in the process. I slowly continued for the next several miles. By the time I hit the last water stop, my back was becoming stiff and painful, so I decided it would be better to sacrifice the rest of that run in hopes of saving the marathon. I caught a ride in from the person manning the water stop. Within a few days my back felt better, and from then on I ran with my eyes open.

Here is how some other past participants experienced flow:

Jennifer Haglund:

> *I was running alone. When I hit the flow experience was after I started repeating over and over again, "I am strong. I am tough. I am awesome. I am healthy. I create my own reality. I love to run. I love to run. I love to run!" Sometimes I was saying it to myself and sometimes out loud. It had this incredible timing to the beat of my steps and it gave me an amazing sense of strength. When I got to my Grandma's for a water break, I didn't want to stop. I felt like I was running about six inches off the ground and my feet weren't even touching. This was the most extraordinary moment of the whole training for me, partly because I did it completely by myself. It was this experience that really made me believe in myself.*

Although he had participated in athletics in high school, Don Greene had been fairly inactive for several years until the age of 37 when he began training for the marathon. He remembers his best experience of flow as happening this way:

> *There were four of us. The headwind was pretty strong that day and we were on a 9-mile straight stretch of road, so we decided to run single-file and take turns leading the way. We had 18 miles to do that day and we*

agreed that we would change leaders every mile, so the first person would go to the back, the second would take over the lead, the third would move up to and so forth. We chose an 8-minute-per-mile pace and we all agreed that whoever was in front would be responsible to keep that pace. I have never had a better run. Our rhythm was perfect. We moved along with what seemed to me to be no effort at all. I was unaware of cars passing, of time passing, or of anything at all except the feeling of flowing along. Suddenly, we were done with the whole 18 miles. It was great!

Kathy Schneider also reported a terrific ending to a flow experience:

During a 16-mile run, I was floating along feeling great when two high school aged kids on bikes followed me for a while making rude remarks. I just kept on going, they soon lost interest and disappeared ahead of me. Quite a while later I caught up with them as they lounged beside a drinking fountain smoking cigarettes. I wish I had had a camera! Their chins dropped to the ground. They couldn't believe I had run all that way! Their expressions made it a great experience.

Prior to starting to train for the marathon, 20-year-old Todd Hixson had no running experience other than what he had done during high school football and basketball. He remembers one particular flow experience this way:

One time we were running on a Saturday morning and it was really cold. We were going straight north, right into the wind. A friend and I were running together and we had a 16-miler to do. The temperature was about 10 below zero. The first eight miles (into the wind) were really tough, but we had a good pace going, we were perfectly synchronized, our paces and stride length were the same and we were just rolling along. Then we got to the turn-around point. We made a U-turn and started back for town with the wind at our backs. It seemed so easy, so effortless. We increased our pace even more and it was like floating. The time passed so quickly! We were like one smooth, well-oiled machine, side-by-side...or like a team of horses, and the feeling of power was incredible. I felt like I could have done the whole marathon that day and it would have been easy.

Despite having previous marathon experience, Ron Steele noted real change in his running style as a result of having participated in the marathon class:

I definitely became more inwardly focused during my running and it made a real difference. If you've never experienced this, it's hard to appreciate. It's almost like mentally blacking out. It's like when you are driving along and all of a sudden you realize that you missed seeing a bunch of stuff. You didn't cause any accidents, but it's like somebody else was driving for you. Running can be the same kind of thing. When you are in that state, you can just kind of go on automatic pilot. The feeling is so hard to describe, but maybe it's like ...freedom. There is a feeling of tremendous durability. It's like you could run right through a wall and not even feel it. There is no pain threshold. When I go into this state, it is an all-encompassing thing. You hear experts talk about the runner's high, that physiological thing that sometimes happens when you run long distances. I don't know much about it, but I do know it exists. I have been there.

Michelle Roland remembers that one day she was...

...doing a 10 miler. I had to be home for the weekend, so I couldn't do it with the class. I was a little concerned about doing it all alone, but I had not missed a training run during the whole semester, so I felt confident that I'd be OK I started out about 8 a.m. on a Saturday morning. The route I picked wound along some bike paths through woods and fields. The air was cool and there was almost no wind. I started slowly and, as I got warmed up, I started to feel really strong. It seemed so easy. It didn't seem to matter if I was going up a grade or not. It took no effort. My breathing was regular and smooth. My legs didn't get tired. My feet hardly seemed to touch the ground. I felt fluid and powerful and like I could run forever! I know I wasn't supposed to, but I actually ran an extra two miles that day just because I didn't want it to end.

As you can tell from these accounts (or maybe from your own experience), flow is a wonderful experience. If you haven't been there yet, you can get there by relaxing and drawing upon the mental techniques you have been developing. Have fun with it. Experiment to find out the best way for you to achieve it. But take my advice....keep your eyes open.

	Scheduled Distance	Actual Distance	RPE
Day 1	4		

Comments:

| **Day 2** | 6 | | |

Comments:

| **Day 3** | 4 | | |

Comments:

| **Day 4** | 14 | | |

Comments:

Total Miles This Week_____Cumulative Total_____

Chapter 9:

Week Nine
Crossing the Emotional Plateau

PART 1

Why Trying Harder Isn't Helpful

We called this chapter "Crossing the Emotional Plateau" because it has been our experience that this week in the training is often a very difficult one for the people who have taken our class. It is your ninth week of training. You're going to exceed 30 miles this week for the first time. You are going to go 16 miles this coming weekend! And you look at the training program for the next couple of weeks and you are going to go 16 miles again the next two weekends, and you still have seven weeks of training to go....and....and...and. For many people, it is sort of a flat spot. You've come a long way, but you still have a long way to go. And you are probably going to be REALLY tired at the end of that 16-miler this weekend. So, you may have trouble keeping your spirits up. What a lot of good people do at this point, though, is to rededicate themselves to the goal. They say something like, "Hey, I can do this. I've come this far and I'm doing OK I'll just have to TRY HARDER!" By this they mean the kind of trying that involves gritted teeth, steely-eyed gazes and clenched fists. But that won't help. What WILL help is what we call "trying easier." Trying "harder" often means a kind of grim determination that ends up taking all the fun out of marathon training. Now, you may be thinking, "Fun? What fun?" And, if you ARE thinking that, then you need to go back to Part One of Chapter 8 and reread the paragraph about the relationship between flow and fun. If you are not having any fun during this training, you are probably not running as well as you could and you are probably finding it difficult to hang in there and complete the training. Trying harder can make it even less fun, so that's not what we want to see you do.

As we said earlier, what we want you to do is try easier. What does that mean? Well, first of all, it does mean continuing to try. It means continuing to put a lot of effort into both the physical and mental training. It means going out to run on the days the schedule calls for even when you don't feel like it. But trying easier also means adopting an approach to the training that includes keeping this thing in perspective. Running this marathon is not something you HAVE to do. It is something you HAVE CHOSEN to do, something you WANT to do. In the great scheme of things, it is not that important that it be THIS marathon. Now, it may sound to you like this would be the last attitude we would want you to have. But that is not the case. We believe that if you adopt this approach, you will be more likely to complete the training and therefore the marathon, than you would if you adopt the "I must do this. My value as a human being depends on it" type of attitude. That is the trying harder approach and it will kill the fun, and when the fun goes, so does the motivation.

Trying easier includes learning to relax and we will give you some help with that in the next chapter, but at this point we want you to work on maintaining a perspective on this that allows you to enjoy the training and to look forward to the stretching and to your runs. As strange as it may sound, it will sometimes help to take your mind OFF the goal of running the marathon and to remind yourself that this training is for you and your self-development and that it is contributing to your physical and mental health. If, for whatever reason, you don't complete the whole program this time, it will still have contributed to your well-being and you can choose another marathon and restart the program later. Cutting yourself some slack in this way will increase the likelihood that you will, in fact, finish the training and the marathon. As we discussed in Chapter 1, you make your own reality and you make your own decisions. You don't HAVE to do anything. You are doing this because you chose to.

PART 2 | Physical Preparation

> ### Week 9 Training
> Day 1: 4 miles
> Day 2: 7 miles
> Day 3: 4 miles
> Day 4: 16 miles
> ### Total for Week: 31 miles

Another barrier comes crashing down this week, the 30-mile-per-week barrier. The three-mile increase over last week comes from 1 mile added to the medium distance run and 2 miles to the long run. After completing the 16-mile run this week, you just have one more distance increase on the long run. In other words, after you successfully complete the 16-mile run this week, you will be only two miles short of your longest run prior to the marathon. You do 16 miles this week, 16 miles next week, and then the bump up to 18 miles for the next two weeks. Remember, one of our basic premises is that if you can run 18 miles on a training run, you can run a marathon. This has been true in 99% of the cases when runners have used this training schedule.

Training the Cardiorespiratory System.

Which body system is the most important in running a marathon? Is the cardiorespiratory system more important than the muscular system? Are the muscular system and cardiorespiratory system more important than the skeletal system? In some ways it is a little nonsensical to talk about which system is most important because we have to have all the systems functioning at some minimal level in order to run a marathon.

However, if you had to prioritize the importance of each system, one way to do it would be to see which system differs most when comparing an average runner to an elite runner. In other words, how much difference is there in each of the three systems between an average runner and an elite runner. To be an elite runner, do you have to have certain capacities in the systems? The answer is yes.

The system that is most different between an average runner and an elite runner is the cardiorespiratory system. The cardiorespiratory system refers to the heart, the lungs, and the miles and miles of vessels which carry blood around the body. Specifically, the part of the cardiorespriatory system that is different is the heart. The capacity of the heart to pump blood is the primary difference between an average runner and a world-class runner.

Why is the capacity of the heart to pump blood so important? Remember when we discussed the concept of oxygen transport and how oxygen is used to make ATP? Well, the ability to deliver oxygen to the muscles so they can make ATP is a direct function of the heart's ability to pump blood. The more blood the heart can pump, the more oxygen can be delivered to the muscles and the more ATP can be made.

The amount of blood the heart can pump per beat is the stroke volume. The amount of blood the heart can pump in 1 minute is the cardiac output. The number of times the heart pumps in one minute is the heart rate. The relationship of between stroke volume, cardiac output and heart rate is expressed by this equation:

Cardiac Output = Heart Rate x Stroke Volume

For any individual, the maximal heart rate and maximal stroke volume determine how much blood the heart can pump (i.e., the maximal cardiac output).

However, when you compare one individual with another, the major factor accounting for performance differences is the maximal stroke volume. The reason is that the maximal heart rate is primarily a function of age. Two individuals the same age will have approximately the same maximal heart rate, regardless of whether one is more or less fit than the other. However, as one becomes more fit, the maximal stroke volume increases, which increases the maximal cardiac output even though there is no change in the maximal heart rate.

Table 9.1 illustrates the types of differences you typically see in maximal values for cardiac output, stroke volume and heart rate when comparing a normal untrained 30-year-old individual before and after training with an elite endurance athlete of the same age. Because maximal heart rate is determined by age, the effect of training and the difference between the two individuals is easily seen. Training can increase the maximal stroke volume and cardiac output by about 25%. But the elite athlete has a maximal stroke volume and cardiac output that is almost twice that of the average trained individual and considerably more than twice that of the average untrained individual. This is exactly why the elite male and female marathoners can run 26 miles at around a five or six minute-per-mile pace whereas the trained "average" runner can only run a marathon at maybe an eight minute-per-mile pace. Most of us would have a very difficult time running one mile at a five- or six-minute pace much less 26 miles at that pace. The ability of the elite runner is determined in large part by genetics. It is not something that is trainable. In other words, the average individual could not train long or hard enough to ever be able to run a marathon at a five or six minute-per-mile pace. However, the average individual, with training, can significantly improve his or her ability to run a first marathon, and then to run subsequent marathons at a faster pace. Much of this improvement is due to an increase in the heart's ability to pump blood.

Also note in Table 9.1 that, on average, females are lower in all the variables listed except maximal heart rate when you compare a male and female at the same level of training or genetic endowment. In other words, the figures for an untrained female are lower than those for an untrained male, the figures for a trained female are lower than those for a trained male, and the figures for a genetically endowed female are lower than those for a genetically endowed male. These physiological variables (stroke volume, cardiac output, heart rate, oxygen consumption) explain why females, on the average, perform at a lower level than males in aerobic activities. It is because of the basic differences in these cardiorespiratory variables. A female's heart just can't pump as much blood as a male's heart. Another factor contributing to the lower maximal oxygen consumption in females is that their hemoglobin values are lower so not as much oxygen can be transported to the muscles.

Table 9.1 Differences in Stroke Volume, Cardiac Output, Heart Rate, and VO$_2$max Due to Training and Genetics				
Variable	Gender	Untrained*	Trained**	Elite Athlete***
Maximal Heart Rate (beat per minute)	Male	190	190	190
	Female	190	190	190
Maximal Stroke Volume (fluid ounces per beat)	Male	2.6	3.5	7.0
	Female	2.0	2.8	5.6
Maximal Cardiac Output (quarts per minute)	Male	15.5	21.0	41.5
	Female	11.8	16.6	33.3
VO$_2$max (ml/kg/min)	Male	40	50	75
	Female	35	44	65

Normal untrained 30-year-old
**Normal trained 30-year-old*
***Genetically endowed 30-year-old*

How does training improve the heart's ability to pump blood? When you first start running, the initial runs force the heart to pump more blood than it is used to pumping. This is an overload on the heart and the heart adapts to the overload by getting better at pumping. This is primarily accomplished by the heart pumping more blood each beat because the heart becomes a stronger muscle and can contract with greater vigor and force. The more you run, the more the heart adapts and it becomes easier and easier to run at a certain pace. If you increase the pace, the heart is forced to pump more blood, your heart adapts more and it gets even better at pumping blood.

Another interesting relationship that helps explain some of the differences observed between runners is the relationship of heart rate to the ability of the heart to pump blood. The major factor that determines the maximal heart rate is age. A rough estimate of your maximal heart rate can be made by using the formula

Maximal Heart Rate = 220 - your age

At any aerobic work effort your cardiac output is determined by the combination of your heart rate and stroke volume. Therefore, your maximal cardiac output, which is the major factor determining your greatest capacity to perform aerobic work, is determined by your maximal heart rate and maximal stroke volume. As you get older and your maximal heart rate declines, your maximal cardiac output also declines as does your capacity for performing aerobic work. That is why, in general, a 30-year-old can perform better in endurance exercise than a 60-year-old can. Your level of cardiorespiratory fitness has virtually nothing to do with your maximal heart rate but it does affect your stroke volume. This fact explains why a 60-year-old could perform better than a 30-year-old if the 60-year-old were well trained and the 30-year-old untrained.

Determining Your Appropriate Training Intensity

In determining the appropriate intensity of training in an endurance activity, the heart rate is often used as an objective measure of intensity. But the heart rate that is used is always a percentage of the maximal heart rate, not an absolute heart rate. For example, a heart rate of 150 would not be the same level of intensity for a 30-year-old and a 60-year-old. For the 30-year-old it represents about 79% of the maximal heart rate (maximal heart rate = 190) and for the 60-year-old it represents about 94% of the maximal heart rate (maximal heart rate = 160). Therefore, running at a heart rate of 150 would be much more difficult for the 60-year-old and the subjective sense of effort would be much higher.

What is an appropriate training intensity? The training schedule in this book is written in terms of mileage and says nothing specifically about the intensity or how fast you should be running. The intensity of training, which is reflected in how fast you run, should be determined by your heart rate and confirmed by your subjective feelings of effort. The use of the heart rate is referred to as the training heart rate and the use of subjective sensation of effort is referred to as the rate of perceived exertion (RPE). Although the training heart rate is the more objective measure of the two, the RPE can be quite accurate when it is used repeatedly.

For the typical individual, the appropriate training heart rate should be 70-80% of the maximal heart rate. This is a heart rate that, as training progresses, should be sustainable over the distance of the long training runs. As you become more trained over the duration of the training program, the pace necessary for you to reach your training heart rate will probably increase. You will have to run faster to achieve your training heart rate. This is because your stroke volume increases and therefore your heart doesn't have to beat as often to supply the necessary cardiac output. This is a consistent training effect and should be viewed as a positive sign.

There needs to be some caution with this type of training heart rate assignment because it uses an estimated maximal heart rate determination (220-age). This estimated maximal heart rate can be wrong by as much as 20-25 beats per minute in either direction for certain individuals. For example, a 30-year-old would have a predicted maximal heart rate of 190 (220-30 = 190). However, any given 30-year-old could actually have a maximal heart rate of 170 or 210. The consequences of the actual maximal heart rate being higher or lower than the age-predicted maximal heart rate is that the person would be training below or above his or her desirable level. In the above example, the 30-year-old's training range based on the age-predicted maximal heart of 190 would be 133-152. If in fact this person's true maximal heart rate were 170, his or her training heart rate range should be 119-136, significantly lower than the range based on the age-predicted maximal heart rate. Likewise, if the true maximal heart rate were 210 rather than 190, the training heart rate range would be 147-168. In one case the runner would be undertraining and in the second case he or she would be overtraining.

There are two potential solutions to the problem with the age-predicted maximal heart rate. The first solution is to actually measure your maximal heart rate. Measuring your maximal heart rate requires you to perform a maximal effort for about 4-5 minutes, such as running as fast as you can for 4-5 minutes. The only problem with this is that you have to do a maximal effort and this could be risky for someone who has undiscovered heart disease.

A second way to solve the problem is to use the RPE scale to corroborate the appropriateness of the computed training heart rate range. The RPE scale is a scale from 0-10 with 0 being no effort at all and 10 being a maximal effort. The scale is depicted in Table 9.2. The category indicators on the right of the numbers indicate how people should interpret the number ratings and are meant to reflect a whole-body sensation of effort. The RPE scale is not specific to any one muscle group, like the calf muscle, or to just your breathing, but is generalized to the overall sensation of effort throughout the body. On the RPE scale, a rating of 3-5 correlates to a training heart rate of 70-80% of maximal heart rate. So, if you are running at a heart rate of 70% based on an age-predicted maximal heart rate but your RPE rating is 8, then something is wrong. Either you are not a very good perceiver of subjective effort or your training heart rate is too high because your age-predicted maximal heart rate has underpredicted your actual maximal heart rate. The best strategy is to slow your pace and see if your RPE comes down to a more appropriate level.

Table 9.2 Ratings of Perceived Exertion (RPE) Scale

Rating	Subjective Sensation
0	Nothing at all (resting)
0.5	Very, very easy effort
1	Very easy effort
2	Easy effort
3	Moderate effort
4	Somewhat hard effort
5	Hard effort
6	
7	Very hard effort
8	
9	
10	Maximal effort

Maximal Oxygen Consumption (VO$_2$max) and the Anaerobic Threshold

Maximal oxygen consumption is one of the most measured physiological variables in sports medicine. It is a measure of aerobic capacity and cardiorespiratory functioning and is defined as the greatest amount of oxygen a person can use to produce ATP. In order to achieve VO$_2$max you have to do a maximal, exhaustive work effort. In the exercise science laboratory, the work effort is normally performed on a treadmill or bicycle.

There is a fundamental relationship between VO$_2$max and the variables of stroke volume and cardiac output. All these variables are directly related and are indicative of the same type of capacity. Maximal oxygen consumption indicates what the cardiac output is doing. Here is the overall picture — As muscles are stimulated to do more work, such as running, there has to be an increase in oxygen delivery to the muscles in order for ATP to be produced. The increase in oxygen delivery is due to an increase in cardiac output. As the oxygen is delivered to the muscles, the muscles extract the oxygen and use it in the aerobic energy processes to make ATP so you can keep running. Without an increased cardiac output which delivers more oxygen to the muscles, oxygen consumption could not rise to the levels necessary to support the increased work effort.

Trained skeletal muscles have a tremendous capacity to extract oxygen from the blood and make ATP. In fact, trained muscle has the capacity to extract pretty much all the oxygen that can be transported to the muscle. Therefore, the limitation in a person's VO$_2$max is the ability to deliver oxygen to the muscle or in the cardiac output, as was emphasized earlier. From a functional standpoint, VO$_2$max and cardiac output are measures of the same capacity — the capacity to provide oxygen to the muscles and the capacity of the muscles to use the oxygen to make ATP. Individuals with high maximal cardiac outputs will have high VO$_2$max values. The higher your VO$_2$max, the greater is your aerobic capacity. Table 9.1 lists representative values for VO$_2$max for an untrained individual, the same individual after training, and an elite endurance athlete.

Another factor that is highly related to how you perform in endurance activities is the anaerobic threshold. The anaerobic threshold is the percentage of your maximal oxygen consumption that you can work at for an extended period of time. If you work at or just below the anaerobic threshold, lactic acid does not accumulate and you can continue working for quite some time. When you begin to work above your anaerobic threshold, lactic acid begins to accumulate because you are doing more of the work anaerobically. Because of the accumulation of lactic acid, you cannot continue to work very long.

A typical untrained adult has an aerobic threshold of about 50-55% of VO$_2$ max whereas a trained individual may have an aerobic threshold as high as 70-80% of VO$_2$ max. For any value of VO$_2$ max, a higher anaerobic threshold simply means you can do more work for an extended period of time, like run at a faster speed. A high anaerobic threshold can offset a low VO_2max and a high VO_2max can offset a low anaerobic threshold. The best scenario is, of course, to have both a high VO^2max and a high anaerobic threshold. Training increases the anaerobic threshold, just as it increases VO_2max. In fact, the type of training you are doing in the program recommended in this book is the type that increases your anaerobic threshold.

Effects of Endurance Training

Endurance training increases your capacity to perform aerobic work, whether it be running, bicycling, swimming, or any other type of aerobic activity. Specifically, endurance training will result in the following types of adaptations in the cardiorespiratory system and the muscular system.

1. Increase maximal cardiac output, stroke volume, and VO_2max.
2. Increase in stroke volume and decrease in heart rate at any submaximal work effort.
3. Increase in stroke volume and decrease in heart rate at rest.
4. Increase in capacity to perform endurance exercise.

As it relates specifically to running, over the course of the marathon training schedule, you should see a decrease in your resting heart rate and a decrease in the heart rate at any submaximal running speed. For example, if your heart rate while running at a 10 minute/mile pace is 160 at the beginning of the training program, it may be 130 at the end of the training program. In order to keep running at a particular heart rate throughout the training program, you will have to increase your pace. In the example just mentioned, at the end of the training program you may have to run a 9 minute/mile pace in order to stay at a heart rate of 160.

PART 3 | Mark Block's Story

Given the potential difficulty of this week's training, instead of sharing comments from several past participants, I would like to focus on one in particular whose story I think you will find especially inspirational. When I was collecting names of past participants to interview, Dave said to me, "There's this guy who was in the class a few years back, and I think you should interview him. His name is Mark Block." So I called him up, and on one of the coldest days of the winter showed up at his door with tape recorder in hand. I wasn't sure what to expect, but I had a feeling that it would be worth hearing. I took two tapes. I'm glad I did.

This is his story.

A high school track star in both cross country and the 2-mile, Mark set track records in the state of Iowa that stand to this day. After high school, he went to the University of Northern Iowa on a cross country scholarship, and between two workouts routinely ran 14 miles per day. After his first year of college, Mark began questioning the direction he wanted his life to take. So, at the age of 20, he decided to enlist in the Army rather than return to college in the fall. To keep himself in condition during the summer, he ran on the river roads near his hometown of Fort Dodge. Two days before he was to leave for boot camp, his whole life changed.

It was August 3, 1986. He and a friend were driving down a road that had only recently been reopened after construction. Mark planned to take a run on that road the next day and he wanted to scope it out ahead of time. It was late — 2:00 a.m. They had not been drinking. They zipped through the darkness reminiscing about their night and their friendship in preparation for Mark's departure.

Suddenly, they missed a turn in the road. The small car Mark was driving went into the ditch and flipped several times. Mark was not wearing a seat belt. As the car flipped, Mark was thrown through the windshield but stopped by the metal of the hood and engine as they crumbled in front of him. The car continued flipping until it smashed into a tree and stopped.

Both men lay unconscious.

After the friend regained consciousness, although dazed and disoriented, he managed to crawl out of the car and walk to a farmhouse for help. Shortly after, a 911 call went out to the volunteer paramedic squad to respond to a one-car accident in which there was one fatality. The coroner was notified.

When the paramedics arrived they crawled inside the car but could not locate a pulse on Mark. Although all initial indicators pointed to his death, they started resuscitation efforts and to their surprise managed to get a pulse. As quickly as possible, Mark was stabilized at the scene, extricated from the car, and transported to the nearest hospital.

A CT scan revealed head trauma, a broken neck, and a partial cut of the spinal cord. As the trauma of the injuries settled in his body and swelling increased, his condition worsened. He needed more sophisticated care than the local hospital was able to provide. In grave condition, he was airlifted by helicopter to Des Moines. En route, Mark suffered cardiac arrest. The transport team managed to revive him, but things looked very bleak for him as the helicopter landed.

For the next several days, Mark's condition continued to deteriorate. As the swelling around his brain and spinal cord increased, spinal shock set in and he stopped breathing. He was resuscitated again and hooked to a respirator. He had shattered his second, third, fourth, and fifth vertebrae and desperately needed surgery to repair them and the cut in the spinal cord. But his condition was so tenuous that he would not have survived the surgery. For two weeks he lay in a coma paralyzed from the ears down with a respirator breathing for him.

When surgery could finally be performed, the vertebrae were so badly damaged that they could not be repaired — only realigned and reinforced. For the next month, Mark lay paralyzed from the neck down, respirator dependent, and extremely disoriented due to the severe head trauma.

It was at this point that Mark started the recovery process. He remembers it this way:

> *You wake up and you're surrounded by people of authority, doctors and nurses, telling you what you can't or won't be able to do: "you're paralyzed from the neck down, we'll have you in the hospital for three to four months, and when you leave you'll be in a wheelchair — hopefully, an electric wheelchair if you can regain some use of your hands. You'll require assistance in all activities of daily living; basically you'll be totally dependent on somebody else."*

> *At that point in time, once I came out of the coma, all I could do was lie there. I couldn't do a thing. My lungs were gone. I couldn't talk above a whisper. Anytime they'd try to sit me up I would pass out.*

> *That was the crucial moment, for me. Being totally out of control of myself; being totally dependent upon others. It was terrifying. The fear of living that way the rest of my life motivated me. I remember thinking, "What do I have to lose?" I turned the energy of fear into the energy for recovery.*

> *If I would have listened to all those people telling me what I couldn't or wouldn't do, then I wouldn't have even tried. I remember thinking, 'Well, if that's the way it turns out then I'll accept it and live with it, but that doesn't mean I'm not going to try.' Don't get me wrong, I'm not saying I knew more than those people. They're wonderful professionals and when you are in that type of situation, you need them. But all they wanted to see were the probabilities — not the possibilities. By focusing on my limitations, they were limiting me. And I fought against it.*

Mark refused to accept the prognosis offered by the medical staff, and informed the doctors that when he left he would walk out. It was nothing they hadn't heard before from other people with similar injuries. Denial and unrealistic optimism were common initial reactions in cases such as Mark's. A psychiatrist was added to Mark's medical team to help him accept the reality of his situation and prepare him for the normal recovery process with spinal injuries.

What happened next was anything but normal.

Mark's recovery process started with him unable to move or feel anything below his ears. His goal was to walk again. The only major part of his body that still seemed to be working was his brain. So that's what he started exercising first. He began with what he referred to as kinetic visualization. Although at the time he could not get his body to walk, he could walk in his mind. He practiced remembering what it felt like to walk. He lay in bed and visualized feeling his legs, his feet, how it felt to pick up first one leg and then the other and feel the pressure of the ground as it met each foot. Like an athlete mentally rehearsing a performance, Mark mentally practiced moving his fingers and toes. It was a mental process of kinetic reeducation by which he hoped to reconnect the neural pathways running from the brain to the intended muscles. As Mark puts it, "I still had the control center — my brain. It was just a matter of getting the connections going again...finding the "phone lines" that were down and getting them hooked up again so that the message could flow through. I would lay there and visualize something as simple as moving a finger or toe."

The first thing Mark moved was the big toe on his right foot. The nurses told him it was a spasm, and that he shouldn't get too excited about it. Besides, they added, that would be impossible since recovery of movement in cases such as his always happened from the neck down. But at Mark's insistence they went and got the doctor. He, too, said it was a spasm. At Mark's request, the doctor bent directly over the toe in order to watch very carefully...and Mark nearly kicked him!

Initially, movement was not something Mark could repeat at will, but it was a start. As Mark puts it:

> *You start with just a little flicker, and you make it grow through reeducation and increased range of motion. I was able to move before I was able to feel. I could move the toe, but I couldn't feel it. The more I moved it, then the feeling started coming back. Once that happened is when things got really painful, because it felt like pins and needles. But it felt good, because it gave me reference points. When I first started, I couldn't tell where my arms or legs were — there was just dull pain from the neck down.*

Victories were found in reclaiming the ability to do the simplest things. Going from being flat on his back to being able to sit up without passing out took months. Being able to hold a spoon or a glass meant the difference between being dependent on others or being able to feed himself. Being able to push the elevator button was a huge step!

Mark reflects:

Think about the activities of daily living...the things you do and just take for granted. Like brushing your teeth, being able to feed yourself. There are just so many things involved with doing anything — it's never just an all or nothing situation.

When you are surrounded by people constantly telling you, "No, you can't do that," there comes a definite point where you have to make a decision, "OK, I'm going to go for it and do it, or I'm going to believe what they tell me and accept my limitations." It's up to you. Are you going to accept the limitations they are putting on you through their beliefs, or are you going to find out for yourself what you may or may not be able to do?

After a while the doctors threw up their hands in exasperation, and left Mark alone to do it his way. And he did just that. He set his own recovery goals and charted his physical therapy course. Some days, Mark would stay in physical therapy all day. With hard work, prayers, resisting the negativism of others and staying focused on the goal, Mark surpassed everyone's expectations (except his own) and on Christmas Day walked out of the hospital with only a cane for support and a person on either side for stabilizing.

For the next nine months, Mark lived at home and worked a desk job in the family business. That spring, he helped coach the track team at his old high school. He really enjoyed being around the kids and the running again, even though he was still dependent on the cane in order to walk.

One year after his accident, Mark returned to the University of Northern Iowa to resume his studies. According to Mark, that was a very good decision but a very difficult adjustment. Needing the cane in order to be mobile made this 22-year-old former track star extremely self-conscious, and adjusting to college life as an independent adult in his current condition was an extremely difficult transition for him. It was a transition he wasn't handling very well until the day he read an article in the university newspaper about a class which was to be offered the following semester called the "Marathon Class." An informational meeting was being held that week for all interested persons.

The minute he read about it, he knew that this class was just what he needed. He needed a structured mental and physical challenge of this type to help him get his self-confidence back. He just had to get into that class.

He left for the meeting way ahead of its scheduled start time. He wanted to be there before others started arriving so that he wouldn't feel embarrassed when he walked in with his cane. As he parked in the handicapped parking area nearest to the meeting site, he became more and more frustrated with his situation. What was he doing? How could he expect to run a marathon when he couldn't even walk 20 feet without a cane? This was absolutely ridiculous! This just wasn't possible given his limitations.

Suddenly, the irony hit him like a lightning bolt. Here he was doing to himself what he had perceived his doctors and nurses doing to him in the hospital: accept your limitations and learn to live with them. Because he hadn't accepted it then, he was walking when he should have been in a wheelchair. And if he didn't accept it now, who is to say that he wouldn't find a way to do the marathon? He was going! He reached for his cane...and stopped. "Screw it," he thought. "I'm not walking into a marathon meeting with a cane. If I can't get there without it, then I don't belong in the class."

Staggering 20 feet at a time, Mark inched his way the few hundred feet to the meeting site by balancing himself against the outside of buildings and the walls of the hallways. He barely made it in time to find an empty seat. By the time the meeting started, the room was packed. There were over 80 people there hoping to get into the class but fewer than half that many available slots. The instructors, Forrest Dolgener and David Whitsett, explained the class requirements: Students would train for and run a full 26.2 mile marathon. You either finished or you didn't. If you finished, you got an A; if you didn't, you got an F. Training was provided for both physical and mental components. If you followed it, you would finish. If you didn't follow it, you wouldn't. It was that simple. Only those who were serious should stay; once you were in the class, they wanted you to be committed.

Most people stayed, including Mark. Thirty names were chosen from the hat. Mark's was not one of them. After the meeting ended and the room started to clear, Mark stayed behind hoping to talk with the instructors to see if they would reconsider letting him in. He told them briefly what he had been through.

"Can you run at all?," Dave asked him.

"Well, not yet," Mark replied.

"What's your current level of activity?," questioned Forrest.

"Right now, I can walk about 20 feet without having to stop," answered Mark.

Dave looked at the young man standing in front of him. He remembered Mark from his year of collegiate cross country, and now knew why he hadn't been back on the team since. If this young man, who wasn't even supposed to be walking wanted to try a marathon, he sure wasn't going to tell him no. After consulting with Forrest, Dave told Mark, "Here's what we'll do. You go home and think about it overnight. Tomorrow, if you still want to try this, be in my office at 2:00 and we'll talk more about it. OK?"

"OK," beamed Mark. He didn't even need to think about it — he'd be there.

It was a few minutes after 2:00 and Dave was starting to wonder if Mark had reconsidered, when he heard a strange sound coming down the hall. Unable to place the step-slap-drag sound, he listened as it slowly approached his office. When it stopped, there stood Mark in his doorway loaded down with what appeared to be files of paperwork.

"I'd started to think maybe you weren't coming," Dave teased.

"Couldn't find a handicapped parking place, so it took me a little longer to get here," Mark said, smiling.

"What do you have there?" Dave asked, nodding at the stack of papers Mark was trying to balance in his free arm.

"Medical records," Mark replied. "Thought I better bring them in case you had specific questions about my condition."

As his guest sat down, Dave looked at the huge stack of paperwork Mark had just deposited on his desk in wonder at all that this young man must have gone through. Over the next hour, as the details of Mark's story unfolded, Dave's respect and admiration for Mark's determination deepened. While he had concerns about how Mark would hold up under the physically demanding training, he certainly wasn't going to deny Mark the chance to try after all he'd come through to get to this point.

Throughout the course of their conversation, it became clear to Dave how important it was to Mark that he be measured by as many of the same criteria as possible as were expected of the rest of the class. Mark needed to have an A or F goal just like the rest of the students, although an entire marathon in just one semester of training was clearly unrealistic for Mark given his present level of activity. As a way to test the waters Dave said, "Well, you know we're not going to let you off easy."

"Good! I don't want you to...that's why I'm here," Mark answered with a sense of relief. He was so tired of everyone trying to impose their negative limitations on him, that being challenged is exactly what he needed and hoped he would get from Dave and Forrest.

"I've thought about this, and I'll let you in the class, but we have to decide on what would be an reasonable goal. If you're not able to run, can you walk?" Dave said.

"Well, yeah, I've walked two miles, but with lots of stops to rest," Mark replied.

After some discussion about realistic but challenging goals and possible alternative training methods, the two agreed that Mark's goal would be to walk a 10K (6.2 miles). He would train with the rest of the class, and while they would run, he would walk.

Dave recalls:

So, we sent Mark home with the same pretraining instructions as all the other students: by the time the semester began in mid-January they had to be able to jog (or, in his case, walk) for 30 minutes without stopping in order to be ready to begin the formal training.

On the first day of class we met in the UNI-Dome [the university's indoor stadium], and they all did it...including Mark. A leg brace had replaced the cane, and he was very unsteady. He dragged his right leg with every step and was very slow, but he did it.

From then on, every Saturday when we took the class out for their long run Mark was there and he walked over the same course that everybody else ran. We adjusted his distance commensurate with his goal, but he was on the road for at least as long (usually longer) as the rest of the class.

Under Forrest's supervision, Mark cross-trained by lifting weights and riding a stationary bike. But for Mark, the main thing was the walking and he pushed himself — occasionally beyond his capabilities. There were a few times when he got himself in trouble:

I would walk on a straight road out into the country, so that there was only one way to get back and that was to walk back. Often on the way back my legs would start shaking so badly I would have to stop and stretch and rest before I could continue. One time I walked out so far that I couldn't make it back. I had to stop at a farmhouse and ask for help. They must have been able to tell I was in pretty bad shape, because they gave me a ride back into town.

At mid-semester, the class did a 13-mile run — a half marathon — as a kind of mid-term progress check. As usual, everyone started together that morning and headed out into the country for the out-and-back run. Afterward Dave and Forrest sponsored a get-together for the class with soft drinks and sandwiches to celebrate their accomplishment. As Dave remembers:

We were all sitting around talking and laughing when somebody asked where Mark was, and I realized that he hadn't come back yet. It was getting pretty late and I started to get worried because he should've been back by then, so I drove out along the course we had used that day to check on him.

When I found Mark, he was on his way back and extremely tired, but still walking. I pulled up alongside him and said, "Mark, what are you doing? It's almost noon!"

"Well, I'm not done yet," he replied.

I asked him to tell me where he'd walked. As he described his route, I mentally calculated his mileage. "Mark, that's seven miles!" I informed him. "Get in the truck...you're done for today," I laughed.

As we headed back into town, I said smiling, "You know what this means, don't you?"

"What?" Mark asked.

"Well, you just walked your final exam, so you're going to have to increase your goal. Do you think you can do 10 miles?" I challenged.

"Well, I don't know," he answered.

"Good, let's do 10 miles then," I said. And that became his new goal for the marathon, and he continued to train with the rest of the class.

As the marathon approached, Mark got excited and nervous. He was going to be walking among hundreds of runners down the streets of Iowa's largest city. What if something happened? And yet, he felt that he could do more than his goal. He talked with his parents about it and they encouraged him to just walk his 10 miles and get his A for the class. The high school team he had helped coach during his year of recuperation was there for the Drake Relays and they encouraged him to do the same. Suddenly he felt he was being confronted by the same limiting attitudes he had been working to beat since his accident. And it made him mad. He decided he was going to do 13.1 miles...if everyone else was doing a marathon, he would do a half-marathon. When he informed Dave of his decision, after first reminding Mark that his goal was to do ten, Dave added, "But if you want to do 13, great. Go for it!"

They decided that Mark would start at the half-marathon point, and walk to the finish line. After everything was in place, Mark started telling people that he intended to walk 13.1 miles. Everyone encouraged him to just stick with the first goal of 10 miles and get his A. But as Mark explained, "They missed the whole point. I wasn't doing this for a grade. I had taken this class as a challenge to better myself."

Later that night, Mark decided that he wasn't going to start at mile 13 after all. He was going to start at mile 11, and walk 15 miles! In all honesty, Mark wasn't sure he could make it that far, but decided he would either defy all expectations, including his own, or fall flat on his face trying. Mile 11 it would be. He told no one, except for a new friend from Des Moines, Bill Kunz. After reading Mark's story in the local newspaper, Bill had contacted him with a request to meet him and help him in any way possible. A wheelchair user himself, Bill had a special empathy for Mark and what he was trying to accomplish.

The next morning at 7:00 a.m. (one hour before the official start of the marathon), Mark met Bill and another friend, Carol, at mile 11. With Bill cheering him on, and Carol walking with him, Mark began his "marathon." Before too long, the leaders caught and passed him, and sometime after that the fastest of the class members caught up to Mark and passed him as well. Pretty soon, Dave Whitsett, who was running the marathon along with the class, came running up beside Mark. "How are you doing," he asked. "Great," Mark answered.

Dave looked at his watch and looked at Mark. "Where'd you start?" he asked.

Mark only smiled. Dave knew something was up, but he didn't say anything. He just smiled at Mark before he pulled away.

Hours later, Mark was still walking. He remembers the last few miles this way:

Most of the course was closed up. The water stops had been taken down. Traffic control had been terminated. Normal traffic had resumed and cars were flying by me; people were yelling at me to get off the street not realizing that I was in the marathon. Most of the other runners had finished hours before. I'd already been walking for eight hours. I was getting dehydrated, weak and wobbly. My legs were really aching. Carol was still walking with me, and the pastor from the student center on our campus had come to help me, too. At this point, he was driving ahead of me helping to control traffic at the intersections so that I didn't have to stop, plus he brought me water which was a big help because I was starting to get dizzy from dehydration.

When I got to the last mile, some of the people from the class were still there to cheer me on. At Dave's insistence, the marathon officials had kept the finish line set up and were there waiting for me. As I walked that last mile, my family, friends, and some classmates walked with me to show their support and encouragement. By that time I was so fatigued that I had to concentrate very hard just to keep going. I had to consciously think left, right, left, right to keep my legs moving...since the accident, walking had never been an automatic thing — every step required deliberate thought. It was getting really tough. My legs were continuing to shake and wobble, I was getting nauseated from dehydra-

tion, and my whole body was tingling from fatigue. But I could see the finish and there was no way I was not going to finish. Even if I had to crawl, I was going to cross that finish line.

It took me 8 hours and 33 minutes to do it, but I made those 15 miles and got my medal. Afterwards, Dave came up to me and asked, "How far did you go?"

"Fifteen miles," I said.

He gave me a look that seemed somewhere between reproach and happiness and, for a second, I didn't know if he was going to knock me out or hug me! Then, with a huge grin on his face, he proclaimed, "Fifteen miles!" and gave me a big hug.

Mark about to get his finish-line hug from Dave.

"Yeah, I knew if I started there, I'd finish," Mark explained. "There was no way I wasn't going to finish."

Still smiling, Dave told him, "I knew something was up because when I passed you, I knew you should've been further along if you had started where you were supposed to. Fifteen miles! Congratulations, Mark."

In retrospect, Mark had this to say about the whole experience:

The moral of my story is that you never know what you can do until you try. If you listen to what others say, you may not try at all. If you listen to your body, you may quit too soon. What your mind believes, your body believes. Your mind is the key.

I gained so much confidence from that class. Here I was caught in this mode of everyone telling me what I couldn't do. I can't tell you how many times I heard, "Accept your limitations...this is the way you are and you just have to deal with that." And then you go into something like this class where people are telling you what you can do if you set your mind to it. It was awesome! It was exactly what I needed. I wish more people would do that — focus on the possibilities, not the probabilities. That's what Dave and Forrest do in this class. They don't tell you what you can't do...they guide you through what you didn't know you could do, and with their help, you do it. This class is about a lot more than just running a marathon. It teaches you a different way to think — about yourself and your goals. It's really about life and how to really live!

Now 32 years old, Mark is happily married and has a young daughter. He travels regularly as a sales associate for a medical supply company. He no longer needs a brace to walk and is able to run short distances. He credits the experience of this class as a key turning point in his life and level of self-confidence, and continues to employ the techniques he learned during the class in all aspects of his life.

Running Log for Week Nine

	Scheduled Distance	Actual Distance	RPE	
Day 1	4			
	Comments:			
Day 2	7			
	Comments:			
Day 3	4			
	Comments:			
Day 4	16			
	Comments:			

Total Miles This Week_____Cumulative Total_____

Chapter 10:

W e e k   T e n
Moving Into the
High-Mileage Weeks

Learning to Relax

In the last chapter we discussed the idea of "trying easier" and we said that a part of it is learning to relax. The goal is to learn to achieve at will a condition of no, or at most very little, muscle activity. In this section, we are going to offer you some techniques to help you do that, but first let's talk about the physical and psychological benefits of being relaxed.

From a physical point of view, there are several benefits of having relaxed muscles. Injury is less likely. Fatigue is less likely. Soreness and stiffness after exercising are less likely. Obviously these are all things we want to avoid, especially during marathon training. From a psychological point of view, the ability to relax at will produces feelings of reduced anxiety and tension, as well as increased self-confidence and a sense of overall well-being. Finally, being able to relax helps induce onset of sleep and this has clear physical and psychological benefits.

There are a number of techniques available to achieve a relaxed state. If you already know and use one or more of them successfully, we recommend that you continue to do so. However, if the ability to relax at will is not yet one you have acquired, you should consider trying one or more ways to develop the ability. We will discuss two approaches. Each illustrates one of the two routes to relaxation. You can either learn to relax the muscles first and let that move on to your mind, or you can learn to calm the mind and let that go to the muscles. One may work much better for you than the other so you should probably try both.

The muscle-to-mind approach we will describe is called progressive relaxation. It was originally developed by Edmund Jacobson of the University of Chicago back in the late 1920s. He called it progressive relaxation because you move or progress from one muscle group to another as you develop the skill.

Here's how to use progressive relaxation. The muscle groups on which we want you to focus, in this order, are as follows:

1. Dominant hand and forearm
2. Dominant biceps
3. Nondominant hand and forearm
4. Nondominant biceps
5. Forehead (this one may seem irrelevant to you, but it involves a muscle called the frontalis which goes across your forehead kind of like a headband and it is a very important one to learn to relax)
6. Chest, shoulders and upper back
7. Abdominal region
8. Dominant thigh
9. Dominant calf
10. Dominant foot
11. Nondominant thigh
12. Nondominant calf
13. Nondominant foot

For each of these muscle groups, you should perform the following exercise:

1. Focus your attention on the muscle group.
2. Give yourself a verbal signal, such as "now" or "tense" and immediately tense the muscle group. The tension should be in the focused-on muscle group only. Practice until you can isolate the tension in each muscle group.
3. Maintain the tension for 5-7 seconds.
4. Give yourself the verbal signal "relax" and immediately relax the muscle group, maintaining your focus on the muscle group so that you can clearly feel the relaxation.

With thirteen muscle groups, and less than 10 seconds for each one, you can see that you can do one cycle of this exercise in about two minutes. It works best for most people if they repeat the cycle 2 or 3 times, and you can do it even more if it seems to work well for you. If you are interested in reading more about this kind of process, we have included a reference to a book by Jacobson on the topic in a reading list at the back of this book.

There are also a number of relaxation techniques that begin with learning to control the amount of stimulation from the central nervous system to the skeletal muscles. We are going to suggest that you use a variation on the visualization approach that we described back in Chapter 5. If you have been doing what we asked you to do at that point, you should be pretty good by now at "making pictures in your head." If you have not been doing that, you should go back and read Section One of Chapter 5 before going on.

If you have mastered the technique of visualization, and have been using it in the way we suggested in Chapter 5, you may be able to use it to relax as well. Begin by thinking about what kind of situation would generally seem relaxing to you. For some people, it is lying in the warm sun. For some it is being in some quiet mountain setting. For others, it involves being near water such as a river or a lake. Whatever it may be for you, try to imagine it in complete detail. For example, if it is lying on a floating dock in the warm sun with your eyes closed, imagine the feeling of the sun on your skin and the sound of rhythmic lapping of the water against the dock. Think of what you would be wearing, perhaps of the smell of lotion on your body and of the gentle movement of the dock as the water undulates slowly beneath you. Imagine opening your eyes and watching a bird circle slowly above you, riding with motionless wings on the breeze. Close your eyes again and feel the warmth of the sun and listen to the breeze move through the trees on the banks of the lake.

Whatever scene works for you is the right one to use. It will take some practice, but if you continue to work at it and continue to use the same well chosen scene, you will be able to use this technique at will, anytime or anyplace. And when should you use it? Whenever you want to, of course. But times when it (or the progressive relaxation technique, if that is what you are using) may be especially useful would include when you are trying to get to sleep or before particularly anxiety-producing events such as the long run of the week or before the marathon itself.

One last comment. A good time to practice your relaxation skills is right after your runs. We are often naturally relaxed after periods of exercise and your practice sessions may be particularly successful at these times.

 Physical Preparation

> ## Week 10 Training
> Day 1: 5 miles
> Day 2: 8 miles
> Day 3: 5 miles
> Day 4: 16 miles
> ## Total for Week: 34 miles

Each of the three short days is increased by 1 mile. These increments will hardly be noticed because 5 and 8 miles are really short compared to 16 miles. The long run is the same as last week, your second 16-miler in succession.

Remember to take a day off before and after the long run.

Should You Walk?

By now you may have had to walk periodically during the long training runs. Walking should NOT be construed as a big no-no. Periodic walking can be useful in the overall training scheme. Certainly, if you can run the entire distance, you should do so. Everything else being equal, the less you walk the better. But, if walking for periodic short distances during the training runs helps you to complete the entire distance, then walking is really a training aid. When you get to the point you feel you have to walk, then walk at a brisk pace. This brief interruption of your running can be enough for a little recovery so you can resume running. The temporary physiological reprieve from the trauma of running can mentally help you get back to running.

The need or feeling that you can't continue running and that you need to walk a bit is due to fatigue, either physiologically or mentally. After decades of research, the specific cause of fatigue has escaped discovery. It is known that fatigue can occur in either the muscle (called peripheral fatigue) or in the nervous system (called central fatigue). Depending on the length of your training run, a real possibility as a cause of fatigue is running out of energy. If your training run requires more than 1.5 hours, energy may be a problem. If you have not been consuming enough carbohydrates, energy may also be a problem. If you are not consuming any carbohydrates during the training run itself, energy may also become a problem.

A second cause of peripheral fatigue is a buildup of lactic acid during the training run. If you are running too fast early in the run, lactic acid can be a problem later in the run. By slowing down and/or walking, lactic acid can be reduced and its contribution to fatigue can be eliminated.

Your mental condition including the thoughts that you have can have significant impact on central fatigue. Thinking the kinds of positive thoughts and using the various mental techniques described in other chapters in this book can strongly influence central fatigue.

Since there are many potential causes of fatigue, this feeling at any point during a training run is probably due to a combination of factors. Regardless of the causes, the effects of fatigue can be devastating to a runner. Learning how to deal with fatigue, from using mental techniques to walking, will enhance your success during the marathon. Use the opportunities when fatigue confronts you during training to practice your mental techniques and try to battle through the feeling. However, remember that there is a point at which walking may be your best immediate solution.

Patti Hasty Rust:

One thing I really remember from the class is that trying harder is not always the answer. It's kind of ironic, but that is really true. Ever since I was young and participating in athletics that seemed to be the essence of what coaches would tell you..."Work harder, try harder!" But as was pointed out in the class, that carries the negative connotation that you're not trying hard enough already. It causes you to battle with yourself and to tense up; when your muscles are tense they utilize more energy than when you are relaxed. So I guess I would tell people, as we were told in the class, that it really does work to try to relax, welcome the challenge, and enjoy what you're doing, rather than to create a battle within yourself.

I couldn't have said it better myself. Following are examples of both the muscle-to-mind and the mind to muscle approaches to relaxation. As you will see, the direction of the approach isn't as important as is the fact that you practice one of them.

Twenty-three-year-old Michelle Roland was already running about 30 miles per week on her own when she started training with the class. Although not officially enrolled in the class, she trained with us every chance she got, and had this to say on the subject of relaxation:

Relaxing has always been a problem for me. I guess you'd say I am kind of high-strung. So when they started talking in class about the importance of relaxing, I was thinking this was going to be difficult for me. And it was. But, I actually got pretty good at it after a while. What helped the most was practicing right after my training runs. Every time I could, I would go off by myself right after running and just sit quietly and enjoy the feeling of fatigue. I also used those times to learn what it felt like to have relaxed muscles (I had no choice since I was so tired). Once I was able to tell the difference between tense muscles and relaxed muscles, I started to get better at relaxing my muscles voluntarily.

"Absolutely none" was how 20-year-old Scott Hazelton described his running experience prior to taking the "marathon class." Relaxation was a new concept to him as well:

I found the best time to learn to relax was when I was trying to go to sleep. I sometimes have trouble getting to sleep and so learning to relax had a double benefit for me. What I did was to start with my toes and work up. I tried to tighten the muscles in my toes without tightening the muscles in my calves. I concentrated really hard on doing it. If I succeeded, I would try to tighten the muscles in the arch of my foot without tightening the muscles in my legs. And so on up my body. I became very aware of how tight or relaxed my muscles were, and in the process, I also became better at getting to sleep.

Tricia Tuttle, a 22-year-old who had never run more than three miles before starting this program, found that the mind-to-muscle approach worked best for her:

I used the relaxation exercises in both the training and outside of running. What worked best for me was to imagine the ocean or sunny breezy days.

This approach also worked well for Ron Steele:

At this point in the training, I really started to get into using visualizations and it was a turning point in the training for me. It really helped me to believe for myself the positive self-talk they were instructing us to use. Through the use of visualizations I wasn't getting as tired during the daily and long runs which served to reinforce the self-talk. I could see both physical and mental improvement, and it was very progressive in nature right up to the day of the marathon itself.

Jane Mortenson reflects:

Doing the runs gave me time to think. I can get so busy just trying to keep up with everything (motherhood, career, homemaking, etc.) that making time for prayer and personal reflection is sometimes challenging. When I ran, I had this undisturbed time during which no one could bother me. If you choose to use it that way, running can provide a lot of time (and I had more than most!) to focus on rebuilding or strengthening the spiritual aspect of your life and celebrating all you have to be grateful for.

Jane's comments raise an issue that crossed my mind several times over the course of training, and perhaps has crossed yours as well. Can a person operate from an internal locus of control (ILOC) and still believe in a higher power? That's a huge question, and not one most college students (including me) would have the guts to ask while surrounded by a classroom of peers — and I'll ask almost anything!

I raise it now, not because I claim to have the definitive answer, but because I think it is a legitimate question and an important issue to address. And while I won't tell you what to think, I will share with you what I have decided: Do you have to believe in a higher power to be able to run a marathon? No. Does it help? Well, it did me, but that's because the presence of a higher power is part of my belief system. Is it possible to operate from an ILOC and still believe in a higher power? Yes, much in the same way that one is still the child of his or her parent(s) even after becoming an adult.

This issue also crossed Jane Mortenson's mind and she graciously shared the following thoughts on the subject:

While I'm not always able to control all that happens to me, I am in control of how I react to the things that happen to me. I can have a pity-party or I can be aware of and celebrate my blessings. I have a great life. Yes, I am fighting cancer, but the cancer isn't my life. It's just an obstacle I have to work to overcome and I believe I will.

We may not be able to control all the circumstances of our lives, but once they happen God gives us choices. We are the ones who choose what to think. We even choose whether or not to believe in a higher power. But the choice is ours and that's how we exercise internal locus of control — through our choices. You can either choose to experience life, or you can choose to sit back and let life happen to you. For me, I'll choose life. And with God's help, I'll live it to the fullest.

If this question is one that you have been struggling with, perhaps this has helped you to reconcile the issue. If not, you might consider discussing it with your pastor or spiritual leader.

When we're talking 26.2 miles, walking is not a sin or a crime. As Section Two stated, walking can be beneficial, especially to first-time marathoners. This was an issue that Geraldine Zapf Hall initially struggled with. To her, having to walk was a sign of defeat and one which she felt bad about until the instructors explained to her that periodic walking was actually beneficial and increased her chances of successfully completing the marathon. After that her attitude toward walking totally changed and there was no stopping her:

There had never been any other group I was involved in where every-body was so nice, so young and so energetic. Even though I think I was the oldest person to participate with that class, I never felt like I was old. That I was old enough to be every one of those kids' mother didn't seem to matter to them. It was like we were all one close-knit group. Even though during the training runs, most of them would already be coming back while I was still going out, I never felt bad or ashamed about it. I never felt like I couldn't do it. There was one time when I ran by myself, the rest of the group had already come in, and one of the instructors came out and took me the rest of the way in. But I never felt bad about that, either. There was a positive attitude about everything that kept me going. Even when I would have to stop and walk, that positive attitude kept me going. I'm not saying I couldn't have run the marathon without that group support, but it sure helped in the only one I ran.

General Tips from the Marathoners — Week Ten:

- One of the easiest and quickest ways to relax while you are running is to drop your arms. The next time you are running and start feeling fatigued, notice where your arms are. If there is any tension in them at all, drop them and shake them out. Then make a point to keep them swinging loosely by your side at the same angle as is being formed between your hips and knees with each stride. You'll be surprised how much this simple adjustment will help relieve tension and slow the development of fatigue.

	Scheduled Distance	Actual Distance	RPE
Day 1	5		

Comments:

	Scheduled Distance	Actual Distance	RPE
Day 2	8		

Comments:

	Scheduled Distance	Actual Distance	RPE
Day 3	5		

Comments:

	Scheduled Distance	Actual Distance	RPE
Day 4	16		

Comments:

Total Miles This Week_____Cumulative Total_____

Chapter 11:

Week Eleven

Getting Used to the Long Runs

PART 1 — Associative and Dissociative Mental Techniques

In Chapter 7, we talked about learning to focus and said we would return to the topic again in Chapter 11. Also, in Chapter 8, in our discussion of flow, we talked about the advantages of thinking about your running form, your breathing, etc. while running and that will be relevant here as well.

So, what do you usually think about while you are running by yourself? Do you "space off" and think about other things or do you think about what you are doing? When you are spacing off, we say you are dissociating; that is, you are disconnecting your physical self from your mental self. When you are thinking about what you are doing (in this case, about running), you are associating or maintaining a connection between your physical and mental selves. What about when you are running with others? What do you talk about? When you talk about running, you are associating. When you talk about other things, you are dissociating.

Some people prefer the dissociative approach because, they say, "It makes the runs seem to go by so much more quickly." And, if your objective is to make the runs go by quickly, dissociation is probably the way to do that. However, if you enjoy running or even succeed in achieving flow while running, then you probably don't want the runs to go by quickly. In fact, they may be one of the highlights of your day and you do not want to "miss" them by dissociating. Another consideration is that we want you to be training both your body and your mind and, when you are dissociating, your mind is no longer part of the training. As we have discussed in earlier chapters, practicing visualization and concentration, as well as focusing on what you are doing are important aspects of your marathon preparation. It seems to us, then, that dissociating while you are running constitutes training only your body. It is almost as if, when you find it necessary to dissociate during your runs, you are "putting up with" the training runs in order to achieve the goal of running the marathon.

Our recommendation is that you use the associative approach. Work on focusing on the running itself, on developing the feeling that you are an inexhaustible machine, on achieving that feeling of flow we have been discussing. When you become skilled at it, it will feel like you are "on automatic pilot," as one of our students put it, and you will be able to emotionally sit back and watch yourself glide along effortlessly. One of your authors particularly enjoys the image that he is a giant steam engine with huge lungs (cylinders) that are capable of taking in and processing massive quantities of air, producing endless power. He sometimes says it makes him feel "bulletproof" and "indestructible." Feelings like this are not achieved by dissociating or by listening to tapes or to the radio on a headset. So, lose the walkman, forget the daydreaming and work on investing yourself in the activity...learn to love the running for its own sake. And, in only five more weeks, you will cruise through that marathon and go on to enjoy many more miles of flow.

 Physical Preparation

> ### Week 11 Training
> Day 1: 5 miles
> Day 2: 8 miles
> Day 3: 5 miles
> Day 4: 16 miles
> ### Total for Week: 34 miles

This week is the last of the 16-milers. The longest runs, 18-miles, will be the next two weeks. After that it is all down hill to the marathon. If you have stuck to the training schedule, at the end of this week you will have run 250 miles!

This is the third 16-miler so you have a good idea what to expect. Think about how you have done on the previous 16-milers. Before you run the 16-miler this week, think about whether you have optimized your preparation. Have you rested the day before? Did you eat appropriately all week? Did you drink enough fluid before and during the runs? Were you mentally prepared? All these factors can affect how you do on these long runs. If there is a potential problem area, now is the time to address it.

Let's briefly review the physiological factors that can have such a dramatic affect on running these long runs. On a comparative basis, the short runs of the week, five and eight miles, probably seem like a breeze. What happens when you stretch an eight-mile run into a 16-mile run?

To run 16 miles at an 8-12 minute-per-mile pace requires approximately 2-3 hours, give or take a few minutes. Two to three hours is a long time to keep the body continuously functioning at a high level. Remember what was said regarding fatigue in an chapter 10. For each of you, the level of fatigue you experience and the cause of the fatigue may be very different. For some, fatigue may result from inadequate fluid consumption which drives up the body's temperature. For others it may be inadequate carbohydrate stores which reduce the fuel availability to the muscles. For still others it may be more related to the central nervous system, perhaps partly physiological or partly psychological. The point is that your experience during the 16-mile run may be substantially different from someone else's. Each runner needs to assess his or her own preparation in all the areas that can be controlled. You can certainly control the physiological. It is more difficult to control the psychological so all the tools you have learned up to now become quite important.

PART 3 To Be (Associative) or Not To Be...

This is a decision you need to make for yourself. Of course, you already know that our recommendation is to utilize the associative approach since it will help encourage a more thorough integration of the physiological and psychological conditioning. Association can happen to varying degrees. It can be as multifaceted and encompassing as accomplishing the state of flow or as simple as "running with your shadow" (a technique used by Julie Stone during the 1995 class). You decide how much to include in the association; the more extensive the association, the more thorough the mental/physical integration.

For Todd Hixson, focusing on bodily movements and sensations was the avenue to effective association:

> *My best runs often included focusing a lot on how I felt. I would concentrate on my stride, my breathing, the way my feet hit the ground, or where I was carrying my arms. Sometimes I would think about remaining relaxed and I would focus on loosening my shoulders or my neck muscles.*

Chris Henle's approach was decidedly more mental:

> *I pictured a good run in my mind. Initially, I would talk with my run-*

ning partners. Later, running became a time of personal reflection. My turning point came when running became more fun. I used to hate to run; it was a chore at first. Now it was easier.

Even years later, Ron Steele remembered some of the associative techniques he used while running:

Dave suggested that while we ran we try to think of 25 reasons for running. That can keep your mind occupied for a while! Something else I found helpful was to mentally connect myself to whomever was ahead of me. As long as they move forward, then I move forward. In a subconscious way, it helped keep me going.

Some people utilize both associative and dissociative approaches, depending on the situation. This was the case for Jane Mortenson who had several suggestions to share:

I was fascinated by the rhythm of my breathing and the feel of my heart beating, and in awe over how magnificent the body is. For me, the first three miles were always the hardest; this never seemed to get any easier over the course of training. Even as we neared the end of the program, there were still times at the start of a run when it felt as though I had never run before, and might not be able to make even one mile! To combat these negative thoughts, I compared trying to get my body going to having trouble starting a lawn mower or getting an old treadle sewing machine going. After those first three miles, it was as if everything became automatic and magical. I just followed the rhythm of my own machine and ran at a comfortably slow pace.

In all honesty, the activity of running was never actually fun for me. My fun started when the endorphins kicked in. Until then, I usually thought about anything but running. I would recite the Lord's Prayer, the Apostle's Creed, and sing songs in my mind. Our training route went by some stately old homes and I would always sing the Beverly Hillbillies theme song in my mind as I passed them.

Another activity that always helped me get through several miles, would be to go through the alphabet and think of things I was grateful for, such as "A" for Active, "B" for Bold, etc. I could pass a lot of time just doing that. For me, the real fun started once I finished my run. I felt terrific and enjoyed the rest of the day celebrating what I had done. My ritual of being with friends and taking a relaxing bubble bath were great rewards to look forward to.

Amy Kepler took a decidedly dissociative approach:

I took a dissociative approach by utilizing mental images of beautiful scenery, the smell of flowers, and rolling hills which I would greet by saying, "Come on hills, come run with me," as the theme song to Flash Dance played in my head.

Heidi Brandt also found songs to be inspirational and would pass the miles by singing to herself:

I would imagine all my muscles working together as I sang to myself Queen's "We are the Champions," & "When I Come Around" by Green Day. I would also sing cheers from high school like "We got spirit." There were certain chants I would say over & over. I would tune out and not realize that a mile had gone by. I also talked a lot of the time — it made time go by faster.

Kathy Schneider reflected:

The dissociative approach worked well for me. Rather than focusing on the running, I would think about significant people and/or events in my life such as family members or times spent with friends. I would find myself running faster; the miles seemed like footsteps.

While the associative approach is what we recommend, as you can see different things work for different people. Experiment. Once you figure out what works best for you, use it. Practice it during every run and try to become more efficient and effective in its use. Believe me, you will need these skills during the marathon.

	Scheduled Distance	Actual Distance	RPE	
Day 1	5			
Comments:				
Day 2	8			
Comments:				
Day 3	5			
Comments:				
Day 4	16			
Comments:				

Total Miles This Week_____Cumulative Total_____

Chapter 12:

Week Twelve
Knocking Down the Wall

PART 1 · What Happens (Psychologically) at the Wall?

To begin with, the psychological effect of the wall will be minimized if you know what to expect physically and understand what is occurring. That is why we are going to explain it in the next section of this chapter. Understanding something helps to give us the feeling that we can control it and therefore keeps us from panicking. But, even though you understand it, expect it and are therefore not surprised when it occurs, hitting the wall can be a demoralizing experience if you are not prepared for it psychologically.

Part of being psychologically prepared for the wall is to have accepted the idea that, in spite of all your training (even if you run every mile the training schedule calls for), your body will not really be ready to run 26.2 miles. "What?" you may be saying, "Isn't that what all this training is about?" Yes, it IS what it's about. It's just that most people's bodies are not capable of storing enough fuel to go for as long a time as first-time marathoners usually take to complete the marathon distance. World-class marathoners don't usually hit the wall the same way we mortals do, and one reason is that they are only taking half the time we are to finish the marathon! So, you may be thinking, if I just train more, run more training miles, I can avoid hitting the wall. No, it won't work that way. If you try to increase the mileage, there is a strong possibility that you will injure yourself and not get to start the marathon, let alone finish it. So forget about increasing the training mileage.

So, what are you going to use for energy when you hit the wall? The answer is, you're going to use all that mental preparation you have been doing. Look at it this way. How did you feel late in that 16-mile run last week? If you felt strong, then we are really happy for you. But most of you probably felt REALLY tired. A lot like you will feel at the wall on marathon day. But you kept going, didn't you? Even if you walked some, you kept going, right? And you finished the 16 miles, just like you will finish the marathon. You are probably going to be even more exhausted this week when you run that first 18-miler. But when you feel that fatigue coming, you will go on anyway. We know you will. We have seen our students do it week after week. And every time you push through that barrier of exhaustion, you get better at knocking down the wall! You've already been doing it for weeks. Remember the first time, way back in week 1, when you first ran 5 miles? You were exhausted THEN! Now your SHORT runs are 5 miles long and it seems like you barely get warmed up, right?

What happens to some people psychologically when they hit the wall in the marathon is that they "give up." They allow their minds to fill up with defeatist self-talk and they simply quit mentally. Then they begin shuffling along with their heads down, then walking, still with their heads down, like they are ashamed of what they are doing and, finally, many of them drop out and don't even finish or they stumble in to the finish looking and feeling as if they wish they had never started the marathon in the first place. You are not going to be one of those people. Those people include some who set time goals in the marathon and then, when they hit the wall and realized, at the 18- or 20-mile mark, that they weren't going to achieve their goal, they gave up. But you haven't made that mistake, have you? (If you have, you have not been paying attention...so go back and read the part in the Introduction about why you should have no goal other than finishing.) Some of those people decided early on in their training that they were not going to walk a single step in the marathon and so, when they found it necessary to walk at mile 20, they felt defeated and gave up. But you didn't do that because, as we discussed in Chapter 10, you know the value of periodic walking during a marathon. And some of those people only trained their bodies and so, when the fatigue came, they had nothing else to rely on. But you didn't do that either.

So, when the fatigue comes, you will use your visualization and your positive self-talk and your concentration. And you will go on. And if you need to walk, you will walk with your head up and a steady, proud look in your eyes because you will know that you are doing what you set out to do, and that is complete this marathon. And you will not feel defeated. You will feel triumphant and you will go all the way to the finish line and you will cross it with joy and ecstasy and a feeling of achievement like you've never felt before. And that's the way it's going to be, because you have already decided that is how it's going to be and you make your own reality.

So, what is the answer to the question of what happens psychologically at the wall? Whatever you decide will happen, that's what. And what you have decided is that you are going to knock that wall down. You always do. You have been doing it every week. And you will do it again on marathon day. Because you are a marathoner.

 Physical Preparation

> ## Week 12 Training
> Day 1: 5 miles
> Day 2: 8 miles
> Day 3: 5 miles
> Day 4: 18 miles
> ## Total for Week: 36 miles

This is the beginning of the end — the end of the long runs which are preparing you for the really big one, the marathon. The long run this week and next week is 18 miles, 75% of the marathon distance. In marathon tradition it has been often said that if you can run 18 miles you can run 26.2 miles. In our experience, this has always been true. There are several factors that can explain why you only need to run up to 18 miles in order to run a marathon.

On the day of the marathon, several things will be different from going out on your usual training runs. First, you will be mentally fired up because of the realization that this is what you have prepared for past 16 weeks to do. Most marathons have a degree of pageantry and party atmosphere that simply adds to the hoopla. There is a feeling of camaraderie with hundreds, thousands, or even tens of thousands of people you don't even know. You have the same objective, a common interest, and a mutual respect.

In addition to being mentally ready to go, you will be physiologically ready to go. The engine will be full of premium fuel and you will have had a recent major tune-up. The tune-up will be the result of the tapering you will do the last two weeks. The reduction in the training mileage will allow you to be fully rested, recovered and ready to go. The tapering process will fine tune your muscles so that they will be functioning at an optimal level.

What Happens (Physiologically) at the Wall?

Many marathon runners hit the proverbial "wall" at about the 18-mile mark, give or take a mile or two. You may have already experienced this feeling on one of the longer runs or you may experience it on the 18-milers. What is the "wall" and what is causing the sensation you feel if you crash into the wall?

Most believe that "hitting the wall" coincides with the point of glycogen (or carbohydrate) depletion in the active muscles and liver, resulting in inadequate blood sugar for the brain and inadequate carbohydrate for the active muscles. The sensation of hitting the wall is described as being total fatigue, exhaustion and inability to maintain the pace you had been running. This is the feeling one would expect to experience if he or she were glycogen depleted.

If muscle glycogen is depleted, the muscles must rely almost exclusively on fat to manufacture ATP which dramatically reduces the amount of ATP that can be made per unit of time. This decrease in the rate of ATP production forces the runner to slow to a pace that can be maintained with approximately half the ATP compared to when carbohydrates were available. For typical recreational runners, this speed is nothing more than a brisk walk at best. For some, a walk becomes difficult.

Four factors determine whether or not you ever hit the wall in a marathon. The factors are your level of glycogen in the muscle at the start of the marathon, the amount of carbohydrates you consume during the run, your level of conditioning and the pace you run during the marathon. Let's see how each of these factors contributes to "the wall" and how you can effectively reduce the likelihood you will hit the wall.

It seems pretty logical that the more glycogen you have stuffed in your muscles at the beginning of the marathon, the less likely you are to run out. This factor is almost totally related to nutrition and how much activity you do in the 12-18 hours prior to the marathon. By maintaining a high carbohydrate intake throughout the week of the marathon, you are keeping the muscles stuffed with glycogen. By tapering your mileage down the week of the marathon and by not doing any significant activity the day before the marathon, you are reducing your use of the glycogen stored in the muscles. The combination of stuffing the muscles with glycogen and then preserving the glycogen by not doing a lot of physical activity will ensure maximal amounts of glycogen at the start of the marathon.

Once you begin the marathon, you start to deplete the carbohydrates you have stored. You need to begin to consume carbohydrates early during the run so they will be available to help conserve the stored carbohydrates. By consuming carbohydrates during the run, you are adding fuel to the fuel tank so the tank doesn't drain to empty as rapidly. Most runners prefer to do this by consuming a liquid form of carbohydrates, usually contained in a fluid replacement drink like Gatorade. This is discussed more fully in Chapters 5 and 6. It should be once again emphasized that carbohydrate replenishment during the run needs to be done early and frequently. Don't wait until you hit the wall because it takes some time for the carbohydrates to become usable to the body.

For the past 12 weeks you have been training your muscles to be efficient in using fuel and producing ATP. One of the specific adaptations that has occurred, primarily as a result of the long runs, is an increase in the ability of the muscle to use fat as a fuel source to produce ATP. The more fat the muscle can use, the less carbohydrate it has to use. If you can use more fat in order to run at any given pace, you will be conserving your carbohydrates so you will not use them up as fast. By conserving your carbohydrates, you will be less likely to run out and "hit the wall."

The last factor under your control that can have a significant impact on whether or not you will hit the wall is the pace at which you run the marathon. You can decrease your chances of hitting the wall by simply running at a slower pace. Recall in an earlier chapter we said that running faster requires that you use more carbohydrates to make ATP than does running slower. The slower you run, the easier it is for the muscle to use more fat and less carbohydrate. If the other two factors discussed above are held constant, running at a slower pace uses less carbohydrates which will effectively conserve the carbohydrates so they will last longer. If you reduce the use of carbohydrates sufficiently, they will last throughout the marathon.

Obviously, the ideal situation for the marathon runner is to have the carbo-hydrates run out just as you cross the finish line. If this were to occur, you would have received maximal energy yield from your carbohydrates and you would have run the distance at the fastest pace you could have. Unfortunately, this is a difficult task to achieve because all the factors discussed above vary from day to day and from marathon to marathon. Even elite marathon runners don't run the same way each race. Some days are better than others.

However, experience does provide valuable lessons and marathoners get better at running marathons just by having run several. But, if this is your first marathon, you only have the experience of your long runs and the knowledge and experience of others to rely on. Remember your primary objective — to finish and have a successful experience. The objective is not to run as fast as you can. There-fore, the pace at which you run the marathon should be a comfortable pace for you to maintain. You should even back off from the pace at which you run your 18-mile runs, at least early in the run. You have to be far-sighted and recognize what is going to be happening those last six to eight miles. Most marathoners feel petty good the first half to three-fourths of the 26.2 miles. It is the last part of the run that really determines success or failure. In fact, there is an old marathon saying that all too often is true — "the last 6 miles is the last half of the run." The last six miles does seem like the last half and you need to do everything you can to reduce your chances of "hitting the wall."

PART 3 | The Wall

Remember the childhood classic *The Little Engine That Could* that we re-ferred to a few chapters ago? For those of you who might have forgotten, this is the story of the train full of toys and good food that was on its way up a mountain when the engine that had been pulling it stopped. Even though the engine wanted to go on it could not get its wheels to turn anymore and the whole train stopped. It looked like the toys and good food were going to be stranded until a little blue engine came along and agreed to try pulling them over the mountain to the town of boys and girls that awaited their arrival. Even though she was a very small engine normally used only in the train yard and had never been over the mountain, the little blue engine managed to pull the train over the mountain by telling herself, "I think I can, I think I can, I think I can...."

So what does this children's story have to do with the wall, you ask? Everything. Let me give you the updated "marathon" version:

There once was an engine pulling a train from east to west across the state of Colorado. Although the cars were fully loaded when it started on the eastern plains, they had not felt heavy to the engine. The engine's furnaces blazed hot from the coal burning in them and starting had been easy on the flat land. Before long, the engine was flying across the grassy prairie with the train rolling easily behind it. It knew that its destination lay on the west side of the state and that it would have to cross a mountain range to get there, but the engine wasn't worried. Its coal car was loaded to the brim and there were water stops along the way. Besides, if it needed to lighten its load, it could always dump the extra car of wood positioned behind the coal car. Had it been up to the engine he would have left the wood car behind altogether for he was sure there would be enough coal for the trip, but the older engines had insisted. Since this was his first time to run this route, the young strong engine obliged although he was sure the wood would not be necessary since he was so new and strong.

At first, the climb was so gradual the engine hardly noticed it. In fact, the engine was rather enjoying the feel of its wheels turning fast and strong against the rails. The day was perfect, the track was clear; the run was going so well that the engine relaxed and enjoyed the breathtaking view of the approaching snow-capped mountains. The closer the engine got to the mountains, the more excited he became. He had never seen anything like them, and he couldn't wait to actually be in them and see their beauty up close. In his hurry, he bypassed a couple of water stops and kept the furnace stoked with coal, and the train flew across the prairie.

Being in the mountains was like no other experience the engine had ever had. Climbing through the switchbacks as they wound their way up and through the beautiful landscape was exciting and challenging, and the engine relished this new experience that the flatlands could not offer. He was a little surprised by how much coal climbing these mountains took, but he was sure that there was enough to get the train through. He remembered that the older engines had told him to start throwing in some wood along with the coal at this point in the route, but he didn't want to contaminate the fast-burning coal with the slow-burning wood when it didn't appear that would be necessary. Surely, he thought, this must be the last peak and it will all be downhill from here. So, he ignored the advice and continued to use coal to power up the mountain at full tilt.

What he thought would be the last peak hadn't been, and he was trying to figure out where he was on the map when the train jerked and rapidly started to slow. Quickly, he checked the furnace. In his distraction, he had let the fire run low. He called for more coal, but there was no response. The coal car was empty. Now all that was left was the slow-burning wood to power the train through the rest of these seemingly unending mountains. Not only that, burning wood required more water than did coal, and because he had bypassed some water stops they were low on water. How could he have let this happen! Why had he ignored the advice of the older, more experienced engines? Now the whole train was in jeopardy of being stranded because he had allowed himself to become so caught up in the excitement of the trip. He frantically tried to remember the stories he had heard the older engines tell about their runs through the mountains in hopes that they would help him know what to do.

"Pack the furnace with wood and keep her stoked," he remembered one old engine saying. "Back off your throttle and take her slow and steady," another had quipped. "Conserve your water until you get to the next stop and then fill 'er up," a third had warned. As the engine hurried to act upon these suggestions, the train continued to slow and was nearly to the point of stopping when he remembered what the wisest of all the engines had said. "The most important thing is to never give up. As long as you have wood and water you can make it. But you'll never know that if you quit. Once you leave the track, it's over. You'll probably never make that run again...a train without an engine is no good to anyone; an engine without a train has no purpose. Just stay together, use one another's strengths, give the wood and water a chance to do their job, and finish the run."

Until the wood started to really burn, the engine did his best to keep the train moving by using the rise and fall of the mountains and the momentum of the attached cars. Before long the furnace glowed red-hot with the crackling wood and black smoke billowed from the stack. The engine shuddered as the throttle was opened and the wheels strained to respond to the flow of energy from the furnace. Gradually the train picked up speed, and before long it was slowly winding its way through the scenic switchbacks.

To the engine, the mountains seemed to stop as quickly as they had started. Before long he was once again rolling through a breezy prairie surrounded by waving grass. They were on a gradual descent and the momentum of the attached cars became an asset as they helped to push the entire train toward its destination. As the train station came into view, the engine vowed to share his own story with the other engines once he returned to the roundhouse — especially the oldest engine. It would have been a great mistake not to have finished, for it had been quite a run, indeed.

The parallels between the two stories are obvious, as are the parallels between my version and the typical experience of the first-time marathoner. The wall is the point at which your engine runs out of coal (glycogen) and has to switch to wood (fat). Not everyone hits the wall. But as was stated earlier, most first-time marathoners run at a slow enough pace (and should) that they will have run out of glycogen before they run out of marathon. If you have been following the training program as it's been given, and if you run the marathon according to the instructions you will be given, the only dangerous thing about the wall is letting it stop you before your body can make the fuel source switchover. And that would be a real shame after all you will have gone through. So, just accept right now that you will probably hit the wall, but decide that you will not let it stop you.

I know that sometimes saying you are going to do something and then actually doing it when the time comes, are two different things — especially if it involves something you've never done before. Maybe the following stories will help you anticipate what the wall will be like, and how you will handle it if you do encounter it..

Prior to signing up for the "marathon class," the extent of Eric Stoneman's previous long distance running had been limited to "one 600-yard run in the Presidential Fitness Test." Here's what this 6'2", 230 pound, 21-year-old had to say about the wall:

> There is no question in my mind that the wall is real. When it comes, the feeling of fatigue is overwhelming. But what gets you through it is that you have felt that kind of fatigue many Saturdays before. It happened the first time I ran 10 miles. At about eight, I thought, "I am dead. I can't finish this." But I did. It happened again in the 16-milers and the 18 milers. But each time, I found that my body was wrong, because each time I reached down mentally and found a way to keep going, so that by the time it happened at mile 18 in the marathon, I knew I could go on....and I did, all the way to 26.2 miles.

Jeri Kurtzleben, who thought anyone who regularly ran more than three miles qualified as a world-class runner, admits:

> At about mile 18 my blisters really started to bother me. It was like I had to push, push, push myself to finish...but I did it..

Jane Mortenson used a unique mental strategy which paid her huge dividends during the entire race:

> *I did something during the marathon that really seemed to help me have a successful and enjoyable run, plus I think it was a major reason why I never hit the wall. During the training, once I completed the first 18-miler nonstop at my slow pace, I felt I could do anything and could definitely do the marathon. When it came time to actually run the marathon, I mentally ran the last eight miles first. Since I knew I could do 18 miles with no problem, my mental strategy was to get those extra eight miles out of the way first, and then just do 18 like I had done before. It worked wonderfully! After eight miles, I was feeling so good it was as if I had just gotten warmed up. At a water stop, I reached down and massaged my bunions for a few seconds, washed down a couple ibuprofen with AllSport, ate a candy lifesaver, and said to myself, "Well, it's a new day. Now, I'm just going to go out and run that Saturday morning 18-miler." It was a mental game that really worked for me. I never hit the wall. Since mentally I never ran further than 18 miles, I never got psyched out about running farther than I ever had before. Physically, I know I ran 26.2 miles, but mentally I didn't. It sounds absurd, I know, but it worked.*

Todd Hixson summed up his experience this way:

> *The wall is exactly as big as you think it is.*

Sometimes the wall has more mental aspects than physical as Ron Steele's account reflects:

> *I never once hit the wall in any of the races I did. Instead, my trouble spot seemed to be getting through mile 14-15. I developed a kind of mental block about that particular place in the marathon as the result of an experience I had while running another marathon and was totally exhausted at this point and had real problems. Ever since, I've had trouble at this particular place in all the rest of marathons I've run. But I keep going and get through it and then I'm fine.*

Chris Henle remembers:

> *As we were standing there bunched together in the dark waiting for the marathon to start, I suddenly got really nervous. All at once it hit me*

that it was actually here and I was going to run a MARATHON! I didn't know whether to throw up or cry. We started out slow, like Forrest and Dave had suggested. For the first half, I ran with people. By mile 15, I was running by myself and I felt better. It had taken me a long time to feel warmed up and relaxed, but now I just cruised along. I never hit the wall. At mile 22, I caught up with classmate Eric Johnson, and we ran the rest of the way together. Before I knew it, I was in the stadium and just one lap away from the finish line. Those last 400 yards were the hardest. It was so close, yet so far. I wanted it to be over, and at the same time I wanted it to never end. When I finally did stop, I felt great! So great, in fact, that I celebrated later that night by going to a concert.

Unlike Chris, I did hit the wall and I hit it hard. This was what hitting the wall was like for me:

I had already been running for nearly five hours when at mile 20 I simply ran out of gas. It literally felt like my body was out of fuel, and even though my mind said, "Go!" my body would not respond. All I could do was walk. I was among the last group of runners and as even they began passing me I was engulfed by a wave of discouraging negative thoughts. I was only at mile 20, there were six miles left, and it was beginning to drizzle. I was getting passed by the slowest of the slow. My body was out of fuel. I suddenly felt very alone. I guess I panicked that I might not be able to finish. And I started to cry. In spite of all the negative thoughts, I remembered that we were to walk with our heads held high no matter what happened. So with head up and tears streaming, I kept walking. A couple of women came up beside me and seeing my tears asked if I was OK Although I managed a sob-racked, "Yes," my mind was screaming, "NO!" They must have sensed the discrepancy, because they walked with me for a few minutes until I had stopped crying.

After they left, I tried to regain my composure by assessing the situation. I realized that this must be the infamous "wall," and I tried to remember what we had been told to do if we hit it. I was already running at a slow pace...any slower would be to walk. I had taken advantage of every water stop and I drank as much as I could. I had some dried apricots with me which I took out and ate. As I walked, I stretched out my upper body, arms, and neck in order to try to re-lease pent-up tension. I tried to relax by breathing slowly and deeply. I wasn't feeling as panicky, but I still didn't feel like I could start running again. So I did something that the instructors hadn't discussed in class — I prayed. "God, I've come this far, but now I need your help. Please give me the strength I need to finish this. Amen."

I barely had my eyes open when I felt an arm come around my shoulder. I looked to my left to see fellow classmate, Adam Boesen, standing beside me.

Where he had come from I had no idea. He ran at a faster pace than me, and I hadn't seen him all day. But suddenly, here he was giving me a hug.

He asked me how I was doing and I told him I was having a hard time. He listened attentively and then said, "I think I have something that might help." From his fanny pack he pulled a condiment-size silver packet. As he handed it to me he instructed, "Eat this. It's like concentrated Gatorade. They call it power food and it's supposed to boost your energy. It might help."

"But aren't you going to need it?" I asked.

"No, I just had one. This is an extra," he assured me.

I looked at the packet of energy in my hand and suddenly knew my prayer had been answered. By way of this seemingly mortal man, God had delivered the fuel my body needed in order to be able to finish the marathon. To me, Adam's wings couldn't have been any more real had they been visible.

"How does it feel to be an angel of God?" I asked him with all sincerity.

"What do you mean?" he asked, looking puzzled.

As I told him about my prayer, all the tension and fatigue seemed to drain from his face and he brightened. By the time I finished with, "So you see, you really are an angel," he was beaming.

"You know," he said, "I was feeling really discouraged myself. About mid-way I started having bad leg cramps and had to stop several times and stretch. I've had to walk quite a bit. Before I saw you I was feeling pretty low because I thought everyone else was way ahead of me. I have been struggling with why this had to happen to me and feeling pretty badly because of it, but I don't anymore. Thanks."

We hugged and quietly walked in the drizzle warmed by each other's company and the magical moment we had just shared. After a few minutes Adam asked, "Will you be OK?"

"I'll be fine, " I answered, knowing that I would be.

"Then I'll see you at the finish," he said.

"Yes, you will," I answered. And he was gone. I remembered the packet in my hand, opened it, and swallowed the jell-like goo. Within minutes I could feel raw energy start surging through my body. About that same time I came across a port-a-potty. I went to the bathroom, and rubbed vaseline on the areas that were starting to chafe. At a nearby water station, I washed down two ibuprofen I had tucked into my fanny pack. I shortened my chant to "I am a marathoner and I am doing this because...." I narrowed my focus and increased my concentration. And I started running again...and I didn't stop.

	Scheduled Distance	Actual Distance	RPE

Day 1 | 5

Comments:

Day 2 | 8

Comments:

Day 3 | 5

Comments:

Day 4 | 18

Comments:

Total Miles This Week_____Cumulative Total_____

Chapter 13:

W e e k   T h i r t e e n
The Last of the BIG Weeks

We talked about goal setting in the Introduction when we discussed the importance of setting the appropriate goal for the marathon: FINISH IT. We hope you haven't modified that goal. One reason we are revisiting the subject of goal setting at this point is that we know that as some people near the end of the training period they start to consider modifying the goal. Sometimes, especially if the training is going well, first-time marathoners start to feel a little TOO optimistic. If they feel OK after the first 18-miler, they start saying to themselves, "I think I can do this marathon in under four hours." Have you said something like that to yourself? If you have, we think you should stop it. If you have forgotten what can happen when you do that, you need to go back and read the part of the Introduction on "Choosing the Goal." We are serious. Do it now if you are starting to think of the goal as anything other than finishing. Go ahead. We will wait here until you are done reading.

Oh good, you are back. (Or maybe you didn't even need to reread that part again, since we had just reminded you of it in Chapter 12.) Either way, you are ready to go on. There are a few other things about goal setting that would be useful to keep in mind as we get close to the marathon. One of them has to do with the practice of setting interim goals during the marathon. Sometimes, even though people seem to have succeeded in maintaining the overall goal of finishing the marathon, they find themselves thinking things like, "I need to be at the five-mile point under one hour," or "I need to maintain a 10-minute-per-mile pace." What this causes them to do is to try to accomplish those goals in their training runs during these last few weeks of training and then, if they are unable to do it, their motivation starts to nose-dive.

What you have been doing over the last three months or so is following a training program which is made up of a series of goals. The goals are stated in terms of daily and weekly distances. We have emphasized that your goals should simply be to complete those runs. We have suggested that it is important for you to keep a training log and to record the distances and elapsed times of your runs because this will allow you to chart your progress. In all cases, the important measurement is your current performance compared to your own past performance. So, the appropriate overall goal is simply to get better. That is, to go further. And that is exactly what you have been doing. Your long runs have gone steadily up from five miles to 18 miles and your weekly totals have more than doubled from 16 miles to 36 miles.

So, think of the marathon as the long run for week 16. How should you handle it with respect to goal setting? The same way you have handled all the other weekly long runs. The goal is to complete it. No overall time goals. No interim goals. Just finish.

Later on, in other marathons, you can set overall and interim goals if you want to and, to increase the liklihood that you will achieve those goals, you may even want to set time goals for your training runs. But for now, keep that one goal in mind. Finish this marathon.

 Physical Preparation

> ## Week 13 Training
> Day 1: 5 miles
> Day 2: 8 miles
> Day 3: 5 miles
> Day 4: 18 miles
> ## Total for Week: 36 miles

This is the last long one — the last 18-miler. The long run next week is cut in half so this is the last opportunity for your body and mind to adapt to the long run. You did it last week, you can do it again this week. Just remember the importance of these long runs. This is how your body learns to keep going, mile after mile. The changes occurring in these long runs are preparing your body to go the distance — to run the marathon.

After this last week of high mileage, the physiological training begins to take a back seat to your nutrition, fluid replacement, and the mental training. After this week, your actual training mileage begins to decrease dramatically and the effects of the training will have already occurred. The reduction in the training mileage, called tapering, is going to fine-tune your engine, fill your gas tank, and get your brain excited about running the marathon. After this week, the actual run training becomes less important and your eating, drinking, and thinking become the focus.

Foods and Fluids

As you approach the end of the long training runs, some review of the important nutritional principles will be useful. What you do nutritionally from now until the marathon will have a big impact on your success. The training is almost done, but the nutrition continues to be important until the marathon is finished.

Here are the three basic principles you should follow between now and the marathon.

Maintain a high consumption of carbohydrates throughout the next three weeks. This does not mean overconsuming calories, but of the calories you are consuming, 55-70% should be carbohydrates, with most of those being complex carbohydrates. You should not be gaining or losing weight over these last three weeks. You want to consume enough total calories and fluid to maintain your weight.

Consume enough fluid each day to maintain a slightly yellow-tinted urine and to bring the body weight to within one-half pound (plus or minus) of the preceding day. To achieve this, most runners need to be drinking a minimum of 8 glasses of fluid each day. If the weather is warm and you are losing significant water through sweating, a higher consumption of fluid will be necessary.

Drink on the long run. Consume about 6-8 ounces of fluid (preferably a fluid replacement beverage with sodium and carbohydrate, like Gatorade) every 2 miles.

PART 3 Tortoise or Hare?

As you know, you create your own reality. In your reality, are you the tortoise or the hare? I hope you said tortoise, for in that classic story, he is the one who finishes and that is what we want for you. If you find yourself having "hare-like" thoughts, revisit your reality or your story may not end like you want it to.

Keith Wendl admitted:

I started out really competitive at first. But then Dave advised us not to do that, so I backed off and started to have fun with it.

What happened to Keith happens to most people. In our culture, we are raised to be competitive, not complacent. But as Keith discovered, running becomes more fun when it's done under less pressure. And we want you to have 26.2 miles of fun.

Todd Hixson is another person who had to consciously assess his attitude and restructure his goals when it came to training for the marathon. He shared the following thoughts on the subject of goal setting:

I use goals a lot now. I have used them in swimming, in biking and I used them in training for the marathon too. Before I learned how to use goals, I got injured the first time I tried to train for a marathon because I made the mistake of trying to train too fast. I was setting time goals for certain distances. Later on, I learned that wasn't a good thing to do, and when I just set the goal of finishing each training run and then of just finishing the marathon, it worked just like they told me it would in the marathon class. Before I started marathon training, I had a background in competitive sports and I entered the training with that competitive frame of mind. I always wanted to train fast and to run at the front of the group when we all trained together. It took me a while to get rid of that, but once I did, I began to focus on goals having to do with getting better, goals based on comparing me to my own past performance. So, for the training program, my goal was simply to go further each week, just like the program requires. And, when it came to the marathon, the goal was simply to go 26.2 miles. And that's just what I did.

Ron Steele had these thoughts on keeping everything in perspective:

Running a marathon is a test of what you can accomplish if you want to...if you are willing to take the time and don't quit. Sure there are lots of other ways you can test yourself, but doing a marathon is one of the most challenging I have found. When it comes right down to it, you have to do it by yourself. You may be running with hundreds or thousands of other people, but it's still up to you, the individual, to do it. There is an element of finality to it. There is a start and finish, and in between you just run. That's when you find out who you are and what you're made of. Most people don't even give themselves that chance.

Running a marathon is not easy. It's not supposed to be. Things that are worthwhile usually aren't. If it was easy, then everyone would do it and it wouldn't mean as much. The important thing is to not cheat yourself out of success by quitting, or saying that it's only a success if you make it by such & such a time.

That's not what's important — just doing it is. The rest is just icing on the cake.

Think of all you've already done in the last twelve weeks. In your wildest imagination did you ever think you would have been able to do all that you already have? Jane Mortenson summed it up nicely when she said:

> *There is no way you can fail when you are in control and the judge of what constitutes success. Anything that you do over and above what you normally do is to your benefit. You're still doing more than before. Everyone who runs a marathon is a winner, regardless of how long it takes.*

If something should happen that interrupts your training, that doesn't necessarily mean that you have to drop out of the program. In the 1995 class, a couple of people hit medical roadblocks, but went on to finish the training and complete the marathon. Here are their stories. If something similar has happened to you during this program, take heart, all is not lost.

Kathy Schneider missed the first 18-miler due to bronchitis and only made seven miles of the second one. Knowing that 18 was the most mileage accomplished prior to the marathon, her anxiety grew when she realized that in the marathon she would be going ten miles farther than her longest run since the most she had done was 16 miles:

> *I knew I had to rest and focus on getting healthy, but part of me was really mad at myself for getting bronchitis. I was really worried about what would happen in the marathon. But I kept the goal clear in my mind...finish. I kept telling myself that it didn't matter how fast I went and that, if I just took it easy, I could keep going. And that's exactly what I did on marathon day. I never let that goal out of my mind. Just finish. Just keep going until you get to the finish. It worked really well.*

In mid-March (at about eight weeks into the training) Rob Leslie underwent emergency surgery to have his appendix removed and was laid up for a month afterwards:

> *Now what was I going to do!?! The doctor said that he could perform the operation so that I could recover faster and still might be able to run the marathon, but that it would hurt more at first. He was right...I couldn't even walk for the first week! When I was able to start running again, everyone else was doing the first 18-miler. I knew I wasn't going to be able to run the full 18, so I ran half-way. My pace was really slow, but I was just happy to be back out there. That next week I pushed myself harder than I probably should have, but by the next long run (which*

was the second 18-miler) I was able to do it all, even though I still had to go really slow.

Each week I tried to run more and more, and work myself back up to my previous pace, but it still hurt when I ran. The closer we got to the marathon, the more panicky I became that I might not be able to do the marathon. I talked to my doctor and he said that while normally he would advise against it, he would leave the decision of whether or not to run the marathon up to me. I talked to Forrest and he said that under the circumstances I could drop out of the class, but still go to the marathon if I wanted to. I thought, "If I'm going to the marathon, then I might as well do it." I talked it over with my parents and they were concerned that I wasn't recovered enough from the surgery to be able to do the marathon, but I wanted to see if I could do it and they didn't try to stop me. So I went, and I'm glad I did.

General Tips from the Marathoners — Week Thirteen:

• Some people find that despite running in all kinds of nasty weather and operating on a tighter schedule time-wise, they enjoy better health while training for the marathon than at any other time in their lives. This was the case for me. During the time that I trained for this marathon, I was never sick. Not even once! That was a first for me. My kids brought home all the same flu bugs that they do every winter, and while they still got sick, I never did. It was great! Running, and the proper nutrition that accompanies it, really does boost your immune system. It sure is a lot cheaper than going to the doctor!

	Scheduled Distance	Actual Distance	RPE	
Day 1	5			
Comments:				
Day 2	8			
Comments:				
Day 3	5			
Comments:				
Day 4	18			
Comments:				

Total Miles This Week_____Cumulative Total_____

Chapter 14:

Week Fourteen
Starting the Taper

Integrating Your Mental Preparation Strategies

Well, you have done all the really long runs now. You will be tapering off this week and the next two weeks as you gather strength for the marathon. Your long run this week is "only" 9 miles. Could you have imagined 3 months ago that you could ever think of a 9 mile run as a short run? But that IS what you are thinking now, isn't it? It is only half what you ran last weekend. No problem, right?

So, physically the next couple of weeks will be easy. But we still have some psychological work to do. You have been working on a number of different mental techniques over the last few months and now it is time to pull them all together. This section will provide a review of those techniques and offer you a way to maximize their benefits by integrating them. As we go along, we'll insert the chapter numbers in which we first talked about each of the techniques so that you can go back and review if you need to.

Let's begin by reminding ourselves that we make our own reality (Chapter 1) and that means you can construct whatever set of expectations about this marathon you choose. It is crucial that you believe that. If you have followed our suggestions, you have built a set of success expectations for the marathon and the specific techniques that you have used for doing that are what we are reviewing in this chapter.

Several of those techniques can be used to maintain the positive outlook that is so important in undertaking a marathon. It was in Chapter 2 that we first talked about the value of maintaining that positive outlook when we suggested that you attach the phrase "..but it doesn't matter" to the end of any negative thought or statement that you found yourself using. We hope that you are so positive by this time that you don't need that technique any more but keep it in mind if you do need it. In Chapter 4 we discussed the way in which behavior leads to attitude and then we suggested that a good way to develop and maintain a strong level of confidence was to do what we called acting "as if.." You'll recall that the idea was that if you behave as if you have strong confidence in your ability to run this marathon, you will come to feel that way. A third technique for remaining positive (discussed in Chapter 6) is to use positive self-talk. We suggested that you use a number of present-tense affirmations for this purpose and we hope you have been doing that for several weeks now. The final technique in this group was discussed in Chapter 5 and it is called visualization. We suggested that you use it in three ways. One was to make a mental "videotape" of your best training run. Another was to make a similar mental video of yourself finishing the marathon. The third was to construct images of a specific nature that you found useful. (The example we gave was the one used by one of your authors about the muscle fibers in his legs.)

In Chapter 7 we discussed the importance of learning to focus and concentrate in order to maintain your form when you become fatigued and in Chapter 8 we described how success in focusing on the activity in which you are involved can produce the "flow" experience that will allow you to run effortlessly. In Chapter 11 we suggested that using an association technique in which you focus on the running itself instead of "spacing off" would also help you to achieve that state.

Now let us give you an example of how to combine several of these techniques. When he was a child, one of the authors was very fond of the book we discussed in Chapter 12 — *The Little Engine That Could*. During the author's long training runs and during marathons he often constructs the following word and image tool to help him run. He imagines himself as a powerful locomotive with a huge boiler (lungs) that has tremendous capacity and pistons (legs) that pump machine-like and tirelessly. He makes pictures of himself in his head running powerfully and smoothly as he would look to spectators along his route. He repeats phrases to himself such as "I feel really strong. I am cruising. This is really effortless. I am so relaxed and loose. I can keep this up all day." Periodically, he chants silently and rhythmically to himself "I know I can, I know I can, I know I can." This technique combines positive self-talk, visualization, concentration and association and it often results in a flow experience and always results in a better and more pleasant run.

As you enter these final days of preparation, review the mental techniques you have been using and look for ways to combine them to help you produce a great result on marathon day.

Physical Preparation

> # Week 14 Training
> Day 1: 5 miles
> Day 2: 8 miles
> Day 3: 5 miles
> Day 4: 9 miles
> ## Total for week: 27 miles

This week you start reducing your mileage, a technique called tapering. The total weekly mileage is cut to 27 miles, with all of the cut coming in the long run. The long run this week is just 9 miles, half of the distance you did last week. At this point in your training, with the longest run being 9 miles, the week should feel pretty comfortable for you physically and mentally.

Why is tapering important? After all, you have spent the last 14 weeks building up your mileage and now you are being advised to reduce the mileage just before the race. Physiologically and psychologically tapering makes a lot of sense. Physiologically, tapering allows your muscles to fully recover from the trauma of high mileage. If you consume adequate carbohydrates, the muscles become saturated with glycogen so you won't hit the wall. The two weeks of taper allows any nagging injuries to recover before the marathon. In general, the entire body becomes more physiologically recovered than it has been since the first week of training. All of this is going to make the body stronger and able to give a maximum effort on marathon day.

Sometimes it is difficult to convince athletes that tapering is really good for them for optimal performance. Faulty reasoning says that if training mileage is reduced, then training effects start reversing. This is not true. The amount of training that you will be doing during the taper combined with the relatively short period of two weeks will maintain your training effects. This has been verified through scientific investigation and testimony of competitive athletes and coaches.

One cautionary note. Since the total training mileage is being reduced by approximately 30 miles over the next 3 weeks, your total caloric intake should also be adjusted downward so you don't gain any unwanted fat these last 3 weeks. On the average you need to reduce your caloric intake by about 3000 kilocalories (150-200 kilocalories per day) over the next 3 weeks. This could prevent an unwanted fat gain of about a pound, an amount that may seem insignificant but over the distance of a marathon could become more significant. Continue to monitor your weight and use this as your guide. If you have been successful in decreasing your fat intake over the period of training so that it is already less than 20%, you may need to reduce these calories from the carbohydrates you are consuming. Your protein intake should remain at 15-20% of your total calories.

 The Seduction of Success

In an earlier chapter, I compared the different components involved in the training program to pieces of a puzzle that you were in the process of constructing. Remember? Well, you now have all the main pieces needed to complete the puzzle, and you are nearly done with the training. Only three short weeks remain and they will feel easy compared to what you have already done. As you taper the mileage but continue to pump in carbohydrates and fluids, you are going to start to feel stronger than ever. As you focus on integrating the mental techniques, you will become convinced of your ability to do this and do it well. You are going to feel mentally and physically stronger than you have at any other time in your life. And that is GREAT! That is what is supposed to happen. You are going to become like a race horse before a race: prancing around full of energy, straining against the bit, anxiously waiting to enter the starting gate. The heightened level of energy is exhilarating; the sense of power is exciting.

As wonderful as this process is, there is the potential of being seduced into believing that you are capable of feats over and above what the conditioning has prepared you for. If you allow your attitude to run away with you, you risk blowing everything you've worked for. If you are thinking that this sounds like more of the "Just Finish" message you got last week, you're right, it is. That should tell you how important the proper attitude and appropriate goal are to your having the kind of peak experience we promised you way back at the beginning of the program.

Let me put it another way. This program is designed to train you for endurance. If you suddenly think you are going to turn out a thoroughbred performance, you will be disappointed. The thoroughbreds of marathoning are the ones who run the world-class times. That's probably not you - and that's OK You're not doing this for a world record - you're doing this for you. Expect yourself to utilize the training components you've worked to become skilled at to successfully complete a marathon, and nothing more. Believe me, after running 26.2 miles, just finishing will be enough!

One of the best ways to keep your attitude in perspective and ensure the most enjoyable run possible, is to focus your energy during the next three weeks on integrating the mental techniques that work best for you. Following are suggestions from three past participants about what they found worked best for them. If you are still struggling to find the integration that works best for you, perhaps these will give you some ideas.

Michelle Roland:

I have had some really awesome runs when I was using all of the mental techniques we learned in the class together. What seems to work best for me is to use the mental video of myself finishing the marathon and to combine it with repeating like a chant, the phrases, "I am an animal. I can run forever." I also pick out a spot on the ground about 15 feet in front of me and focus on it, letting the sensation of the passing pavement be my point of concentration. It also gives me a sensation of speed.

Jennifer Haglund:

The best moment of the entire training happened when I achieved flow. It was during one of the 18-milers. That particular weekend I had to go home, and so I ended up doing the long run by myself. At first I was concerned about how not having the group would affect me, but as I found out the solitude helped me create the best run of the whole semester. I incorporated several of the mental techniques that day. I started repeating over and over, "I am awesome" in synch with the rhythm of my steps. As I did this, I would visualize myself running, smiling, and looking strong and healthy. After a while, I decided to incorporate other people from the class into my visualization. I would say, "She is awesome" and every time I said it I would visualize a different girl in the class running, smiling, and looking healthy and strong. Then I repeated it with the guys saying, "He is awesome" until I ran out of guys. Then I would say "They are awesome," visualizing groups of people who usually ran together. I repeated this over and over again, visualizing everyone to the rhythm of my steps. In a way I think it made me feel the class support even though I was on my own.

When I actually hit flow, I started repeating over and over again, "I am STRONG; I am TOUGH; I am AWESOME; I am HEALTHY; I CRE-ATE my own RE-AL-I-TY!; I LOVE to RUN; I LOVE TO RUN; I LOVE TO RUN; I LOVE TO RUN!!" Sometimes I said it out loud, either whispering it or chanting it; sometimes I yelled it or would say it in my head. It had this incredible timing to the beat of my steps and it made me feel so amazing! I felt like I was running six inches above the ground, like my feet weren't even touching. It was incredible! This was the most extraordinary moment of the entire class. What made it even more special was that I did it completely by myself. It was this experience that really made me believe in myself.

Eric Stoneman:

I remember a time during the marathon when I was using all of the mental techniques we had learned and they were working really well. They carried me well into the 17th mile and it was there that I received a gift from a spectator. I was running with a group of about five others from the class. The novelty of running in our first marathon had worn off and we were using the mental tools to keep going. Although no one had said it, we knew at that point that we truly were marathoners. However, fatigue was creeping up on us. Thoughts of walking had entered our minds. We knew there would be no shame in walking, but no one wanted to give in. As we made our way through a residential area, the only sounds were shoes striking the ground and the heavy breathing of the runners. We were running alone...no one but the five of us was within a quarter mile. Then it happened! A lone spectator stood from her folding chair and applauded us enthusiastically as we passed by. The fact that anyone not a competitor in the marathon would applaud made it seem wonderful, but the fact that this woman looked to be over 80 years old made the applause seem louder than any I had ever heard. We smiled, waved and thanked the lone fan. It was as if someone had hit a switch in all of us...our pace increased and the old form was back. There truly was a new spring in our steps, put there by an elderly woman who helped us all cross the finish line.

	Scheduled Distance	Actual Distance	RPE
Day 1	5		

Comments:

| **Day 2** | 8 | | |

Comments:

| **Day 3** | 5 | | |

Comments:

| **Day 4** | 9 | | |

Comments:

Total Miles This Week_____Cumulative Total_____

Chapter 15:

Week Fifteen
Gathering Strength

Peaking: Having Fun on Marathon Day

Back in Chapter 8, when we were discussing the nature of the flow experience, we also talked about having fun. We emphasized the way in which fun is similar to flow in that both occur when we are focused completely on the moment at hand. The eminent psychologist, Abraham Maslow, called these moments "peak experiences" in his 1962 book called *The Psychology of Being*. That is a particularly relevant term because the training program you have been following is designed to bring you to your peak physical condition exactly on the day of the marathon. In addition, we want to make sure that you have a "peak" experience on that day from a psychological point of view. Put another way, marathon day should be the most fun you've ever had. We want it to be a wonderful, fulfilling, exhilarating experience that you will never forget.

Here are a few suggestions to help insure it is that kind of day for you.

1. First and most important; Reaffirm the goal in your mind. It is to finish the marathon. Period.

2. Read Part Two of the next chapter very carefully and follow the suggestions for last-minute preparations and reminders in complete detail. Nothing can make marathon day less fun than the hassles that result from inadequate time, clothing, hydration, etc. You want this to be a no-hassles day. As usual, you can make it whatever you want it to be. So, take a few extra minutes to make sure you will have what you need and enough time before the start of the marathon to use what you bring.

3. Explain to those who will be going to the marathon to watch and to support you that you are likely to benefit most from their presence if they are very positive, cooperative and supportive. This will include complying with any wishes you may express before and during the marathon. You don't need arguments. You don't even need advice or suggestions, no matter how well intended. What would be helpful is their love and their affirmation. But remember, you are a marathoner and you are going to finish this event, no matter what happens. We are just talking here about how to have the most fun doing it.

4. If you have the opportunity, try to visit the marathon site and see some of the course, especially the start and the finish. Since this is your first marathon, you will be unfamiliar with the experience. Nothing can be done about some aspects of that, but a visit to the course can give you a sense of familiarity with at least some of what to expect. If this is not feasible, don't worry about it, but if it is, we recommend it.

 Physical Preparation

> ## Week 15 Training
> Day 1: 3 miles
> Day 2: 5 miles
> Day 3: 3 miles
> Day 4: 8 miles
> ## Total for Week: 19 miles

Down, down, down comes the mileage. This week is a mere 19 miles. The muscles and brain are getting ready for the long one in just two weeks. The reduction in mileage is allowing the muscles to recover more fully so that by marathon time, they will be well rested and fueled up for optimal performance. Be sure and keep the carbohydrate and fluid consumption high. Don't overeat, just maintain 55-70% of your total caloric intake as carbohydrates.

Eating and Drinking During the Week of the Marathon

Throughout the week of the marathon you want to maintain a high percentage intake of carbohydrates in order to go into the marathon with as much glycogen as possible stored in the muscles. If you have not been doing such a conscientious job up to now, this last week can be really critical to success. Eat a high percentage of carbohydrates throughout the week!! Since long-term nutrition is not a prime consideration this week, you can take in more simple sugars than would ordinarily be recommended. Just don't overconsume total calories and gain weight.

Drinking also takes a high priority during the week so you will be optimally hydrated on the day of the marathon. The worst thing that could happen to you would be to go into the marathon dehydrated. No matter how much training you have done, no matter how many carbohydrates you have eaten, if you aren't hydrated, forget it. It will be a short and terrible experience. Make sure your urine is faintly-yellow (not dark yellow) throughout the week. It is OK to drink more water or fluid than necessary this week because you will just eliminate it.

An important rule as you get closer to marathon day is don't do anything drastically different from what you have been doing for the past 15 weeks. You want to stick to eating and drinking what you know you can tolerate. The marathon day is not the time to find out that a new food or drink causes stomach upset, diarrhea, or worse. If you have been eating and drinking appropriately for the last 15 weeks, the marathon week and the day of the marathon should not be any different.

There has been a lot of importance tied to the evening meal the day before the marathon, usually referred to as the "pre-competition" meal. However, if you have been eating appropriately all week, this pre-competition meal assumes less importance. Again, this is a critical time to eat something you know your body will tolerate. The last meal should be primarily carbohydrates and should be relatively low in bulk (or you need to be sure you can have a bowel movement prior to the marathon). If you eat a lot of bulk and are not able to eliminate it before the marathon, it can cause problems during the run. Many runners like to eat a liquid pre-competition meal so they don't have to worry about having a full gastrointestinal (GI) system during the race. This is not a bad idea, particularly if you are not used to having a bowel movement early in the morning. Probably, you have been trying to mimic marathon day on each of your long runs and if so, you probably have this procedure down by now. Do what you know has worked for you during these training runs.

If for some reason you have not been able to eat high carbohydrates for the two or three days preceding the marathon, the pre-competition meal assumes a more important role. The carbohydrates from the pre-competition meal can be critical to stocking up your muscle glycogen for the marathon. If, however, you have been eating the way you should have two or three days before, the pre-competition meal will only serve to top-off an already existing large carbohydrate storehouse.

Whether you should eat something on the morning of the marathon depends on several factors. If the marathon starts within a couple of hours of when you get up, the need to eat something diminishes. Again, do what you have been doing in your training runs that you know has worked for you. If you do eat something, it should be light in bulk so you don't have a lot in your GI system during the marathon. A liquid carbohydrate drink would be ideal if something is going to be consumed. Consuming about 200-400 kilocalories of liquid carbo-hydrate would help to provide some energy early in the run.

Drink fluids normally up until you go bed the night before the marathon. One thing we are all able to do is eliminate excess fluid when we get up in the mornings so this should not be a concern. You should not drink alcohol the night before because of the diuretic effect it will have. Drink two cups of water or a fluid replacement drink about two hours prior to the marathon.

PART 3 Running Angels

Michelle Roland:

> *I remember that this week was a difficult one for me psychologically. It seemed strange because we only ran 19 miles all week and just eight for the longest run of the week. To me, it seemed too early to be reducing our mileage and I started to worry about whether I would be ready for the marathon. But Forrest and Dave assured us that we needed to taper off in order to be at our strongest and I guess they were right, because we all finished just like they said we would.*

If you find yourself having thoughts similar to Michelle's, rest easy. Dave and Forrest know what they are doing when they say that tapering is necessary and will only increase your chances of enjoying a successful marathon. Any anxiety you may be feeling about the reduced mileage is normal. Remember, for fourteen weeks you have been mentally gearing up to meet the challenge of steadily increasing mileage. Now, just because the mileage has been scaled back doesn't mean your mindset automatically readjusted itself — that takes some effort on your part.

Take a minute and read the first half of Section One of the next chapter — I'll wait.

As you read, this really is the perfect opportunity to practice relaxation techniques. Not only to recalibrate your current level of arousal and anxiety to correspond with the decreased mileage, but also because this skill will come in handy during the marathon (especially at the start) when you are probably going to feel as nervous and excited as a race horse waiting for the gate to open. In fact, right now would be a good time to run through some of these techniques, so take a few minutes and do that.

Now that you are relaxed, I'd like to switch gears. I know the marathon is still two weeks away, but the rest of this section will feature accounts of past participants' marathon experiences. Since the marathon itself is the highlight of training, there are more stories about the actual marathon than will fit into one chapter. So, we're going to start sharing these stories now, and we will finish in the Section Three of the next chapter.

Let's start with Ron Steele:

One thing I love about running marathons is that there are always people in front of you and always people behind you. There is an aspect of anonymity to it. You are just out there along with everyone else and nobody knows who you are or what you do for a living; nobody cares how much money you have or don't have. No one cares about your problems or their problems. You're out there as an individual and yet there is definitely a feeling of camaraderie. At least for a little while, it's as if we're all equal...in the same boat....

As Ron said, marathons have an equalizing component to them. For those few hours, the people out on that course have more in common than not as they become part of the wave of humanity making its way from one end of the course to the other. Often perfect strangers will help one another without ever being asked or expecting anything in return. We call these folks "Running Angels," and when you're the one needing help they do indeed seem to be just that.

Following are stories about running angels past participants either encountered or became to others during the marathon. Perhaps you will find yourself in a similar situation a couple of weeks from now.

Jane Mortenson:

I encountered my "angels" before the race. While we were standing around waiting for the race to begin, I ran into Sandy, one of my best friends from high school, and her family. Sandy, her husband, and her parents were there to cheer on her daughter, who was a member of the class. I had been a bridesmaid in their wedding 25 years earlier! I had known these people forever, and suddenly they were all there! It was like having my own family there, and they ended up cheering me on at different points during the run. It was just the neatest thing when Sandy was waiting at the finish line to give me a hug. I'll never forget what that meant to have those wonderful angels waiting there for me.

The weather was perfect for the marathon. Even the drizzle was good because it kept me cool and moist. It was one time when running was fun! The best part was the crowd and those little kids giving out Gatorade and treating us like we were heroes or Olympians, when actually I was just this old lady tromping down the street. It was kind of like a parade. Everyone was so nice. The whole experience was terrific and it went fast, even though it took me a very long time. It seemed as if all of a sudden it was over, and I was standing with my medal around my neck, holding my rose, drinking Gatorade, and celebrating with my dear friend Sandy whom I hadn't seen in years. It was 26 miles of fun and the memory of a lifetime.

Kathy Schneider:

Some great things happened on marathon day. First of all, my brother ran the marathon with me. He is a more experienced runner than I am and he wasted a lot of energy because of my slow pace, but we wanted to finish together. So he would run ahead and come back, run ahead and come back. He ran more than 26.2 miles just so he could keep checking on me and so that we could finish together. That's love, if you ask me.

During one of the times when I was temporarily separated from my brother, a guy ran up behind me and read my shirt. As he passed me he asked, "Are you really running this for a grade?" I grinned proudly and answered, "Yes!" He said when he was in college he took bowling, not marathoning.

Soon afterwards I came upon a guy who looked like he was having trouble. Right as I caught up to him he collapsed. I helped him up and I said, "Come run with me!" He ran a little while, but still didn't look too strong. I stayed with him until I caught up with my brother, but then he dropped back.

My brother and I ran the last couple of miles together. The closer we got to the track, the more excited I became. When we turned onto the track everyone cheered...I was so pumped I felt like sprinting. All the aches and pains vanished. We finished together — it was awesome!

When I was standing around afterwards, I happened to run into the guy who had collapsed. To my surprise, he gave me a big hug and thanked me for helping him. For me, that was like icing on the cake.

Rob Leslie:

I was really nervous at the start. I was worried that maybe something would go wrong since I had not been able to do some of the training due to my appendectomy. But I blew it all aside because I was just so excited to be there. At the start of the marathon, I felt good. When I got to mile 13, it felt like I hadn't even gone that far because I wasn't tired at all. At mile 19, I hit the wall. My side didn't hurt, but my legs were giving out. I kept running by myself until mile 22 and then I just couldn't keep up the pace, so I fell back with some other runners who kept me going. I walked some because I felt I couldn't run, but I kept my head up! Then a guy came up behind me and grabbed my arm and said, "I'm not stopping, so you're not stopping!" So, I started running with him and I started to feel better because he kept talking to me. We were right at the 26 mile mark and the guy started to fall behind. I said, "Hey, you got me this far. You're not backing down on me now!" So, we finished together. My legs were like noodles. My Dad carried on for about an hour afterwards. It was really great. It boggles my mind that everybody in our class finished.

Eric Johnson:

The first 13 miles was a walk in the park. I was drinking plenty of fluids and that helped a lot. Between 13 and 18, I got a little tired, but still felt strong. Between miles 18-20 I got this sense of deja vu; it felt just like high school football where we had to push ourselves both physically and mentally through the fourth quarter. At mile 22, I started to cramp up and got real tired. Miles 22 and 23 were a real struggle. No one was around and I was running real slow when I crested the top of a hill and saw my whole family holding a big banner that said, "I want to be like Easy" (my nickname) which they had all signed and written inspirational sayings on. At the 24-mile mark, classmate Chris Henle came up behind me. She was running strong and said, "Come run with me, Eric." It was almost like she was picking me up and carrying me. Everything hurt so bad that my body wanted to stop, but with her beside me my mind said, "Go!" She was my angel. I felt like I was just barely stumbling along, but she gave me the notion that it wasn't a problem and I was fine.

I ran the last two miles better than the first two! Crossing the finish line was the first time I felt like an athletic star. In that one moment, I was scampering up the sideline for a touchdown with no time left on the clock; I hit the game-winning home run in the 11th inning; I sank a six-foot putt to save my lead in the British Open; I hit the game-winning spike down the sideline in the Olympic volleyball finals. I did it all right there! Anytime I feel like I can't do something, I think of that moment.

By the way, I still have that banner hanging in my room.

	Scheduled Distance	Actual Distance	RPE
Day 1	3		

Comments:

| **Day 2** | 5 | | |

Comments:

| **Day 3** | 3 | | |

Comments:

| **Day 4** | 8 | | |

Comments:

Total Miles This Week_____Cumulative Total_____

Chapter 16:

Week Sixteen

Marathon Week

 PART 1 | **Relaxing and Reviewing**

Well, this is the week. This weekend you are going to run 26.2 miles. You are strong. You are probably in better condition than you have ever been in your whole life.

However, over the next few days leading up to the marathon, you may begin to feel that you are losing your edge. After all, you are hardly doing any running at all this week. And you only ran 19 miles last week. You may be thinking you are getting weaker. Maybe you peaked too soon. Maybe you should go out for a long run today. Maybe.......?

No. None of that is true. What is actually happening is that the rest you are getting by running less is making you stronger. We know that and let us remind you that the way we know it is that lots of other people in our classes followed exactly the same training program and they did just fine. So relax. And speaking of relaxing, remember our discussion of methods of relaxation in Chapter 10? (If you don't, go back and read over it again.) This week is one of the very best times to use what you learned in that chapter.

First-time marathoners often get pretty wound up and have a lot of anxiety during this last pre-marathon week. That may be happening to you too. We don't want any more of that than absolutely necessary. The reason is that this time is designed to allow you to gather strength. Anxiety and tension produce fatigue. So, spend a lot of time this week using whatever method of relaxation you found most effective when you tried it out in week 10. For example, if you have been taking an hour or so for a run on any given day in the weeks prior to this one, use that same amount of time in progressive relaxation exercises.

Another excellent activity for this week is to review the mental techniques that you plan to use during the marathon. Run those mental video tapes a lot this week. Repeat lots of those positive self-talk items and affirmations. Doing this will have two benefits. One is the usual one of making you feel even more confident and optimistic. The second one is that it will help to keep your anxiety under control.

We want you to arrive at the starting line in peak mental condition as well as peak physical condition. The program you have been following is designed to do exactly that. You are ready. Have a wonderful day! It's going to be the most fulfilling, satisfying day you've had in a long, long time.

There is one more thing we want you to do to help in your mental preparation. There is a section in Part One of Chapter 12 called "What Happens (Psychologically) at the Wall?" Go back and read that section over again. Do it right now. And do it several times this week, including just before you start the marathon.

 PART 2 | **Physical Preparation**

> ## Week 16 Training
> Day 1: 3 miles
> Day 2: 3 miles
> Day 3: Walk 3 miles
> Day 4: 26.2 miles
> **Total for Week: 35.2 miles**

This is the week you have been working so hard for. Your training is over. The two three-mile runs are just to keep you loose and they really aren't supposed to add anything to your conditioning. Just run them at an easy, comfortable pace. You don't want to get injured at this point in the program. Continue to stretch each day this week.

The three-mile walk is primarily to keep you relaxed without running the risk of using up a lot of your glycogen. Throughout this entire week your use of glycogen should be pretty minimal so that your chances of having a full supply on marathon day will be very high. Don't do any running or extended walking on the day before the marathon. Just take it easy, do your stretching, and prepare yourself mentally for the big event.

Preparation on Marathon Day
Preparing for the Weather. There are several last minute things you can

do that can have a dramatic impact on your marathon experience. You want to be prepared for pretty much anything that may happen that day, particularly changes in the weather. As the boy scouts have said for a long time "Be Prepared."

The weather can be a friend or foe in many ways. However, as you well know, you can't control the weather, you can only adjust to it. Depending on the time of year and the part of the country in which your marathon takes place, you have to have appropriate clothing. This becomes a particular problem in the spring and fall in some parts of the country that have four-season climates. During this time of the year, the weather could either be 75 degrees or it could be 40 degrees. Not only might the weather be changeable day to day, it could change from the marathon start time to the finish. If the marathon starts early in the morning, which most do, the weather could be very cool but by the time you finish 3-5 hours later, the weather may be warm. In conditions like these, you need to have clothing that can be taken off and either discarded or managed in some other way like tying it around the waist (this may be a good idea if there is a chance you will need it later in the run). Wearing light layers is the way to go. Even when it is pretty cool, you can be comfortable with just long sleeves once you have warmed up. You may need a windbreaker or other similar outer layer to start the race, but you may want to take it off later as you and the weather warm up. Since the legs can tolerate much cooler weather than the upper body can, wearing shorts and/or running tights usually suffices.

You may experience the need to put clothing on during the marathon as well as take it off. Sometimes the wind may change directions, a front may come in during a marathon, or the change in the direction of running may cause a sudden need for a windbreaker. Tying a windbreaker or similar item around the waist works well in this situation.

Generally, being a little cooler is better than being a little warmer. The cooler you are, the easier it will be to dissipate heat. Being warm and cozy may feel good while you are running but it may also increase your heat load and be a disadvantage at some time later in the run. You don't want to be uncomfortably cold, but at the same time you don't want to overdress.

One trick that has worked well for many runners, (when the weather at the start of the race is cool but once you get going it would be fine), is to wear a large plastic garbage bag (just cut holes for the arms and head and slip it on like a baggy sweatshirt) while you are waiting for the start of the run. Then you can discard it as the marathon begins or after you have sufficiently warmed up. You may get some strange looks but it really does the job and you don't have to worry about taking care of warm-ups or other clothing. Note: We are not suggesting that you litter. You will almost always find trash receptacles near the starting line of marathons.

Another problem related to the weather is becoming hypothermic at the end of the run. Hypothermia (low body temperature) is a possibility , especially on cool days. If the weather is cool you may be very comfortable running but once you stop, you can cool off very quickly, especially if there is a cool breeze. Under these conditions, you need to have something to put on at the end of the run. If you have friends watching the run, leave some clothing with them so you can put it on after you finish. At large marathons where there are substantial crowds, designating a meeting place would be wise. Sometimes it is hard to find someone with everyone milling around at the finish. In lieu of leaving some clothing with someone, you can use the garbage bag again if you carry it with you throughout the run. They can be easily wadded up and put in a pocket or waist band if you may need it at the end of the run.

On bright sunny days, too much sun can be a problem for the runner. If the weather is warm and the sun is out, sun tan lotion/block should be used as appropriate. Remember you are going to be on the course for hours. Too much sun exposure can contribute to sunburn, dehydration and heat illness. Sunglasses are very helpful and appropriate under sunny conditions. Lastly, some type of cap or sun visor can help keep the sun off the head and reduce the chance of sunburn and heat illness.

Pacing During the Marathon. At the start of a marathon for which you have been training for 16 weeks and almost 400 miles, you may be very excited and hyper. You feel great, you are full of energy, there are hundreds or thousands of runners milling around, and you are ready to get going. When that gun goes off to start the run, the tendency for the inexperienced marathoner is to start out at too fast a pace. Sometimes it is difficult for you to realize that you are going too fast because it feels easy for you. In fact it may feel easy for the first 10-15 miles at a pace that is actually too fast for you.

You always want to start at a pace that is too slow rather than too fast. Remember, the longest you have run in training is 18 miles. The absolute fastest you want to go during the first half of the run is the pace you maintained during the 18-mile runs. It is likely that a pace even slower than your 18 mile pace would be appropriate since you have to run eight more miles after you finish the first 18 miles. Going out too fast can often be devastating during the last half of the run. It is not a simple matter of eventually just having to slow down. Going too fast too early can deplete your glycogen, cause accelerated dehydration, and increase lactic acid. The earlier these occur in the run, the more difficult it will be to continue.

Start out at a pace no faster than you know you can finish 18 miles at. You can always increase the pace toward the end of the run if you have something left. Remember the saying from an earlier chapter — "the last 6 miles is the last half of the race."

There is another factor related to pacing and the weather that can make or break a runner. The scenario goes like this: The marathon is in the early spring and it just so happens that the day of the marathon is the first really warm day of spring. You have been training all winter in cold weather and you have not become acclimatized to running in the heat yet. The warm weather may feel real good early on, but it can have devastating effects as the marathon progresses due to your not being acclimatized to the heat. In this situation, you have to recognize your lack of acclimatization from the beginning of the run and slow your pace down compared to what you have normally been running. Being un-acclimatized to running in the heat can really hit you hard and you have to adjust for it. You will also want to drink more fluid than you would normally drink if the weather were cooler.

Preventing Injuries During the Marathon. There is nothing worse than getting injured during the marathon itself. After all the training and time you have spent, not completing the marathon because you injure yourself is a real bummer. You need to be alert and pay attention to a few things that may prevent injury.

You are probably running on unfamiliar roads or trails so pay attention. Watch for uneven surfaces, drop-offs, and curbs. You can get so focused on your running and listening to your body that you completely space-off the running surface. At the least opportune time an uneven running surface can result in a fall or a sprained ankle or foot or worse. Just be aware of the running surface, particularly if it is uneven terrain.

In crowded marathons, it is not uncommon for some early tangle-ups to occur between runners at the start of the race when everyone is packed into the start area. Once you get spread out the likelihood lessens, but be especially alert at the start. Don't try to squeeze between runners if there is not sufficient space. It is better to go around than for you to fall or cause another runner to fall. Sometimes, running in a crowded run is like driving on a crowded freeway. Be a courteous and safe runner. A few seconds lost is not going to hurt you in the end but a trip, a fall, a twisted ankle might take you out of the marathon. One way to avoid this problem is to start at or near the back of the pack. The few seconds or even minutes added to your time is irrelevant and besides, it is a lot more fun to pass people than to be passed.

The worst type of acute injury that can occur is heat injury resulting from dehydration. Recommendations for fluid replacement are contained in Chapter 5 and in the section immediately below. You should be aware of the symptoms of heat illness so you can take appropriate steps should they occur during the race. Remember, heat illness is not something to ignore because it can become deadly.

Listed in Table 16.1 are the signs and symptoms of heat illness. If you begin

Table 16.1. Signs and Symptoms of Heat Illness
Headache
Extreme weakness
Dizziness
Heat sensations on the head or neck
Cramps
Chills and goose bumps
Vomiting, nausea, and irritability
Hyperventilation
Muscular incoordination
Agitation
Confusion
Elevated heart rate

to experience these during the run, don't ignore them. Stop running, get fluid, and find some shade if it is sunny out. Catching symptoms early can allow you to make necessary adjustments and continue the run. Waiting too long to do something can lead to disaster.

Eating and Drinking. During the marathon, it is best to eat and drink at the same time. In other words, drink a liquid fluid replacement drink with carbohydrates in it. Drink early and drink often. The guidelines are to drink at least 6-8 oz of fluid every 15-20 minutes. Well organized runs will have fluids (usually a fluid replacement beverage like Gatorade and water) available at these approximate intervals. Don't pass up the opportunity to drink even if you don't feel thirsty. Remember, during the early part of the marathon, you are really drinking for later on in the run. Some runners prefer to drink their own beverage that they either carry with them or they have available from someone among the spectators. This obviously takes a little more planning and knowledge of the route but it can be worked out. Whether you prefer to drink your own fluid or what the run provides, just make certain you drink enough. Also remember, the warmer it is and the higher the humidity, the more you need to drink.

PART 3 | Marathon Stories

Well, this is it! You've gone through the training program, you have all the tools you need to complete the marathon, and you know how to use them to your benefit. You are ready, and as I promised you way back in the Introduction, it will be one of the peak experiences of your life. Do not allow anything to get in the way of enjoying this — you've earned it. Have fun with it, for you will remember this day for the rest of your life.

Now, on to more marathon stories...and by the way, we would love to hear yours! If you would like to share your marathon experience with us, feel free to write us at the address indicated in Part One of Chapter 17.

Amy Kepler:

We were encouraged to run slower than our usual pace. At first this was frustrating because you feel so ready after all the training that you just want to go out there and take it by storm. But by mile 21 when I couldn't breath anymore, and had to walk it off, I was glad that I had been conservative in the first half. Crossing the finish line was an incredibly emotional experience. I was so glad that my family and friends were there to share it with me.

Patti Hasty Rust:

I would describe the marathon as a really fun, enjoyable and uplifting experience. There were parts that were tough, but overall I never doubted that I was going to finish it and I really tried to just enjoy the day. I had a lot of support from my family which added a lot to the day. My parents were there, along with my sister and her husband. Overall, it was a very positive experience.

Julie Stone:

A friend, who had run with the 1993 class, ran with me. I felt great until my foot started to hurt after mile 18. I never hit the wall, though. On mile 20 we must have looked crazy to the spectators 'cause we were singing and dancing as we ran! On mile 21 my sisters ran with me. It was like a huge party! It was great!!

Eric Stoneman:

The big number 26, signifying the 26 miles I had run, was now up ahead in my sights. I was running with my friend, Rob. He pointed down to my shoe to tell me it was untied. We both stopped so I could tie it. I started to bend over, felt like I was going to black out, and said to Rob, "I can't." If we had been doing anything other than running a marathon, I'm sure he would have given me a strange look and said, "Whatta ya mean, you can't do it?" Most 6'2", 230 pound men are capable of tying their own shoes. But without any hesitation, Rob bent down and tied my shoe for me and we resumed our jog. We rounded the last corner and both saw the finish at the same moment. We looked at each other and, without a word, began a sprint to the finish line. Although Rob could have crossed the line ahead of me, he slowed so we could finish together. Marathoning is definitely not an individual sport.

Tricia Tuttle:

I remember the marathon like it was yesterday. Two other girls from our class and I had done all the training together so we ran the marathon together, too. There was such a sense of camaraderie. We ran a little slower than our normal pace and at the 13-mile point I felt great. At 20 miles I had a real energy rush and picked up my pace, but then at 24 miles I hit the wall and had to use my mental imagery to keep going. My family was waiting for me at mile 26, and they followed me to the track. When I entered the stadium and could see the finish I started to cry...it seemed so close and yet so far.

Ron Steele:

In my opinion, there's no greater feeling than having your family there beside the race course. It is a tremendous lift knowing that they are going to be waiting to cheer you on. It gives you something to look forward to, especially when you are starting to get tired. Just about the time you wonder if you can keep going, you see them standing ahead ready to cheer for you and it's a real inspiration.

Elizabeth Kilgore:

My mom came to see the marathon. We had made mental tapes of ourselves finishing the marathon, and at the end of mine my mom told me that she was proud of me and that she loved me. I had told her about my tape. All through the marathon, she was frantically looking for me so that she could be sure and make my tape a reality for me. She was so afraid that she would miss me that she went early to the finish line and stood there for two hours until I finally ran into the stadium. After I crossed the finish line, she did indeed tell me she loved me and that she was proud of me. I cried for the next thirty minutes. Finishing the marathon was the most emotionally intense thing I have ever accomplished. For me, the marathon was easier than the long runs.

Heidi Brandt:

I told my Dad about the class and he came for the marathon. He was the first person I saw when we got off the bus! Secretly, I was a little worried about not making it, so I went to bed early so that I wouldn't be tired at the start. I guess I didn't have anything to be worried about because by the time we passed mile 13 I felt like I had just started running! It seemed like my Dad was on every corner — he kept moving to stay ahead of me to give me support.

At one point, I came across a girl whose stomach was hurting really bad. I slowed down and ran with her for a while until she felt better. Then I sprinted back to my group. Mile 23 was the worst for me, but from there it seemed to get better and by the time I hit the track I felt like I was in the Olympics. I think I could've tripped over my own smile it was so big! It was awesome...I want to do it again!

Keith Wendl:

The first 10 miles was a party. I was pumped, full of energy, and having a blast! At 10 miles, I ate some Skittles and that helped keep my energy level up. By mile 16, I was starting to hurt. I started running alongside a guy who loved Kentucky basketball. He was like Bubba in the movie Forest Gump who could only talk about shrimp. But for this guy it was Kentucky basketball and he just would not shut up! I loved it, though, because it kept me going. At mile 18 I was really hurting because I was going against what we had been told about not setting time goals and trying to finish in less than four hours. I heard it was a big accomplishment to finish your first marathon in under four. I regret it now, because I didn't enjoy it as much as I could have if I hadn't put that pressure on myself. But the finish was great. When I got to the end, there was a guy laying on the finish line and everyone thought he had collapsed, but he was kissing the ground! I'll never forget it.

Jeri Kurtzleben:

It was still dark when we started which I thought was really neat. I couldn't believe it when we got to the third mile mark — it felt like nothing. It was a piece of cake until 13 miles. Then it got harder, but I was OK until 18 miles when I started to get blisters. From there I had to just push, push, push and will myself to finish. I ran the last several miles with a guy from our class and he did a great job of keeping me going by telling me goofy stories. By the last mile I really felt like stopping, but he helped me stick it out. Crossing the finish line was a wonderful feeling! I cried. I had never felt like that before; had never pushed myself that hard. I felt like I discovered a part of me that I hadn't known existed.

I, too, remember starting in the dark. Even though the light of day had yet to break, the starting area was packed and diehard spectators lined the streets to cheer us on. We had been instructed to go out slower than our normal pace and to start at the back of the pack. Several members of the class started together in this group. Hearing the command, "Runners, take your places," and then hearing the gun go off was so exciting…and we were on our way!

As I have said, I run at a very slow pace. So slowly, in fact, that there are people who walk faster than I run! I didn't know this until the marathon had started and everyone was finding a pace and settling in for the long haul. I will admit, it is a rather rude awakening to think that you are out there running only to be passed by speed-walkers! And usually they were women half-again my age! Initially, that was a little demoralizing, but I just kept telling myself, "It doesn't matter" until I got past those first few awkward miles and started to get into my mental routine.

The first eight miles are a blur in my memory. They went by so fast (even at my slow pace). I guess I was just so busy trying to take it all in that I really didn't even think much about the running. There were so many people. It was dark. I was on strange streets trying to watch for potholes, traffic, other runners, and make sure that I didn't get lost and wander off course. Once it started getting light, I enjoyed looking at the houses in the neighborhoods we were running through. It was early May and the trees, yards, and flowers were just starting to come into full bloom. It was beautiful, peaceful, and refreshing.

It wasn't until mile nine that I remembered I had decided ahead of time to dedicate a different mile to those people in my life who were or are most significant. As I ran each mile, I would spend that time thinking about that person, what they meant to me, and how they were important in my life. I started with God. Next came my maternal grandmother who had died just six weeks prior. Then came each of my parents, etc., etc. As I did this, my chant played in my mind like background music. I focused my gaze on the ground about ten feet ahead of me (yes, I did have my eyes open!) and I floated along on automatic pilot.

There isn't a whole lot I remember between mile nine and twenty — just bits and pieces here and there. But one thing I do remember was the water stop at 13.1 miles — the half-marathon point. Suddenly I was now the one passing all those walkers who had initially passed me back at the start, for they all quit and I kept going! The tortoise wins again!! I felt vindicated.

As you already know from reading Section Three in Chapter Twelve, it was at mile 20 that I hit the wall and encountered Adam, my running angel. By mile 21, I was running again, albeit very slowly at first. As the carbos hit my blood stream, my strength returned and I was able to resume my normal pace. Suddenly, I was back among other runners and passing a few one by one. We were climbing a long gradual hill. I realized how sore my knees were and hoped that they would hold out for the 1 1/4 hours it would take me to finish. I decided to forego my mental dedications so that I could fully concentrate on the mental techniques necessary to create flow, but before doing that I made a promise. "God, you get me through this, and the last mile's yours."

I crested the hill to find that the water stop stationed there was in the process of being dismantled. Police officers were picking up the pylons they had used to cordon off the intersection. I remember thinking, "Hey, this isn't over yet!" I realized that I would have to finish this thing completely on my own, and I got a little nervous because I wasn't entirely sure about how to get back to the stadium. The flat gray clouds that had blanketed the sky were giving way to larger clouds of dark blue and gray. It didn't look good.

Somewhere between mile 23 and 24, a little boy standing along the route offered me two helium filled balloons. Now they bounced alongside me as I nervously anticipated the storm I could feel approaching. The air had turned suddenly cooler. Lightning could be seen cutting through the wall of black that hugged the horizon. I continued to gain on the few remaining runners, most of whom were now walking. I had shortened my chant to, "Mar-a-thon-er" and only lifted my focused gaze to monitor the approaching storm. It started to sprinkle.

Unknown to me, race officials had decided to pull all remaining runners off the course due to the massive thunderstorm that was bearing down on the city. When they informed Dave Whitsett of their decision, Dave told them he still had one runner out and warned the officials, "You'll never get her off that course; she won't quit no matter what!"

Meanwhile, police cars started pulling up beside the runners left on the course and I watched as one after another either got inside the cars or walked off the course. I guessed what was happening, and it wasn't long before a cruiser pulled up alongside me. "Miss, due to lightning in the area the race is being called. We will be happy to give you a ride back to the stadium."

"No thanks," I politely informed the officers inside, as I kept running.

The two police officers exchanged looks, and then the driver said, "Miss, should you decide to continue you must realize you do so at your own risk. All support services for the race are being pulled due to the dangerous weather in the area."

"I won't quit," I said. From the tone of my voice he must have known there was no point in arguing with me. "But I don't know the way back to the stadium," I continued, "so will you stay with me long enough to show me the way?"

After another exchange of looks, they agreed and the cruiser settled in behind me crawling along at four miles per hour with lights flashing. Not long after, the lightning they had warned me of was all around me. With balloons held tightly against my body, I worked to remind myself that God would not have brought me this far only to have me get struck by lightning! Though it was midday, street lights came on, fooled by the falling darkness. As I approached each intersection, the police car pulled around me and into the intersection, stopping traffic until I had run through. Their presence helped me to stay calm and focused. I took solace in knowing that if anything did happen, they were there and would help.

When the hard rain came, it arrived very quickly. Even though I had my garbage bag with me, by the time I could have gotten it on there would have been no point. It was as if someone had turned on the kitchen faucet and I was running in the bottom of the sink! It was raining so hard I had to continually wipe the water from my eyes so that I could see where I was going. The police car had moved in front of me to alert oncoming traffic of my presence. Water was everywhere! I was soaked to the bone, and there were still 1 1/2 miles to go. The balloons had started to sag, my knees were getting weak and every so often threatened to give way. I fought against the negative thoughts that knocked at the door of my mind by narrowing my focus even more. With the police car to guide and protect me, I looked only at what was directly in front of me. I adopted the chant, "This one's for me." And I kept going.

Though I still wasn't sure where we were, I knew we must be getting closer to the university because of the buildings and streets. Surely this must be the last mile! To anyone watching I must have been quite a sight as I plodded through the pouring rain with my police escort, balloons dragging behind me. There was absolutely nobody else on the street, and I was feeling very alone in the cold rain when I suddenly remembered my promise to God. "This one's for you, this one's for you, this one's for you." It's all I thought as I ran, and the more I said it the stronger I began to feel.

I followed the police car as it made a right turn and up ahead lay the back side of the stadium. I was almost there! It seemed so close and yet so far. A pickup truck which had been approaching suddenly stopped and out jumped Dave Whitsett! With a huge smile on his face, he fell into a jog beside me and asked, "How are you doing?" It was all he had to say to release the flood of emotions stored up inside of me. As we slowly made our way in the pouring rain around the stadium to the track entrance, between sobs I told him all that had happened since seeing Adam at mile 20. Still following the police escort, he told me that the race officials had stayed at the finish line for my arrival. As we approached the entrance to the track, Dave said, "This last lap is all yours," and he headed across the infield to the finish line. Before entering the track, I made a point to thank the police officers for staying with me.

I ran the last lap in the pouring rain, balloons dragging on the ground behind me. My only witnesses were a couple of very cold, wet race officials and one beaming instructor. As I plodded around the same part of the track that I used to set speed records on in high school, I remembered my promise and was saying, "This one's for you" as I watched my foot cross the finish line.

The race officials quickly recorded my number and time, gave me my medal, and handed me two soggy roses. Dave hugged me and told me how proud he was of me for finishing. "What's the matter?" he asked, as I stood sobbing.

It all seemed so unreal. I had been running for six hours 47 minutes. Now I could stop. There I stood in the rain, soaked to the skin, holding two roses that were as droopy as I must have looked, high from the adrenaline and endorphins that surged through my system, and all I could do was cry! "The things a girl has to do for flowers," I replied. As Dave laughed, we walked off the track and toward the field house where everyone else was waiting.

	Scheduled Distance	Actual Distance	RPE	
Day 1	3			
	Comments:			
Day 2	3			
	Comments:			
Day 3	Walk 3			
	Comments:			
Day 4	26.2			
	Comments:			

Total Miles This Week_____Cumulative Total_____

Chapter 17:

Week Seventeen
After the Marathon:
What Now?

 PART 1 **The Post-Marathon High (or Low)**

YOU DID IT! You finished the marathon. We knew you would. So what now? Well, one thing that we would like very much would be for you to take the time to let us know about your experience. If you are willing to do that, you can reach us at the address given at the end of this section.

So, how are you feeling mentally? At this point, most first-time marathoners are feeling as though they can do absolutely anything. You are probably enjoying telling family, friends and co-workers about your experience. Some of them will get bored hearing about it long before you get bored talking about it, but that's OK. You earned the right, so go ahead. Maybe you can get someone to do the next one with you. What? The NEXT one? Well, are you going to do another one? Not everybody does, but lots of our students have continued as marathoners, or at least have continued to train and to participate in other, shorter races.

Think about it. Aren't the feelings you have about yourself pleasant to have? Some of them came from completing the marathon, but lots of them are results of all the hard mental and physical work and weekly achievements that led up to the marathon. You can continue to have those feelings if you do two things. One of them is to maintain the physical condition you have attained by continuing to work out. That's what Section Two of this chapter is about. The second thing is to continue to use the positive, optimistic outlook you developed in preparing for the marathon in other aspects of your life.

You may have realized as you went along in the book and the training program that the marathon has just been a vehicle. A very important and useful vehicle, but a vehicle nonetheless. What we are really interested in is your total approach to life and helping you to adopt a physically and mentally healthy lifestyle. Having the marathon as a goal has served you well, and even if you never again use any of what you have learned from this experience, the experience itself will remain a highlight of your life. But there is still more, much more, to be gained.

We hope you are now convinced, if you were not at first, that you really do make your own reality. You can change your behavior and your perceptions at will. You really CAN do just about anything you set out to do. That's not a cliché. It's a fact. And you know that now. You can apply that knowledge to your work, to your relationships with family, friends and acquaintances, to any aspect of your life you choose. And that is the long-term substantive benefit of all we have been asking you to do in this book. If you would like to tell us how it went for you, write us at:

Marathon Experiences
Psychology Department
University of Northern Iowa
Cedar Falls, IA 50614-0505

 PART 2 Physical Considerations

Recovery From the Marathon

Immediately following your completion of the marathon, you will be exhausted and exhilarated at the same time. You will probably have a few aches and pains but much of the acute discomfort will be masked by the mental high you will be experiencing. What should you do now?

As mentioned previously, there may be some immediate things you need to do within minutes of finishing the marathon. If you are cold, get warm. Change out of your wet clothes as soon as possible, especially if it is a cool day. Begin to drink fluids to start the rehydration process. If it has been warm and you have been sweating heavily, a fluid replacement beverage with sodium would be the best fluid to drink. Take care of any blisters that may have developed during the run so they do not become infected. If you have any joint discomfort or pain, ice the affected area as soon as you can and continue to ice 3-4 times in the next 24 hours. Taking 400 mg of ibuprofen three times a day over the next 48 hours will help manage joint and muscular discomfort.

Even though you have been training for 16 weeks, the marathon you have just completed is very traumatic on your body. Moderate to severe muscular soreness and stiffness will develop within 24-48 hours as a normal consequence of the amount of exercise you did. This is normal and should not be construed as a problem. The soreness tends to develop predominantly in the thigh and calf muscles and you will notice it most when you have to go up and down stairs. Ibuprofen will help the soreness. Stretching will also help the soreness.

For the first 2-3 days following the marathon, don't do any running. You should stretch 2-3 times each day, but running is not recommended. After 3-4 days, the acute muscular soreness and stiffness will fade away and you will begin to feel fairly normal again. Even though you feel pretty good, the muscles still have not fully recovered and are still going through a repair process which may last for several weeks. There are differences of opinion as to when you should resume running again. Some say let your subjective feelings be your guide. This is probably a pretty good recommendation but when you do start back, run slowly and for short distances. You should not feel bad about taking a week or two off. It will certainly not hurt you and it may help with complete recovery.

As you gradually get back into running or other forms of exercise, you need to decide what your objectives are. Are you going to try to run another marathon? Do you just want to stay fit and healthy? Are you trying to maintain a certain body weight? What you should do for exercise will depend largely on your objective.

Running Another Marathon. Following successful completion of your first marathon, you may have a desire to do it again. Some runners get hooked with the idea of running another, and then another, and before long it may become a natural thing for you to do. Many runners can run periodic marathons without any undue consequence as long as there is sufficient spacing between marathons. So, how long is sufficient spacing?

Sufficient spacing depends entirely on your individual capacity to tolerate the training associated with the marathon. It is not the marathon itself that causes the problems, it is all the training leading up to the marathon. Many recreational runners can tolerate marathon training and can run one marathon a year without any major consequences. The closer the marathons are spaced together, the more likely problems will result, normally some type of injury. If you were able to do the training recommended in this book without any significant problems, you could probably run one marathon a year comfortably.

Your training schedule also has a lot to do with the ability to run repeat marathons. The schedule recommended in this book was specifically designed for the first-time marathoner and for a 16-week training period. This schedule is not the best schedule for someone wanting to run their "fastest marathon." When you start considering trying to improve your marathon time, then you get into a whole different set of recommendations. The thing to remember is that increasing distance and intensity of training will increase the likelihood of injury.

Running Shorter Runs. For some, completing one marathon is all the marathoning they want to do. It was something they just wanted to do one time to see if they could do it. But what about shorter runs, like half-marathons, 10-kilometer runs (6.2 miles) and five-kilometer runs? Compared to training for and running a marathon, these shorter distances may seem like nothing. They are, in fact, much easier to train for and much less likely to result in injury.

For the majority of recreational runners, these shorter runs become the focus of their competitive efforts. There is also a lot more opportunity to run the shorter runs because there are more organized runs of these distances. You could probably find a 5 or 10 K almost every weekend in the summer within a reasonable driving distance. The big advantage of these shorter runs, especially the 5 and 10 K runs, is that the amount of training associated with these distances is very similar to the distances recommended for maintaining good health, a topic discussed in the next section.

Exercise and Nutrition for the Health of It. Most people probably don't decide to run a marathon because it is a healthy thing to do. It is not because exercise isn't healthy for you, it is just that the motivation for running a marathon usually goes beyond the health focus. Indeed, exercise is a very healthy thing for almost everyone. In the big picture of life, regular exercise can be a major contributor to attaining and maintaining optimal health.

Regardless of your motivation for running a single marathon or for continuing to run periodic marathons, it is hoped that you adopt a healthy lifestyle that uses regular exercise as one of its main components. Regular exercise significantly contributes to a healthier existence. It decreases the risk of many chronic and debilitating diseases, most notably heart disease, and gives you the energy to enjoy living. When combined with proper nutrition, regular exercise can add quality and quantity to your life.

How much exercise and what type of exercise leads to good health? You should be happy to know that the quantity of exercise necessary to optimize health is far less than you did to train for and run the marathon. Recent scientific studies have found that the amount of exercise necessary is the equivalent of 20-60 minutes, 3 times a week. The exercise can be any type of aerobic exercise, not just running. The intensity of exercise for optimal health benefit should be 55-70% of maximal heart rate. In running equivalents this amounts to running 2-6 miles at a comfortable pace 3 times a week. Compared to what you have just accomplished, this is pretty minimal and something you can sustain for a lifetime.

In addition to aerobic exercise, maintaining good flexibility becomes important to a good quality life. So do flexibility exercise along with your aerobic exercise. The flexibility exercise will not only decrease chances of injury from your aerobic exercise, but it will allow you to do the kinds of things you want or need to do, like other recreational or occupational activities. Good flexibility also decreases the incidence of certain chronic diseases like low back problems.

Maintaining good muscular strength and endurance is important too. Performing regular strengthening activities will help maintain good muscular function throughout life. Good muscular strength and endurance lays the foundation for other activities, like recreational or occupational pursuits. As was the case for both aerobic exercise and flexibility, good muscular strength and endurance reduces the incidence of chronic diseases.

Finally, the last piece of the puzzle is nutrition. Proper nutrition complements a good exercise program and makes an independent contribution to good health. The type of diet recommended for running the marathon in this book is the same type of diet that is recommended for good health. The diet should be low in fat, adequate in protein, and high in carbohydrates. The total calories consumed should be adjusted to maintain weight in those normally weighted. If you need to lose a few pounds, the combination of decreasing your caloric consumption and exercising is by far the best approach.

Regardless of your plans for future marathons, completion of the first marathon sets you apart from most people in this world. You are a member of an elite group that only a small portion of the population will even attempt to join. As a natural outgrowth of your marathon experience, you are motivated to make regular exercise a part of your lifestyle. Regular exercise combined with proper nutrition will lay the foundation for a healthy life in which you have the energy and stamina to do the things that are important to you.

PART 3 So, What Now?

Congratulations!! You did it! I hope it was everything you thought it would be and then some. Remember back in the Introduction when I promised that this would be a peak experience that would change you forever? At the time, you may have wondered how I could make such a bold statement. Maybe you were even a little skeptical that it would indeed have such a profound effect on you. I hope that this experience has made a believer out of you.

If you are feeling a little lost as far as what to do now, that's normal. For the past several months your physical and mental energy have been mutually focused on one goal and you followed a very structured program in order to achieve that. Now that has suddenly come to a end and you may feel a little uncertain about what you want to do next. Following are accounts from several past participants in which they share their post-marathon experiences and discuss the long-term impact that training for and completing the marathon has had upon their lives. Maybe reading them will help ease this time of transition for you and give you some ideas about where to go from here.

Geraldine Zapf Hall:

When I got to work the day after the marathon there were 26 helium balloons waiting for me. There were so many I could barely see my desk! If there was anyone in the office who hadn't known about the marathon before, they certainly knew now! The balloons were from a niece I am especially close to. She had been one of my biggest supporters during the training. Getting those balloons meant almost as much to me as getting the medal for finishing the marathon. I had two very special days back-to-back.

Running the marathon was one of the most rewarding things I have ever done. It was for me. It was something I accomplished that I could put on my resumé, or maybe in my obituary. I did it, and at the age of 55 no less! It took me a long time, but I wasn't ashamed of that. I went and told everybody exactly how long it took me and that I walked part of it, but that I had finished. When I told them, people looked at me and said things like, "I don't know how you did that," or, "Why on earth did you do that?" Still, even though they might have thought I was crazy for doing it, when they would introduce me to others they would say, "She ran a marathon." It may sound strange, but I think down deep, everybody would like to do it. And I did.

Exercising is now a regular part of my life. Whether I run or walk or both, doesn't matter. It's what I do for me, and it has become a big part of my life.

Ron Steele:

After their first marathon some people, myself included, think, "I'll never do this again. Never! This is stupid. Why did I ever do this? I'm so tired!" But then a few days go by and you find yourself thinking, "I think I'll do another one. It wasn't so bad after all." And before you know it, you're looking at the marathon schedule picking out your next one. Marathoning has a way of getting in your blood. Believe me, I know...I've run several!

Even though I don't have any definite plans for another marathon in the near future, I still try to run as often as I can. I run at a very slow pace, but that's OK. I'm doing this for me — not for others or the time clock. I just feel better when I run, plus it helps me to better cope with things in general. The skills we learned in this class don't apply just to marathoning — they apply to life! Just like you never know what the next step in a marathon will bring, so too, you never know what will happen next in life. But if you don't keep going, you're never going to find out. By staying relaxed, centered, and positive you can handle just about anything that comes your way.

Jeri Kurtzleben:

The first three weeks after the marathon, I didn't run much at all. Then I went through a period where I kind of went back and forth between running and not running. But I always seemed to come back to it; I guess I missed the feel of it. For me, it's such a mind-clearing experience. No matter how badly things are going, running always seems to help. By the time the run is over, I'm more relaxed, focused, and things just seem to fall into place.

I have since trained for and run a second marathon. I approached the second one in much the same way as the first, except I basically did it on my own. I guess it was important for me to know that this was something I could do without the added support of the class. To me, doing the second marathon meant that I could do many more should I choose to. It also made me an even more confident person.

I have applied what I learned in the class to my everyday life. I think it is very easy to get negative with yourself. I don't do that anymore. If something goes wrong, I think, "OK, what do I need to do differently next time?" I am definitely a more positive person now. This class was the first time in my life that I had a steady exercise program and regular exercise is now a part of my lifestyle. Recently, I got my cholesterol checked and the results were really good and they asked me if I exercised a lot. I thought, "Wow, it really works!" But the main reason I have made running a part of my lifestyle is not so much for the health benefits, as it is that it's one of the few things I do for me just because I want to.

Kathy Schneider, who has spent most of her life dealing with medical problems, reports:

I have continued to run regularly for enjoyment. The marathon started other adventures for me. My brother and I tried skydiving four months after the marathon and we plan on running the Grand Canyon. My goals just keep getting higher.

Julie Stone, who had some previous long-distance running experience prior to this class, reflects:

If I had to say which had more of an impact on me, the mental training or the physical training, I would definitely say it was the mental training. Whereas before I might have just thought about doing things, now I just DO them because I believe I can. I have a much more positive outlook. I figure if I can run a marathon, I can do anything. Using the class materials, I've even trained three other people to run a marathon, including my sister.

Heidi Brandt admits:

After the marathon I had some back problems and had to lay off the running for awhile. But after that settled down, the doctor said I could start again and I've been running ever since. I do a lot more stretching now, especially my back, and feel great. You know, I used to run to get in shape. Now, I run because it makes me happy. The marathon was such an awesome experience...nothing else has even come close.

Rob Leslie also had some physical problems after the marathon:

After the marathon, I had some trouble with my knee, but worked with a physical therapist and it got better. Running made it feel better, in fact, it seemed to feel worse when I didn't run. Also, running definitely had a positive effect on my mood. I plan on doing more marathons, and someday hope to run the Boston. Going through this experience has definitely changed my perceptions on personal limits. If I start thinking that I can't do something, I remind myself that compared to a marathon, this is a piece of cake. I have a lot more confidence in myself now.

Eric Johnson:

The class did great things for my whole life. I now know that I can do anything I want to — it's just a matter of doing it. If I wanted to be President by the time I'm 55, I could do it...I know that's probably extreme, but it's that kind of a feeling.

I have a picture of the marathon on my wall. People look at it and say "I could never run a marathon." And I reply, "Like I'm some Olympic runner? I'm Joe Schmoe — if I can do it, anybody can do it!"

Amy Kepler reports:

As a result of this experience, my thinking is more positive. I truly believe that I can do anything if I work for it. When I get down, I ask myself, "Am I preparing to fail or preparing to keep going?" I believe that running makes a person stronger not only physically, but mentally. I plan on running another marathon. If I ever coach a team, I will use the techniques we learned in this class because they work and they build winners, regardless of where you finish.

The only thing I've ever done that comes close to running the marathon is standing on a mountain top in Wyoming and seeing the view. Both experiences were outstanding! Limitless. No boundaries — only possibilities.

Patti Hasty Rust:

The marathon was something I was really doing for myself, and the fact that I took on the challenge and did it makes me feel powerful...like I can do anything. This experience showed me that even if there is something that seems insurmountable, with the right preparation and the right kind of attitude, I can do it, whatever it might be. It's one thing to hear it, and another thing to know it. Because of the marathon, I know the only limits that exist are those which I create myself. This knowledge has had a big impact on my life.

The only other thing I've done that even remotely resembles the marathon is have a baby. And since the marathon, I had my second child. The past two years have certainly been filled with peak experiences! Makes me wonder what else lies ahead! Whatever it is, I know I can handle it and I look forward to it.

Tricia Tuttle:

The marathon is something I still tell people about. They are often surprised and seem to think it is something they couldn't do. But I tell them I'm just a normal person like they are, and if I can do it so can they.

After I graduated from college, I mentioned it in job interviews. It showed that I am a hard worker and have dedication. On a recent business trip I told several people about it, and later about half of them came up and asked more about it. On another business trip, I met a guy from Boston who runs a lot but had never done a marathon, and he was asking if I had any tips on marathoning. All of a sudden, it's like I'm a teacher! Now, I run because it makes me feel good. It reminds me that I can accomplish anything I want to. I can't imagine how life would be without the experience of the marathon — nor do I want to! I plan to run another one.

Elizabeth Kilgore:

I still run. When I see people from the marathon class, we always ask each other, "Still running?" — most are.

The next several entries give credence to just how life-changing this experience can be. Remember Chris Henle, the girl who hated to run before starting the class? Here's what she's been up to since:

I still run and did the Rim-to-Rim in September of 1996. (Note: This is a 24-mile run which takes you from one side of the Grand Canyon to the other. Although not quite as long as a regular marathon, it is generally considered more difficult due to the steep slopes and intense climate changes.) It was the same feeling of accomplishment, but I had to have more willpower because doing the Canyon was more of an individual effort and involved hill and stairs training in order to condition for the slope.

Jennifer Haglund, who subsequently married a fellow classmate as a result of this class, expressed insight on the impact this can have on a relationship:

The best thing about the marathon class was meeting Jason. It was a bonding experience like few couples ever share, and it's something we still talk about.

For me personally, it had a great impact on the type of person I am. I became a more internal person (internal locus of control) because I was able to see myself succeed and improve like never before. With each passing day, I came to believe more and more that I had the power to make my own successes and control my own life.

I'm now in a graduate program for counseling psychology, partly because of the huge impact the concepts in the class had on me. I hope to go into gerontology and work with Alzheimer's patients and their families.

Jason Haglund, the other half to the Haglund team, had this to add:

This class changed my life. It wasn't just about running. It was about learning about myself and how to create my own reality; about how to make the most of myself and become the kind of person I want to be. During this class, I made huge strides toward that. I met my future wife in the class, and because of the confidence we both gained from this experience we had the courage to make some decisions about our future and take the risks necessary to make those goals happen that we otherwise might not. We both credit the marathon class with giving us confidence to brave the new and unknown. We are both better people because of this experience.

After the marathon class, I later ran Grandma's Marathon in Duluth, Minn, for which I trained and ran alone. I wasn't as prepared physically as I should have been, but I compensated for that by using more of the mental techniques we learned in the class and I had the best run of my life.

Keith Wendl, who was so enthusiastic about the information presented during class that he brought his lap-top computer to take notes with, hasn't slowed down at all since crossing his first marathon finish line as the following report shows:

This experience changed my life. It's not just about running a marathon. The techniques we learned in this class apply to all aspects of life. One of my long-term life goals is to run one marathon every year in a different state eventually running in all 50 states or until I die — whichever comes first. I'll be in my 70's by the time I'm done. So far I'm on target having conquered Iowa, Minnesota, and Illinois and Virginia. Having a public relations background, I would one day like to coordinate my own marathon. It combines everything that is important to me: fundraising, running, and long-term goals.

Jane Mortenson:

The only thing I know of that compares to the marathon is life itself. The marathon is a little metaphor for life; there are tough spots and easy stretches and getting through it isn't easy for anyone. But if you break it down into achievable segments, it's never as difficult as it may have first seemed.

I have since trained for another marathon with one other person. We had gone through the 18-miler and were within three weeks of the marathon, when pain in my lower back prevented me from continuing. I didn't know it at the time, but the cancer had returned and was in my bones. The running didn't have anything to do with the fact that the cancer had returned. Since I had already run one marathon, I didn't feel like a failure for not continuing the training, but I was very disappointed about not being able to enjoy that experience again.

Now, as I fight cancer a second time, I draw upon the skills and techniques I learned during the marathon training to help me get through it. I take heart in knowing that if I can do a marathon, I can get through just about anything. Taking this battle one step at a time, helps keep me from becoming overwhelmed and to maintain the positive attitude that is so critical when fighting cancer.

As was mentioned at the beginning of this chapter, while finishing the marathon was the goal of this training program, hindsight suggests that it is really just a vehicle by which to learn and practice life-enhancing skills which could potentially have lifelong consequences.

For me, training for a marathon definitely had a positive effect on my self-concept. My perceptions were notably more positive, as was my self-talk and caliber of mental images. I felt better about myself and was more confident of my capabilities than ever before. I had a new sense of strength. To sum it up, I liked who I saw in my mental mirror. I believe that because I could see my self-image more clearly and was happier with it, I did a better job of projecting it for others to see as well. I disagree that beauty is skin-deep. I think it goes all the way to the mind. What our mind sees, our body will display (the concept of visualization… sound familiar?). As with other constructs, beauty is relative…and you're the one who creates your own reality.

Distance is also relative — a marathon is short compared to the journey of life. So, the answer to the question, "What now?" is "Anything you want!" The techniques that helped you finish this marathon can be applied to any other challenge you face. But the transference of knowledge and skills will not happen automatically. You must exercise an internal locus of control to apply what you have learned to other aspects of your life. For some goals, it may be as simple as substituting them for the marathon and you will be able to use the same basic program as it's laid out. Other goals will require you to be more creative in the application of the program components. Even if the structure is not directly applicable, the concepts are. By generalizing them to other goals, your chances for success dramatically increase. And that's what this experience is ultimately about: learning the skills and techniques and developing positive habits that will enhance your ability to be the kind of person you want to be, to create the kind of life for yourself that you want to live, to feel successful in all that you do.

Marathon Calendar

When using this list, please keep the following in mind. First, we have listed the marathons by month, but not by specific date since the exact date changes by a day or so each year. Second, we prepared this list in the fall of 1997 and it was accurate as of that date, but the contact person may change from year to year and, occasionally, a marathon may be discontinued or the name of it may change. Of course, this list is not complete either, so you may know of, or hear of, other marathons as well. For the most part, however, these contact addresses will work for you, and, in any case, you will want to verify the date and place before you start training. For a number of years, *Runner's World* magazine has included, in its January issue, a very useful list of marathons and you may want to consult that source as well. We certainly did when we were compiling this list. If you use the Internet you can get current lists of marathons from *Runner's World* at http://www.runnersworld.com

JANUARY — U.S.A.

CHARLOTTE OBSERVER
   Charlotte, NC Marathon Office, PO Box 30294, Charlotte, NC 28230; (704) 358-5425.
WALT DISNEY WORLD
   Orlando, Fla. Walt Disney World Marathon, PO Box 10,000, Lake Buena Vista, FL 32830; (407) 939-7810.
ENGLEWOOD RESERVE
   Englewood, Ohio. Denny Fryman, 7581 Glenhurst Dr., Dayton, OH 45414; (937) 898-7015.

KING DAY CLASSIC
Tacoma, Wash. H. Douglas Brown, 1115 Martin Luther King Jr. Way, Tacoma, WA 98405; (206) 383-3531.

POINT REYES TRAIL
Point Reyes National Seashore, Calif. Enviro-Sports, PO Box 1040, Stinson Beach, CA 94970; (415) 868-1829.

HOUSTON-METHODIST
Houston, Tex. Houston Marathon Committee, 720 N. Post Oak Rd., Ste. 335, Houston, TX 77024; (713) 957-3453.

MARDI GRAS
New Orleans, La. NOTC, PO Box 52003, New Orleans, LA 70152; (504) 482-6682.

GREAT VALLEY
Chambersburg, Pa. Mike Witter, 5645 Stamy Hill Rd., Waynesboro, PA 17268; (717) 263-5631.

RARITAN VALLEY
Piscataway, N.J. Martin Dolphin, 79 Dayton Ave., Somerset, NJ 08873; (908) 846-2739.

SAN DIEGO
Carlsbad, Calif., In Motion, 511 S. Cedros Ave., Ste. B., Salana Beach, CA 92075; (800) 994-6668.

WINTER FUN
Vandalia, Ohio. Denny Fryman, 7581 Glenhurst Dr., Dayton, OH 45414; (937) 898-7015.

BEARGREASE SNOWSHOE
Duluth, Minn. Barb Van Skike, c/o Shannon Bohr, 13512 Krestwood Dr., Burnsville, MN 55337; (612) 435-8114.

ELLERBE SPRINGS
Ellerbe Springs, NC Doug Dawkins, 129 Springer Mountain Rd., Rockingham, NC 28379; (910) 895-9590.

JANUARY — INTERNATIONAL

TIBERIAS
Tiberias, Israel. Shimon Haviv, Israel Athletic Association, PO Box 4575, 61044 Tel Aviv, Israel; Tel.:972 3 685 6267. Fax: 972 3 685 6270.

BERMUDA
Hamilton, Bermuda. Bermuda Marathon Secretary, PO Box DV 397, Devonshire DV BX, Bermuda; (441) 238-2333. Or Marathon Tours, 108 Main St., Boston, MA 02129; (617) 242-7845.

TRINIDAD/TOBAGO
Barataria, Trinidad. Raffique Shah, c/o Trinidad/Tobago Marathon, Ninth

St. and Ninth Ave., Barataria, Trinidad, West Indies; Tel.: (809) 674-1692.
Fax: (809)674-3228.

VIETNAM

Ho Chi Minh City, Vietnam. Sports Asia Ltd., 26/1 Le Thanh Ton, District
1, Ho Chi Minh City, Vietman; Tel.: 84 8 822 6084. Fax: 84 8 822 6323.

OSAKA INTERNATIONAL LADIES

Osaka, Japan. Kansai Telecasting Corp., 5-17, 6-Chome, Nishitemma,
Kita-ku, Osaka 530, Japan; Tel.: 81 6 315 2601. Fax: 81 6 315 2179.

February — U.S.A.

STINSON BEACH

Mount Tamalpas State Park, Calif. Enviro-Sports, PO Box 1040, Stinson,
Beach, CA 94970; (415) 868-1829.

TALLAHASSEE

Tallahassee, Fla. Dana Stetson, 3218 Albert Dr., Tallahassee, FL 32308;
(904) 668-3839.

MID-WINTER

Huber Heights, Ohio. Denny Fryman, 7581 Glenhurst Dr., Dayton, OH
45414; (937) 898-7015.

CAROLINA

Columbia, S.C. Carolina Marathon Assoc., PO Box 5092, Columbia, SC
29250; (803) 929-1996.

TYBEE

Tybee Island, GA. Anna Boyett, PO Box 15785, Savannah, GA 31416;
(912)232-0070.

MID-WINTER

Huber Heights, Ohio. Denny Fryman, 7581 Glenhurst Dr., Dayton, OH
45414; (513) 898-7015.

DEATH VALLEY TRAIL

Death Valley, Calif. Enviro-Sports, PO Box 1040, Stinson Beach, CA, 94970;
(415) 868-1829.

LAS VEGAS INTERNATIONAL

Las Vegas, NV Al Boka, PO Box 81262, Las Vegas, NV 89180; (702) 876-
3870

LOST SOLES

Talent, Oregon. Jerome Ellison, PO Box 523, Talent, OR 97540; (503) 535-
4854.

METRO-DADE

Miami, Fla. Miami Runners, 7920 S.W. 40th St., Miami, Fla. 33155 (305)
227-1500.

CHARLOTTE OBSERVER

Charlotte, NC, Don King, PO Box 30294, Charlotte, NC 28230; (704) 358-5425.

AUSTIN

Austin, Texas. Austin Marathon, PO Box 684456, Austin, TX 78768; (512) 891-6000.

OHIO RIVER RRC

Oxford, Ohio. Dan Thompson, 1171 Nutmeg Ct., Centerville, OH 45459; (513) 438-5308.

SNOWFLAKE

Vandalia, Ohio. Denny Fryman, 7581 Glenhurst Dr., Dayton, OH 45414; (513) 898-7015.

VALLEY OF THE SUN

Phoenix, AZ. Valley of the Sun Marathon, 6505 N. 16th St., Phoenix, AZ 85069; (602) 277-4333.

WASHINGTON'S BIRTHDAY

Greenbelt, Maryland. Washington's Birthday Marathon, PO Box 1352, Arlington, VA 22210; (703) 271-8959.

BLUE ANGEL

Pensacola, Fla. Blue Angel Marathon, c/o MWR, Bldg. 632, Naval Air Station, Pensacola, Fla. 32508; (904) 452-4391.

COWTOWN

Fort Worth, TX. Jim Gilliland, PO Box 9066, Fort Worth, TX 76147; (817) 735-2033.

SMOKY MOUNTAIN

Townsend, Tenn. Sherman Ames, 4560 Gravely Hills Rd., Louisville, TN 37777; (615) 681-7467.

HUDSON MOHAWK

Albany, NY Lori Christina, 2-A Ramsgate, London Square Apts., Clifton Park, NY 12065; (518) 383-4514.

OLYMPIAD MEMORIAL

St. Louis, MO. Marathon Sports, 13453 Chesterfield Plaza, Chesterfield, MO 63017; (314) 434-9577.

ESCAPE FROM MARIN

Sausalito, CA. Envriro-Sports, PO Box 1040, Stinson Beach, CA 94970; (415) 868-1829.

FEBRUARY — INTERNATIONAL

ANTARCTICA

Artigas, King George Island. Marathon Tours, 108 Main St., Charlestown, MA 02129; (617) 242-7845.

BEPPU-OITA MAINICHI
Tokyo, Japan. RKB-Mainichi Broadcasting Co. Ltd. Tokyo Branch, 5-11-4 Ginza, Chuo-ku, Tokyo 104, Japan; Tel: 81.3.3546.2503 Fax: 81.3.3546.0869.
VALENCIA
Valencia, Spain. Antonia de la Lastra, Pintor Peyro Nr. 10-7A, 46010 Valencia, Spain; Tel: 34.6.369.2071. Fax: 34.6.362.6823.
CARIB CEMENT
Kingston, Jamaica. Brian Breese, Caribbean Cement Co., PO Box 448, Kingston, Jamaica; (809) 928-7530 Fax: (809) 928-6096.
TAHITI
Moorea, Franch Polynesia, David Nordquist, Tahiti Tourism Board, 300 N. Continental Blvd., Suite 180, El Segundo, Calif; (310) 414-8484.
CAPETOWN
Capetown, South Africa. Jack Luker, 13 Belvedere Rd., Claremont Cape 7700, South Africa; Tel: 27.21.616.186 Fax: 27.21.641.687.
CIUDAD DE SEVILLA
Sevilla, Spain. Instituto Municipal de Deportes, Del Ayuntamiento de Sevilla, Prolongacion Avda. de la Salea s/no 41007, Sevilla, Spain; Tel: 34.5.95.452.0033 Fax: 34.5.95.467.5524.
INTRNATIONAL EGYPTIAN
Cairo, Egypt. Basser Riad, Egytrav Travel & Transport, Nile Hilton Centre, Tahrir Square, Cairo, Egypt; Tel: 20.2.575.5029.

MARCH — U.S.A.

NANTUCKET
Nantucket, Mass. Paul Daley, PO Box 401, Norton, MA 02766; (508) 285-4544.
TRAIL'S END
Seaside, Oregon. Gordon Lovie, Oregon RRC, PO Box 549, Beaverton, OR 97075; (503) 646-7867.
B & A TRAIL
Severna Park, Maryland. Tom Bradford, 746 Mimosa Ct., Millersville, MD 21108; (410) 987-0674.
HYANNIS
Hyannis, Mass. Jack Glennon, 28 Barnstable, Hyannis, MA 02601; (508) 778-6965.
LOS ANGELES
Los Angeles, CA. Los Angeles Marathon, 11110 W. Ohio Ave., Suite 100, Los Angeles, CA 90025; (310) 444-5544.
MENDOCINO TRAIL
Russian Gulch State Park, CA. Enviro-Sports, PO Box 1040, Stinson Beach,

CA 94970; (415) 868-1829.

NAPA VALLEY

Calistoga, CA. Dave Hill, PO Box 4307, Napa, CA. 94558; (707) 255-2609.

MARCH MADNESS

Vandalia, Ohio. Denny Fryman, 7581 Glenhurst Dr., Dayton, OH 45414; (513) 898-7015.

MAUI

Kahului, Hawaii. VIRR, PO Box 330099, Kahului, HI 96733; (808) 871-6411.

BIG BASIN REDWOODS

Big Basin Redwoods State Park, CA. Enviro-Sports, PO Box 1040, Stinson Beach, CA. 94970; (415) 868-1829.

CATALINA

Two Harbors, CA. California Athletic Productions, 304 Stonecliffe Aisle, Irvine, CA. 92715; (714) 737-1495.

MUSIC CITY

Nashville, TN. Greater Nashville Athletic Club, PO Box 150867, Nashville, TN 37215; (615) 298-3435.

SHAMROCK

Virginia Beach, VA. Jerry Bocrie, 2308 Maple St., Virginia Beach, VA 23451; (804) 481-5090.

SUFFOLK COUNTY

Brookhaven, NY. Nick Morris, PO Box 1543, West Babylon, NY 11704; (516) 957-7346.

GREAT SOUTHWEST

Abilene, TX. Mike Osborn, YMCA Box 3137, Abilene, TX 79604; (915) 677-8144.

TRAIL BREAKER

Waukesha, Wisconsin. Trail Breaker Marathon, 2949 N. Mayfair, Suite 106, Wauwatosa, WI 53222; (414) 453-7600.

ATHENS

Athens, Ohio. Tom Wolf, 44 Grosvenor St., Athens, OH 45701; (614) 594-3042.

MARCH — INTERNATIONAL

PYRAMIDS

Cairo, Egypt. Marie Frances Productions, 7603 Newmarket Dr., Bethesda, Maryland 20817; (301) 320-3663.

LAKE BIWA MAINICHI

Lake Biwa, Japan. The Mainichi Newspapers, Osaka Office 3-4-5, Umeda Kita-ku, Osaka 530-51, Japan; Tel: 81.6.346.8371 Fax: 81.6.346.8372.

CHINA COAST
 Hong Kong A.V.O.H.K., PO Box 10368, Central Hong Kong; Tel. and Fax: 852.818.4856.
LAKE SIMCOE
 Orillia, Ontario, Canada. Norm Patenaude, 297 Canice St., Orillia, Ontario, Canada L3V 4J6; (705) 327-3375.
NAGOYA INTL. WOMEN'S
 Nagoya, Japan. Tomomi Suda, The Chunichi, Shimbun 6-1, 1-Chome, Sannomaru, Naka-ku, Nagoya 460-11, Japan; Tel: 81.52.221.0737 Fax: 81.52.221.0739.
TEL AVIV
 Tel Aviv, Israel. Tel Aviv Marathon, Hapoel Sport Assoc., PO Box 7170, 8 Haarboa St., 64339 Tel Aviv, Israel; Tel: 972.3.561.3322. Fax: 972.3.561.0568.
CATALUNYA
 Barcelona, Spain. Marathon Catalunya, C. Jonqueres, 16-9-C, 08003 Barcelona, Spain. Tel: 34.3.268.01.14. Fax: 34.3.268.43.34.
VIGARANO
 Vigarano Mainarda, Italy. Stella Nicola, Via Municipio 1, 44049 Vigarano Mainarda, (FE), Italy; Tel: 39.532.43.196. Fax: 39.532.43.563.
DONG-A INTERNATIONAL
 Kyongju, Korea. Chung-Woong Kim M.B.E., 145-1 Chungjeongno 3ka, Seodaemunku, Seoul 120-715, Korea; Tel: 82.2.361.0730. Fax: 82.2.361.0445
ROME
 Rome, Italy. Norman Ross, Hmbert Travel Agency, 400 Madison Ave., New York, NY 10017; (212) 688-3700.

APRIL — U.S.A.
GOLDEN GATE-HEADLANDS
 Sausalito, Calif. Enviro-Sports, PO Box 1040, Stinson Beach, CA 94970; (415) 868-1829.
ARMY MULE MOUNTAIN
 Bisbee, Arizona. Mule Mountain Marathon, PO Box 12100, Fort Huachuca, AZ 85607; (602) 533-2442.
HOGEYE
 Fayetteville, Arkansas. George Moore, 2466 Sweetbriar Dr., Fayetteville, AR 72703; (501) 442-6488.
BOSTON
 Hopkinton, Mass. B.A.A. Boston Marathon, PO Box 1996, Hopkinton, MA 01748; (508) 435-6905.

CAMP LEJEUNE

Camp Lejeune, North Carolina. Commanding General, Attn: BMWR/ MREC-4, Marine Corps Base, PSC Box 20004, Camp Lejeune, NC 28542; (910) 451-1799.

HIGH PLAINS

Goodland, Kansas. Michael Skipper, 305 W. 10th St., Goodland, KS 67735; (913) 899-5280.

LONGEST DAY

Brookings, South Dakota. Bob Bartling, 410 4th St., Brookings, SD 57006; (605) 692-2414.

NAPA VALLEY TRAIL

Calistoga, Calif. Enviro-Sports, PO Box 1040, Stinson Beach, CA 94970; (415) 868-1829.

GLASS CITY

Toledo, Ohio. Pat Wagner, 130 Yale Dr., Toledo, OH 43614; (419) 385-1072.

PINE LINE TRAIL

Medford, Wisconsin. Pine Line Trail Marathon, PO Box 65, Medford, WI 54451; (715) 748-6450.

ARMY

San Antonio, Texas. John Purnell, 3428 N. St. Mary's St., San Antonio, TX 78212; (210) 732-1332.

BIG SUR

Carmel, Calif. William Burleigh, PO Box 222620, Carmel, CA 93922; (408) 625-6226.

LAKE COUNTY

Zion, Illinois. Lake County Races, PO Box 9, Highland Park, IL 60035; (708) 266-7223.

MICHIGAN TRAIL

Ann Arbor, Michigan. Running Fit, 123 E. Liberty, Ann Arbor, MI 48104; (313) 769-5016.

APRIL — INTERNATIONAL

AALBORG

Aalborg, Denmark. Ole Fibaek, Kaerlundsvej 25, PO Box 614, 91000 Aalborg, Denmark; Tel: 45.98.164.500 Fax: 45.98.137.526.

BELGRADE

Belgrade, Yugoslavia. JSD Partizan, Belgrade Marathon, Jumska 1, 11000 Belgrade, Serbia, Yugoslavia; Tel: 381.11.648.266 Fax: 381.11.651.328.

BRASILIA

Brasilia, Brazil. Joaquim Manoel do Carmo Pires, Brasilia de Atletismo, Av. Pedrio Teizeira, 400 Planalto 69, 040-000, Nanaus, Amazonas, Brasilia,

Brazil; Tel: 55.92.656.5019 Fax: 55.92.656.5345.

LONDON

London, England. NutraSweet London Marathon, Overseas Entry Coordinator, 91 Walkden Rd., Walkden, Manchester M28 5DQ, England. Or contact Marathon Tours, 108 Main St., Boston, MA; (617) 242-7845.

PARIS

Paris, France. AMSP, 8 rue Crozatier, 75012 Paris, France; Tel: 33.1.42.77.17.84. Or contact Marathon Tours, 108 Main St., Boston, MA; (617) 242-7845.

VIENNA CITY

Vienna, Austria. Wolfgang Konrad, Enterprise Sports Promotion, Trautsongasse 6, A-1080 Vienna, Austria; Tel: 43.1.402.6917 Fax: 43.1.403.6241.

MADRID

Madrid, Spain. Maricio Blanco Villen, Mapoma, C/-Linneo 4, 28005 Madrid Spain; Tel: 34.1.366.9701 Fax: 34.1.364.0313.

ROTTERDAM

Rotterdam, Netherlands. Stichting Rotterdam Marathon, PO Box 1627, 3000 BP Rotterdam, Netherlands; Tel: 31.10.417.28.86.

WROCLAW

Wroclaw, Poland. MOSIR Poludnie, Lubinska 53, PL 53-623, Wroclaw, Poland; Tel: 48.71.552.087 Fax: 48.71.555.030.

MAY — U.S.A.

GREAT POTATO

Boise, Idaho. Tim Severa, YMCA, 1050 W. State St., Boise, ID 83702; (208) 344-5501.

SHIPROCK

Farmington, New Mexico. Nancy Krivo, 2800 N. Dustin, #205, Farmington, NM 87401; (505) 327-5595.

WHISKEY ROW

Prescott, Arizona. YMCA, 750 Whipple St., Prescott, AZ 86301; (602) 445-7221.

AVENUE OF THE GIANTS

Weott, Calif. Gay Gilchrist, Six Rivers Running Club, 281 Hidden Valley Rd., Bayside, CA 95524; (707) 443-1226.

BUFFALO

Buffalo, New York. Buffalo Marathon, PO Box 652, Buffalo, NY 14202; (716) 837-7223.

CITY OF PITTSBURGH

Pittsburgh, Pennsylvania. Larry Grollman, Marketing Director, City of

Pittsburgh Marathon, Center for Sports Medicine, 4601 Baum Blvd., Pittsburgh, PA 15213; (412) 578-3320.

CLEVELAND

Cleveland, Ohio. Revco Cleveland Marathon, 1925 Enterprise Pkwy., Twinsburg, OH 44087; (800) 467-3826.

LINCOLN

Lincoln, Nebraska. Nancy Sutton, 5309 S. 62nd St., Lincoln, NE 68516; (402) 423-4519

LONG ISLAND

East Meadow, New York. Patti Kenler, Sports Unit, Eisenhower Park, East Meadow, NY 11554; (516) 572-0251

SPRING FLING

Vandalia, Ohio. Denny Fryman, 7581 Glenhurst Dr., Dayton, OH 45414; (513) 898-7015.

RACE OF CHAMPIONS

Holyoke, Mass. Fast Feet, 231 Elm St., West Springfield, MA 01089; (413) 734-0955.

WILD WILD WEST

Lone Pine, Calif. Chamber of Commerce, PO Box 749, Lone Pine, CA 93545; (619) 876-4444.

HEADLANDS WOLF RIDGE

Sausalito, Calif. Enviro-Sports, PO Box 1040, Stinson Beach, CA 94970; (415) 868-1829.

LAKE GENEVA

Lake Geneva, Wisconsin. Barbara and Frank Dobbs, PO Box 1134, Lake Geneva, WI 53147; (414) 248-4323.

MUIR WOODS

Mount Tamalpais State Park, Calif. Enviro-Sports, PO Box 1040, Stinson Beach, CA 94970; (415) 868-1829.

CAPITAL CITY

Olympia, Washington. Capital City Marathon, PO Box 1681, Olympia, WA 98507; (360) 786-1786.

ANDY PAYNE

Oklahoma City, OK. United National Indian Tribal Youth, PO Box 25042, Oklahoma City, OK 73125; (405) 424-3010.

BAYSHORE

Traverse City, Michigan. Deb Seyler, 1019 Pine St., Traverse City, MI 49684; (616) 941-5743.

GAGE ROADRUNNER

Gage, Oklahoma. Janet Pierce, PO Box 328, Gage, OK 73843; (405) 923-7727.

LONE STAR PAPER CHASE

Amarillo, Texas. Heather Sells, c/o Amarillo Globe-News, PO Box 2091, Amarillo, TX 79166; (806) 345-3451.

COEUR D'ALENE

Coeur d'Alene, Idaho. Coeur d'Alene Marathon, PO Box 2393, Coeur d'Alene, ID 83816; (208) 773-7581.

MADISON

Madison, Wisconsin. Madison Marathon, 449 State St., Madison, WI 53705; (608) 256-9922.

MED-CITY

Rochester, Minn. Wally Arnold, 1417 14th Ave., NE, Rochester, MN 55906; (507) 282-1310.

VERMONT CITY

Burlington, Vermont. Andrea Riha, Key Bank/Vermont City Marathon, POBox 4102, Burlington, VT 05402; (800) 880-8149.

WYOMING

Laramie, Wyo. Brent Weigner, c/o Cheyenne Track club, 3204 Reed Ave., Cheyenne, WY 82001; (307) 635-3316.

MAY — INTERNATIONAL

FLETCHER CHALLENGE

Rotura, New Zealand. Fletcher Challenge Marathon, PO Box 610, Rotorua, New Zealand; Tel. or Fax: 64.7.348.8448.

VANCOUVEVR

Vancouver, British Columbia. Gordon Rogers, Box 3213, Vancouver, British Columbia, Canada V6B 3X8; (604) 872-2928 Fax: (604) 872-2903.

FOREST CITY

London, Ontario. Thames Valley Children's Center., 779 Baseline Rd., E, London, Ontario, Canada N6C 5Y6; (519) 685-8675.

JOHNNY MILES

New Glasgow, Nova Scotia. George Manos, PO Box 7, New Glasgow, Nova Scotia, Canada. B2H 5E1; (902) 755-8363.

NATIONAL CAPITOL

Ottawa, Ontario. Leopold Roberge, PO Box 426, Station A, Ottawa, Ontario, Canada K1N 8V5; (613) 234-2221.

TALLINN

Tallinn, Estonia. Rein Raspel, Haabeeme, Ranna tee 2-102, Harju, m/k ee 3006, Tallinn 203006, Estonia; Tel: 372.2.238.231.

TURIN

Turin, Italy. Turin Marathon, C.so Unita d'Italia 133/A, 10127 Turin, Italy; Tel. or Fax: 39.11.663.1231 or contact Norman Ross, Humbert Travel

Agency, 400 Madison Ave., New York, NY 10017; (212) 688-3700.

COPENHAGEN

Copenhagen, Denmark. Copenhagen Marathon, Aarhusgade 85, DK 2100 Copenhagen, Denmark; Tel: 45.35.26.69.00 Fax: 45.31.38.79.63.

OKANAGAN

Kelowna, British Columbia. Running Room, 115-2463 Hwy. 97N, Kelowna, British Columbia, Canada, V1X 4S2; (604) 862-3511.

LAKELAND RUNAWAY

Vermilion, Alberta. Lakeland Runaway Marathon, Recreation Department, Lakeland College, Vermilion, Alberta, Canada T0B 4MO; (403) 853-8471.

MUNICH

Munich, Germany. Michael Schultz-Tholen, Freizeitverein fur Sport e. V. Heckenrosenstr. 17, 8022, Grunwald, Germany; Tel: 49.89.641.06.16 Fax: 49.89.641.06.21.

JUNE — U.S.A.

GOD'S COUNTRY

Coudersport, Pennsylvania. Potter County Recreation Department, PO Box 245, Coudersport, PA 16915; (814) 435-2290.

GOVERNOR'S CUP

Helena, Montana. Governor's Cup Festival, PO Box 451, Helena, MT 59624; (406) 447-3414.

RIDGERUNNER

Cairo, W. Virginia. John Hendley, North Bend State Park, Rt. 1, Box 221, Cairo, WV 26337; (304) 643-2931.

GOLD COUNTRY TRAIL

Nevada City, Calif. Nick Vogt, 1025 Grange Road, Meadow Vista, CA 95722; (916) 878-0697.

NIPMUCK TRAIL

Ashford, Conn. David Raczkowski, PO Box 285, Chaplin, CT 06235; (203) 455-1096.

STEAMBOAT

Steamboat Springs, Colo. Chamber Resort, PO Box 774408, Steamboat Springs, CO 80477; (303) 879-0882.

PALOS VERDES

Palos Verdes, Calif. Palos Verdes Marathon, PO Box 2856, Palos Verdes, CA 90274; (310) 828-4123.

SUNBURST

South Bend, Indiana. Carter Wolf, 615 N. Michigan St., South Bend, IN 46601; (219) 674-0090.

HOOSIER

Fort Wayne, Indiana. Bob Hockensmith, 3732 Thyme Ct., New Haven, IN 46774; (219) 749-1237.

SUGARLOAF

Eustis, Maine. Chip Carey, Sugarloaf USA, RR 1, Box 5000, Kingfield, ME 04947; (207) 237-2000.

TAOS

Taos, New Mexico. Bruce Gomez, PO Box 2245, Taos NM 87571; (505) 776-1860.

VALLEY OF THE FLOWERS

Lompoc, Calif. Valley of the Flowers Marathon, PO Box 694, Lompoc, CA 93438; (805) 735-3255.

MARATHON TO MARATHON

Storm Lake, Iowa. Tami Horsmen, PO Box 234, Marathon, IA 50565; (712) 289-2246.

FILA SKY

Aspen, Colo. Allan Taylor Communications, 505 8th Ave., New York NY 10018; (212) 714-1280.

HIGH SIERRA

Truckee, Calif. Sky High, PO Box 20963, Wl Sobrante, CA 94803; (510) 223-5778.

GRANDMA'S

Duluth, Minnesota. Grandma's Marathon, PO Box 16234, Duluth, MN 55816; (218) 727-0947.

MAYOR'S MIDNIGHT SUN

Anchorage, Alaska. John McCleary, Municipality of Anchorage Parks & Recreation, Box 196650, Anchorage, AK 99519; (907) 343-4474.

PARK OF ROSES

Columbus, Ohio. Denny Fryman, 7581 Glenhurst Dr., Dayton, OH 45414; (513) 898-7015.

JUNE — INTERNATIONAL

STOCKHOLM

Stockholm, Sweden. Stockholm Marathon, Box 10023, S10055 Stockholm, Sweden. Tel: 46.8.667.19.30 or contact Marathon Tours, 108 Main St., Boston, MA 02129; (617) 242-7845.

MARATHON DELA BAIC DES

Charlo, New Bruswick. Jeannita Caron, Box 8, Site 10, Charlo, New Brunswick, Canada E0B 1M0; (506) 684-5133.

MELBOURNE

Melbourne, Australia. AusFit Events Management, PO Box 2045 KEW, Melbourne V1C 3101, Australia; Tel: 613.853.2768. Fax: 613.853.2721.

YUKON GOLD MIDNIGHT
Whitehorse, Yukon. Run Yukon, 4061 Fourth Ave., Whitehorse, Yukon, Canada Y1A 1H1; (403) 668-4236.

MANITOBA
Winnipeg, Manitoba. Manitoba Marathon, 200 Main St., Winnipeg, Manitoba, Canada R3C 4M2; (204) 925-5751.

TWENTE
Enschede, Holland. International Twente Marathon, Wim Verhoorn, PO Box 104, 2678 Z] De Lier, Holland; Tel: 31.17.451.7273 Fax: 31.17.451.0129.

MIDNIGHT SUN
Baffin Island, Northwest Territories. Ellen Herie, 20 Toronto St., 12th Floor, Toronto, Ontario, Canada M5C 2B8; (416) 869-0772.

MOUNT KILIMANJARO
Tanzania, Africa. Marie Frances Productions, 7603 Newmarket Dr., Bethesda, MD 20817; (301) 320-3663.

JULY — U.S.A.

GRANDFATHER MOUNTAIN
Boone, North Carolina. Harry Williams, 460 Deerfield Forest Pkwy., Boone, NC 28607; (704) 265-3479.

OHIO/MICHIGAN
Toledo, Ohio. Tom Faldey, 3743 Woodmount Rd., Toledo, OH 43613; (419) 475-0731.

SAN FRANCISCO
San Francisco, Calif. San Franisco Marathon, PO Box 77148, San Francisco, CA 94107; (415) 391-2123.

MOSQUITO
Leadville, Colo. Chamber of Commerce, PO Box 861, Leadville, CO 80461; (719) 486-3900.

UNIVERSITY OF OKOBOJI
Pike's Point State Park, Iowa. Herman Richter, Univ. of Okoboji Marathon, Box 3077, Spencer, IA 51301; (712) 338-2424.

DESERET NEWS
Salt Lake City, Utah. Deseret News/Granite Furniture Marathon, PO Box 1257, Salt Lake City, UT 84110; (801) 237-2135.

KILAUEA VOLCANO
Hawaii National Park, Hawaii. Kilauea Volcano Marathon, PO Box 106, Hawaii National Park, HI 96718; (808) 967-8222.

JULY — INTERNATIONAL

CALGARY STAMPEDE

Calgary, Alberta. Jill Hamilton, Box 296, Station M, Calgary, Alberta, Canada T2P 2H9; (403) 270-8828.

PAAVO NURMI

Turku, Finland. Paavo Nurmi Marathon, Urheilupuisto FIN-20810, Turku, Finland; Tel: 358.21.2503.526 Fax: 358.21.2503.106.

FRIENDLY VOYAGEUR

Massey, Ontario. Leslie and Liz Gamble, RR 1, Massey, Ontario, Canada P0P 1P0; (705) 865-2655.

GOLD COAST

Gold Coast, Queensland, Australia. Gold Coast Marathon, PO Box 5251, Gold Coast Mail Centre, Queensland 4217, Australia; Tel: 61.75.911.2404 Fax: 61.75.914.599.

HELSINKI CITY

Helsinki, Finland. Helsinki City Marathon, Radiokatu 20, 00240 Helsinki, Finland; Tel: 358.0.158.2405 Fax: 358.0.149.6731.

NOVA SCOTIA

Barrington, Nova Scotia. Raymond Green, PO Box 100, Barrington, Nova Scotia, Canada B0W 1E0; (902) 637-3254.

AUGUST — U.S.A.

DRAKES BAY TRAIL

Point Reyes National Park, Calif. Enviro-Sports, PO Box 1040, Stinson Beach, CA 94970; (415) 868-1829.

FRANK MAIER

Juneau, Alaska. Ben Van Allen, 6731 Gray St., Juneau, AK 99801; (907) 586-8322.

CRATER LAKE RIM

Crater Lake, Oregon. Crater Lake Rim Runs, 5830 Mack Ave., Klamuth Falls, OR 97603; (503) 884-6939.

PAAVO NURMI

Upson, Wisconsin. Chamber of Commerce, 207 Silver St., Hurley, WI 54534; (715) 561-4434.

MAMMOTH MOUNTAIN TRAIL

Mammoth Lake, Calif. Sky High, PO Box 20963, El Sobrante, CA 94803; (510) 223-5778.

SUMMER SPREE

Vandalia, Ohio. Denny Fryman, 7581 Glenhurst Dr., Dayton, OH 45414; (513) 898-7015.

PIKES PEAK

Manitou Springs, Colo. Nacy Hobbs, PO Box 38235, Colorado Springs, CO 80937; (719) 473-2625.

UNION TERMINAL
   Cincinnati, Ohio. Denny Fryman, 7581 Glenhurst Dr., Dayton, OH 45414;
   (513) 898-7015.
KONA
   Kailua-Kona, Hawaii. Jim Lovell, PO Box 5316, Kailua-Kona, HI 96145;
   (808) 329-4661.
SILVER STATE
   Reno, Nev. Ski Pisarski, Silver State Marathon, 1460 Prospect Ave.,
   Sparks, NV 89431; (702) 849-0419.
SAUSALITO
   Sausalito, Calif. Enviro-Sports, PO Box 1040, Stinson Beach, CA 94970;
   (415) 868-1829.

AUGUST — INTERNATIONAL

SIBERIAN
   Omsk, Russia. Siberian Marathon, PO Box 41, Glavpostampt, Omsk,
   Russia 644099; Tel: 7.3812.311.844 Fax: 7.3812.310.007.
FESTIVAL-BY-THE-SEA
   Saint John, New Brunswick. Canada Games Aquatic Centre, 50 Union St.,
   Saint John, New Brunswick, Canada E2L 1A1; (506) 696-4922.
REYKJAVIK
   Reykajvik, Iceland. Sigurdur Sigmindsson, Lyngmoar 3, 210 Gardaber,
   Iceland; Fax: 354.1.626.385.
DAIHATSU ADELAIDE
   Adelaide, Australia. S.A. Road Runners Club, 1 Sturt St., Adelaide, South
   Australia 5000; Tel: 61.8.213.0615 Fax: 61.8.211.7115.
EDMONTON FESTIVAL
   Edmonton, Alberta. The Running Room, 8537 109th St., Edmonton,
   Alberta, Canada T6G 1E4; (403)433-6062.

SEPTEMBER — U.S.A.

BLACK HILLS
   Rapid City, South Dakota. Black Hills Marathon, PO Box 9243, Rapid City,
   SD 57709; (605) 348-7866.
MONSTER TRAIL
   Virgil, N.Y. Joe Dabes, 86 Lake Rd., Dryden, NY 13053 (No phone calls)
SCOTTY HANTON
   Port Huron, Mich. Doug Seville, PO Box 611628, Port Huron, MI 48061;
   (519) 542-2153.
SNOWGOOSE
   Anchorage, Alaska. Anchorage Running Club, PO Box 211923, Anchorage,

AK 99521; (907) 258-4964.

TUPELO

Tupelo, Miss. Johnny Dye, 1007 Chester Ave., Tupelo, MS 38801; (601) 842-2039.

HEART OF AMERICA

Columbia, Missouri. Joe Duncan, Columbia Track Club, PO Box 1872, Columbia, MO 65205; (314) 445-2684.

TURTLE

Roswell, N.Mex. Bob Edwards, 715, E. Linda Vista Blvd., Roswell, NM 88201; (505) 624-8830.

AMERICAN ODYSSEY

Marathon City, Wisconsin. Roger Ross, 3842 Crestwood Dr., Wausau, WI 54402; (715) 675-6977.

BISMARCK

Bismarck, N. Dakota. Bill Bauman, YMCA, PO Box 549, Bismarck, ND 58502; (701) 255-1525.

JACKSON

Jackson, Wyo. Jill Harkness, Teton County/Jackson Parks & Recreation, PO Box 811, Jackson, WY 83001; (307) 733-5056.

MUIR BEACH TRAIL

Muir Beach, Calif. Enviro-Sports, PO Box 1040, Stinson Beach, CA 94970; (415) 868-1829.

DUTCHESS COUNTY

Fishkill, N.Y. Irvin Miller, 11 Manor Dr., Poughkeepsie, NY 12603; (914) 471-0777.

MARATHON OF THE ROSES

York, Penna. Clay Shaw, 3035 Raintree Rd., York, PA 17404; (717) 764-1181.

NORTHERN SHUFFLERS

Marquette, Mich. Bud Velin, 2015 E. M-28, Marquette, MI 49855; (906) 249-9603.

BURNEY CLASSIC

Burney, Calif. Don Jacobs, Box 217, Dept. M, Burney, CA 96013; (916) 335-2825.

ERIESISTIBLE

Erie, Penna. Rick Godzwa, PO Box 8311, Erie, PA 16505; (814) 459-8381.

BETHEL MOUNTAIN

Bethel, Alaska. Mary Wilda Warner, PO Box 1258, Bethel, AK 99559; (907) 543-2110.

EQUINOX

Fairbanks, Alaska. Running Club North, PO Box 84237, Fairbanks, AK

99708; (907) 452-8351.

SUGAR RIVER TRAIL

Brodhead, Wisconsin. Chris Roberts, 601 17th St., Brodhead, WI 53520; (608) 897-4516.

WALKER NORTH

Walker, Minn. Leach Lake Area Chamber of Commerce, Box 1089, Walker, MN 56484; (800) 833-1118.

FALL FANTASY

Vandalia, Ohio. Denny Fryman, 7581 Glenhurst Dr., Dayton, OH 45414; (513) 898-7015.

CLARENCE DEMAR

Cilsum, New Hampshire. Rich Sanford, PO Box 6257, Keene, NH 03431; (603) 357-5891.

DUKE CITY

Albuquerque, N. Mexico. Duke City Marathon, PO Box 4543, Albuquerque, NM 87196; (505) 890-1018.

EAST LYME

East Lyme, Conn. Way Hedding, Box 186, East Lyme, CT 06333; (203) 739-2864.

PORTLAND

Portland, Oregon. Les Smith, PO Box 4040, Beaverton, OR 97076; (503) 226-1111.

SEPTEMBER — INTERNATIONAL

BEAVERLODGE TO GRAND PRARIE

Grand Prarie, Alberta. Bill Turnbull, 6913 97A Grand Prarie, Alberta, Canada T8V 5E5; (403) 532-7138

TWIN CITIES

St. John's, Newfoundland. Brian Mulchahy, 47 Victory Lane, Mount Pearl, Newfoundland, Canada. A1N 3Z3; (709) 368-1728.

GOLDEN EAGLE

Canmore, Alberta. Running Room, 321A-10 St., NW, Calgary, Alberta, Canada T2N 1V7; (403) 270-7317.

OILSANDS

Fort McMurray, Alberta. Ann Locke, PO Box 5792, Fort McMurray, Alberta, Canada T9H 4V9; (403) 791-4027.

SASKATCHEWAN

Saskatoon, Saskatchewan. Ray Risling, 128 Ottawa Ave. S., Saskatoon, Saskatchewan, Canada S7M 3L5; (306) 382-2962.

YELLOWKNIFE

Yellowknife, Northwest Territories. France Benoit, Arctic Runners Club,

Box 1841, Yellowknife, Northwest Territories, Canada X1A 2P4; (403) 920-3128.

AMSTERDAM CITY

Amsterdam, Holland. Amsterdam City Marathon, PO Box 94610, 1090 GP Amsterdam, Holland; Tel: 31.20.663.0781 Fax: 31.20.663.0561.

MONTREAL

Montreal, Quebec. CDRM, Montreal Marathon, POBox 1383, Station Place d'Armes, Montreal, Quebec, Canada H2Y 3K5; (514) 284-5272.

BERLIN

Berlin, Germany. Sport-Club Charlottenburg, Berlin Marathon, Waldschulallee 34, D-14055, Berlin, Germany; Tel: 49.30.302.53.70 Fax: 49.30.392.23.82.

PRINCE EDWARD ISLAND

Charlottetown, Prince Edward Island. Fred Hughes, YMCA, 252 Prince St., Charlottetown, Prince Edward Island, Canada C1A 4S1; (902) 566-3966.

OCTOBER — U.S.A.

NEW HAMPSHIRE

Bristol, N.H. New Hampshire Marathon, PO Box 6, Bristol, NH 03222; (603) 744-6273.

ORCAS ISLAND TRAIL

Eastsound, Washington. Enviro-Sports, PO Box 1040, Stinson Beach, CA 94970; (415) 868-1829.

ST. GEORGE

St. George, Utah. Leisure Services 86 Main St., St. George, UT 84770; (801) 634-5850.

FOX CITIES

Neenah, Wisconsin. Fox Cities Marathon, 835 Valley Rd., Menasha, WI 54952; (414) 954-6790.

JOHNSTOWN

Johnstown, Penna. Johnstown Marathon, YMCA, 100 Haynes St., Johnstown, PA 15901; (814) 535-8381.

MAINE

Portland, Maine. Don Kent, PO Box 8654, Portland, ME 04104; (207) 774-5795.

SACRAMENTO

Sacramento, Calif. Ron Sturgeon, PO Box 995, Dixon, CA 95620; (916) 678-5005.

TWIN CITIES

St. Paul, Minnesota. Twin Cities Marathon, 708 N. First St., Suite CR-33, Minneapolis, MN 55401; (612) 673-0778.

WINEGLASS
Painted Post, N.Y. Mark Landin, PO Box 98, Corning, NY 14830; (607) 936-8736.

YONKERS
Yonkers, N.Y. A.J. Cambria, Yonkers Parks & Recreation, 285 Nepperhan Ave., Yonkers, NY 10701; (914) 377-6430.

CITY OF GALLUP
Gallup, New Mexico. Randy Stokes, 3405 W. Hwy. 66, Gallup, NM 87301; (505) 722-4301.

HARTFORD
Hartford, Conn. Beth Shluger, c/o Hartford Restaurant Assoc., 221 Main St., Hartford, CT 06106; (203) 525-3435.

ATLANTIC CITY
Atlantic City, N.Y. Barbara Altman, Boardwalk Runners, PO Box 2181, Ventnor, NJ 08406; (609) 822-6911.

BATON ROUGE BEACH
Baton Rouge, Louisiana. Jeff Ravlin, 13380 Greenview Ave., Baton Rouge, LA 70861; (504) 275-1576.

GREATER KANSAS CITY
Kansas City, Missouri. Steve Noll, PO Box 10220, Kansas City, MO 64171; (816) 561-1087.

BAY STATE
Tyngsboro, Mass. Bill Smith, 6 Proctor Rd., Townsend, MA 01469; (508) 597-5204.

LAKEFRONT
Milwaukee, Wisconsin. Steve Hartman, c/o Badgerland Striders, 9200 W. North Ave., Milwaukee, WI 53226; (414) 783-5009.

PUEBLO RIVER TRAIL
Pueblo, Colo. Ben Valdez, YMCA, 700 Albany St., Pueblo, CO 81003; (719) 543-5151.

RICHMOND
Richmond, Virginia. Dewayne Davis, Richmond Times/Dispatch Marathon, POBox 85333, Richmond, VA 23923; (804) 649-6738.

STEAMTOWN
Scranton, Penna. Scranton Cultural Center, 420 N. Washington Ave., Scranton, PA 18503; (717) 346-7369.

TOE TO TOW TRAIL
North Cuyahoga Valley, Ohio. Michele Angermeier, 5525 Warrensville Center Rd., Maple Heights, OH 44137; (216) 663-2282.

CAESAR CREEK

Caesar Creek State Park, Ohio. Denny Fryman, 7581 Glenhurst Dr., Dayton OH 45414; (513) 898-7015.

GREEN MOUNTAIN

South Hero, Vermont. Howie Atherton, 6010 Main Rd., Huntington, VT 05462; (802) 434-3228.

WICHITA

Wichita, Kansas. Clark Ensz, 393 N. McLean Blvd., Wichita, KS 67203; (316) 267-6812.

CHICAGO

Chicago, Ill. Chicago Marathon, 54 W. Hubbard St., Chicago, IL 60610; (312) 527-2200.

COLORADO

Denver, Colo. Lesley Fuller, Colorado Marathon, 2126 S. Kalamuth, Denver, CO 80233; (303) 727-8700.

DETROIT FREE PRESS

Detroit, Mich. Detroit Free Press Marathon, 33 Stroh River Pl., Suite 4000, Detroit, MI 48207; (313) 393-7749.

HUMBOLDT REDWOODS

Weott, Calif. Barbara Edwards, 351 Roundhouse Creek Rd., Trinidad, CA 95570; (707) 443-1220.

MOHAWK-HUDSON RIVER

Albany, N.Y. Mohawk-Hudson River Marathon, PO Box 4022, Albany, NY 12204. (No phone calls)

ST. LOUIS

St. Louis, Missouri. SLTR, 2385 Hampton Ave., St. Louis, MO 63169; (314) 781-3926.

SKYLINE TO THE SEA TRAIL

Santa Cruz, Calif. Enviro-Sports, PO Box 1040, Stinson Beach, CA 94970; (415) 868-1829.

CAPE COD

Falmouth, Mass. Courtney and Carolyn Bird, PO Box 699, West Falmouth, MA 02574; (508) 540-6959.

MARINE CORPS

Washington, D.C. Marine Corps Marathon, PO Box 188, Quantico, VA 22134; (703) 784-2225.

OCTOBER — INTERNATIONAL

TWIN LAKES

Orillia, Ontario. Norm Patenaude, 297, Canice St., Orillia, Ontario, Canada L3V 4J6; (705) 327-2643.

CANADIAN INTERNATIONAL

Toronto, Ontario. Jay Glassman, Running First Ltd., RR 1, Uxbridge, Ontario, Canada L9P 1R1; (416) 485-5815.

ROYAL VICTORIA

Victoria, British Columbia. Rob Reid, Vicoria Marathon Society, 182-911 Yates St., Victoria, British Columbia, Canada V8V 4X3; (604) 382-8181.

VALLEY HARVEST

Kentville, Nova Scotia. Steve Moores, RR 1, Wolfville, Nova Scotia, Canada B0P 1X0; (902) 542-1867.

ATHENS

Athens, Greece. Paul Samara, 1235 Pearl St., Denver, CO 80203; (303) 863-0066.

TORONTO

Toronto, Ontario. Toronto Marathon, 240 Heath St., Suite 802, Toronto, Ontario, Canada. M5P 3L5; (416) 972-1062.

DUBLIN

Dublin, Ireland. Marathon Tours & Travel, 108 Main St., Charlestown, MA 02129; (617) 242-7686.

FRANKFURT

Frankfurt, Germany. Frankfurt Marathon, PO Box 180 309, D-60084 Frankfurt, Germany.

ITALIAN INTERNATIONAL

Italy, Carpi. Ivano Barbolini, PO Box 330. 41012 Carpi, Italy; Tel: 39.59.650.297. Fax: 39.59.651.330.

VENICE

Venice, Italy. Venice Marathon Club, via Felisati 34, 30170 Venzia Mestre, Italy; Tel: 39.41.940.644. Fax: 39.41.940.349.

NOVEMBER — U.S.A.

ANDREW JACKSON

Jackson, Tenn. Bob Saffel, Jackson Roadrunners, PO Box 3832, Jackson, TN 38303; (901) 668-1708.

ARKANSAS

Booneville, Ark. Chamber of Commerce, 2nd and Bennett Sts., Booneville, AR 72907; (501) 675-2666.

BIG SUR TRAIL

Big Sur State Park, Calif. Enviro-Sports, PO 1040, Stinson Beach, CA 94970; (415) 868-1829.

CHEROKEE STRIP

Ponca City, Oklahoma. John Friess, 903 E. Central Ave., Ponca City, OK 74601; (405) 767-4339.

MORGAN HILL

Morgan Hill, Calif. California Sports Marketing, PO Box 794, Morgan Hill, CA 95038; (408) 776-3035.

LEPRECHAUN

Vandalia, Ohio. Denny Fryman, 7581 Glenhurst Dr., Dayton, OH 45414; (513) 898-7015.

NEW YORK CITY

New York, N.Y. NYRRC, 9 E. 89th St., New York, NY 10128; (212) 860-4455.

OCEAN STATE

Narragansett, Rhode Island. Ocean State Marathon, 5 Division St., East Greenwich, RI 02818; (401) 885-4499.

OMAHA RIVERFRONT

Omaha, Nebraska. Gary Meyer, 5822 Ohio St., Omaha, NE 68104; (402) 553-8349.

WARWICK

Warwick, N.Y. Warwick Marathon, PO Box 561, Warwick, NY 10990; (914) 986-8572.

CHICAMAUGA BATTLEFIELD

Chickamauga, Georgia. The Front Runner, 3903 Hixon Park, Suite C, Chattanooga, TN 37415; (615) 875-3642.

CITY OF SANTA CLARITA

Santa Clarita, Calif. Santa Clarita Runners, Box 800298, Santa Clarita, CA 91380; (805) 259-5441.

COLUMBUS

Columbus, Ohio. Columbus Marathon, PO Box 26806, Columbus, OH 43226; (614) 433-0395

HAMPDEN-SYDNEY

Hampden-Sydney, Virginia. Hampden-Sydney Marathon, PO Box 158, Hampden-Sydney College, Hampden-Sydney, VA 23943; (804) 223-6185.

HARRISBURG

Harrisburg, Penna. Harrisburg Marathon, 7912 Umberger St., Harrisburg, PA 17112; (717) 652-2521.

SAN ANTONIO

San Antonio, Texas. San Antonio Marathon, 1123 Navarro, San Antonio, TX 78215; (210) 246-9652.

VULCAN

Birmingham, Alabama. Birmingham News, Vulcan Run, PO Box 530363, Birmingham, AL 35253; (205) 995-5344.

PALM DESERT

Palm Desert, Calif. Greg Carel, 73-350 El Paseo, Suite 207, Palm Desert, CA 92260; (619) 346-8070.

PHILADELPHIA
  Philadelphia, Penna. Joe Callan, Memorial Hall, PO Box 21601, Philadelphia, PA 19131; (215) 685-0054.
TULSA
  Tulsa, Oklahoma. Tulsa Marathon, Coneil Larfarlette, 263 E. 45th Place, Tulsa, OK 74105; (918) 744-0339.
HOLIDAY
  Cincinnati, Ohio. Denny Fryman, 7581 Glenhurst Dr., Dayton, OH 45414; (513) 898-7015.
SEATTLE
  Seattle, Washington. Rick Johnston, PO Box 31849, Seattle, WA 98103; (206) 821-6474.
SPACE COAST
  Melbourne, Florida. Bill Dillard, PO Box 2407, Melbourne, FL 32902; (407) 724-2510.
ATLANTA
  Atlanta, Georgia. Atlanta Track Club, 3097 E. Shadowlawn Ave., Atlanta, GA 30305; (404) 231-9065.
MISSISSIPPI BEACH
  Ocean Springs, Miss. Gulfport Rotary Club, 22 Thirty-first St., Gulfport, MS 39507; (601) 865-3071.
NORTHERN CENTRAL TRAIL
  Sparks, Maryland. Northern Central Trail Marathon, PO Box 5464, Towson, MD 21285; (410) 377-8882.

NOVEMBER — INTERNATIONAL
AMSTERDAM CITY
  Amsterdam, Netherlands. Amsterdam City Marathon, PO Box 94610, 1090 GP Amsterdam, Netherlands; Tel: 31.20.663.0781 Fax: 31.20.663.0561.
ADIDAS
  Buenos Aires, Argentina. Maraton Adidas, Avenue Eva Peron 2535, CP. 1650, San Martin, Buenos Aires, Argentina; Tel: 54.1.753.9040, Extension 248.

DECEMBER — U.S.A.
ALMOST HEAVEN
  Charleston, West Virginia. Pat Board, 19 Riverside Dr., South Charleston, WV 25303; (304) 744-6502.
BULLDOG
  Altus, Oklahoma. Can Metcalf, 2610 N.W. Expressway, Oklahoma City, OK 73112; (405) 946-5624.
DALLAS WHITE ROCK

Dallas, Texas. White Rock Marathon, 3607 Oak Lawn, Dallas, TX 75219; (214) 526-5318.

FIESTA BOWL

Scottsdale, Ariz. Rob Wallach, c/o Sigma Fiesta Bowl Race, 6505 N. 16th St., Phoenix, AZ 85016; (602) 277-4333.

HOLIDAY

Vandalia, Ohio. Denny Fryman, 7581 Glenhurst Dr., Dayton, OH 45414; (513) 898-7015.

MEMPHIS

Memphis, Tenn. Kim Cherry, First Tennessee Memphis Marathon, PO Box 84, Memphis, TN 38101; (800) 893-7223.

WESTERN HEMISPHERE

Culver City, Calif. Culver City Recreation Department, 4117 Overland Ave., Culver City, CA 90230; (310) 253-6650.

ALAMAGORDO

White Sands National Monument, New Mexico. Clint Burleson, PO Box 15889, Alamagordo, NM 88311; (505) 382-8869.

KENTUCKY

Louisville, Ky. Stu McCombs, 7004 Beachland Beach, Prospect, KY 40059; (502) 228-1133.

MISSISSIPPI

Clinton, Miss. James Myrick, Mississippi TC, PO Box 866, Clinton, MS 39060; (601) 856-9884.

BRANDON

Brandon, Florida. Brandon Marathon, PO Box 1564, Brandon, FL 33509; (813) 681-4279.

CALIFORNIA INTERNATIONAL

Sacramento, Calif. California International Marathon, PO Box 161149, Sacramento, CA 95816; (916) 983-4622.

CHRISTMAS

Olympia, Wash. Bob Green, Puget Sound Cruisers, 1717 Jacki Court, NE, Olympia, WA 98506; (360) 456-0554.

DELAWARE

Middletown, Del. Wayne Kursh, c/o Schweizer's Delaware Marathon, PO Box 398, Wilmington, DE 19899; (302) 654-6400.

HONOLULU

Honolulu, Hawaii. Honolulu Marathon Assoc., 3435 Wailae Ave., #208, Honolulu, HI 96816; (808) 734-7200.

TUCSON

Tucson, Ariz. Pat Lekacz, 1715 E. Water St., Tucson, AZ 85719; (520) 325-2736.

JACKSONVILLE

Jacksonville, Fla. First Place Sports, 3853 Baymeadows Rd., Jacksonville, FL 32217; (904) 739-1917.

KIAWAH ISLAND

Kiawah Island, South Carolina. Kiawah Island Resort, 12 Kiawah Beach Dr., Kiawah Island, SC 29455; (803) 768-6001.

ROCKET CITY

Huntsville, Alabama. Harold Tinsley, Huntsville TC, 8811 Edgehill Dr., Huntsville, AL 35802; (205) 881-9077.

MARATHON SIX-PACK (THIS EVENT INCLUDES 6 MARATHONS IN 6 DAYS)

Vandalia, Ohio. Denny Fryman, 7581 Glenhurst Dr., Dayton, OH 45414; (513) 898-7015.

NEW YEAR'S RESOLUTION TRAIL

Muir Beach, Calif. Enviro-Sports, PO Box 1040, Stinson Beach, CA 94970; (415) 868-1829.

DECEMBER — INTERNATIONAL

MACAU

Macau, South China. Manuel Siverio, Macau Sports Institute, PO Box 334, Macau, South China; Tel: 853.580.762 Fax: 853.343.708.

Following are summaries of two of the pieces of research we have conducted concerning the effects of marathon training. The first one is a study of the psychological effects of marathon training. It has not been published elsewhere.

Study #1
Effects of Marathon Training on Mood State and Locus of Control
By
Jennifer Dykes, David A. Whitsett and Forrest A. Dolgener

Introduction
We investigated the effects of physical and mental training for a marathon on the general mood state and what is called locus of control of a group of our students. (We discussed locus of control in the first part of Chapter One.) As you will read below, we found that marathon training has significant psychological benefits.

What we did in the study
In the spring of 1995, we asked our students to fill out two questionnaires during the semester in which they were training on our program. The group consisted of 56 people, including 17 men and 39 women. They ranged in age from 17 to 37. They filled out one of the questionnaires, called the Profile of

Mood States (POMS) every week for 14 consecutive weeks. The other questionnaire, called the Locus of Control Scale (LOC), they filled out at the beginning and again at the end of the training. During the semester they followed exactly the same training program as the one described in this book. We also had another group of 53 students (25 men and 28 women) who were not participating in marathon training complete the questionnaires as well so that we could compare their answers to those of our marathon training group.

The POMS is a 65-item questionnaire which measures tension, depression, anger, vigor, fatigue and confusion. The scores on these six scales can be combined into what is called a Mood Disturbance score and that is what we did. The LOC measures locus of control, which, as we discussed in Chapter One, is an indication of the extent to which people feel they are in control of events in their lives. We expected that our marathon trainers would have lower mood disturbance scores and higher internal locus of control scores than the non-marathon trainers.

Results

At the beginning of the training, the two groups had POMS scores that were very similar, but during the semester, the group that was training for the marathon showed less and less tension, depression, anger, fatigue and confusion and more and more vigor (energy). In addition, we noticed that our marathon trainers' scores did not seem to go up and down week to week.. They seemed to show a kind of emotional stability. The scores for the other group showed significant week-to-week variation, but no overall improvement over the semester.

On the other questionnaire, the LOC, the marathon trainers began with scores indicating they were somewhat more internal than the other group and, over the semester the marathon trainers became significantly more internal, while the non-trainers showed no change.

Conclusions

So, what does this mean for you? It shows that training for a marathon may be good for your head as well as for your body. Our marathon trainers felt better emotionally as well as physically and you probably will too. Marathon training seems to help people feel generally less tense, angry, depressed, confused and tired and more vigorous and energetic. In addition, such training seems to increase people's feelings of being in control of their own lives and, from a psychological point of view, we know that feeling that one can influence the events in one's life is part of being psychologically "hardy" and being able to handle life's stresses and challenges.

Study #2

The second article is about the physiological effects of marathon training. This is the study that convinced us that a four-day-a-week training program was the best one for first-time marathoners.

It was first published in a professional journal called the *Research Quarterly for Exercise and Sport* in 1994. If you are interested in the whole article, it was in Volume 65 on pages 339-346 and it was written by Forrest Dolgener, Fred Kolkhorst and David Whitsett. Here is a brief summary of the article.

Introduction

This project was conducted to help answer the question, "How much training is necessary for beginning marathoners to run a marathon?" In our previous classes, we had used a six-day-per-week training program. This had been the traditional approach to training for a marathon with the thought being that the more mileage you do the better off you are. However, most of the research that was telling us that more mileage is better had been conducted with high-ability runners and in our class we were dealing with average ability people training for their first marathon. We knew from our personal experience that there was a point beyond which additional mileage probably only increased the chances for injury and excessive fatigue. The other thought that prompted this research project was that the most important part of marathon training was doing the long runs of each week. We felt that if we cut back our total mileage but still did the same distance for the long runs, the students might recover better, be less prone to injury, feel generally less fatigued during the training and still be able to success-fully run the marathon. We designed this study to see if we were right.

What we did in the study

We divided our class of 51 students into two groups, matched on the results of some physiological testing (treadmill test, blood tests and body fat measures) we had performed before the training program began (so that we could be sure the two groups were about the same running ability). One group (called G6) trained six days per week for the 15-week training program. The second group (called G4) trained for only four days per week for the 15-week program. The G4 group did not run on two of the short-mileage days during the week, which meant they got two more days of recovery per week compared to the G6 group. Over the course of the 15 weeks, the G6 group ran 20% more mileage than the G4 group, but both groups ran the same long run each week. Two weeks before the marathon, the groups were re-tested on the same physiological tests that we had done before beginning training. Their finishing times for the marathon were also used to compare the two groups.

Results

The data showed that the two groups did not differ on any of the tests. The physiological tests and the marathon times were the same for both groups. This means that the four-day-per-week and the six-day-per-week programs had the same effects. It was interesting to note that during the training, some of the students in the G4 group were concerned that they were not doing enough running and we had to periodically reassure them that they were going to be fine (we hoped). You may be wondering as well, if four days a week is enough. This study shows that it definitely is.

Conclusions

We think that the long run each week is the most critical part of the training program. How much more the mileage could be reduced (even beyond the program outlined in this book) is not yet known. It may be that running only three days a week would be sufficient. The answers to this and other questions concerning the best training program for novice marathoners remain for future research projects. But after completing this research study, we are sure that four days a week is enough. That is what we have used in our classes ever since and it is what we are recommending for you.

References and Suggested Reading List

Bernstein, D.A. & Borkovec, T.D. (1973). *Progressive Relaxation Training*. Research Press, Champaign, Illinois

Costill, D. (1986). *Inside Running: Basics of Sports Physiology*. Benchmark Press, Indianapolis.

Csikszentmihalyi, M. (1990). *Flow: The Psychology of Optimal Experience*. Harper & Row, New York.

Csikzentmihalyi, M. (1997). *Finding Flow.* Harper Collins, New York.

Helmstetter, S. (1987). *What to Say When You Talk to Yourself.* Simon & Schuster, New York.

Jacobson, E. (1929). *Progressive Relaxation.* University of Chicago Press, Chicago, Illinois.

Maslow, A. (1962). *Toward a Psychology of Being.* Van Nostrand Co., Princeton, New Jersey.

Newsholme, E., Leech, T. & Duester, G. (1994) *Keep on Running: The Science of Training and Performance.* John Wiley & Sons, New York.

Noakes, T. (1992). *Lore of Running.* Second Edition, Oxford University Press, Capetown.

Piper, W. (1996). *The Little Engine That Could.* Putnam, New York.

Rotter, J.B. (1966). Generalized expectancies for internal versus external control of reinforcement. *Psychological Monographs,* 80, pages 1-28.

Sheehan, G. (1978). *Running & Being: The Total Experience.* Warner Books, New York.

Author Bio Sketches

David A. Whitsett is Professor of Psychology at the University of Northern Iowa in Cedar Falls. He earned his doctorate in Psychology at Case-Western Reserve University in Cleveland. He has been a runner and marathoner for over 25 years and has taught courses in psychology at the university level for over 30 years. He is a co-author of 3 previous books and has written many articles on motivation. Dr. Whitsett lives in Cedar Falls, Iowa.

Forrest A. Dolgener is Professor of Exercise Physiology at the University of Northern Iowa in Cedar Falls. He earned his doctorate in Exercise Physiology at the University of Texas at Austin. He has been a lifelong proponent of exercise and has been a runner and biker for 35 years. He has taught courses related to exercise and wellness at the university level for over 20 years. He has authored many articles dealing with exercise and running and has edited a textbook on personal wellness. Dr. Dolgener and his family reside in Cedar Falls, Iowa.

Tanjala Mabon Kole earned her bachelor's degree in Psychology at the University of Northern Iowa and is currently working on a master's degree in Mental Health Counseling. She was a participant in the marathon class upon which this book is based and completed the 1995 Lincoln, Nebraska marathon. She and her children live in Denver, Iowa.